Praise for the original edition

"A great how-to for teachers!"
—*Washington Post*

"Offers ways to change bullying behavior and prevent potential
victims from being bullied; provides teachers and parents with tools to help
students learn to resolve conflicts appropriately and effectively."
—National PTA's *Our Children* Magazine

"A practical, economic way to make it clear that bullying will
not be tolerated."
—*Educational Dealer*

Parent Council Selection

Teachers' Choice Award
—*Learning* Magazine

THE NEW

BULLY FREE CLASSROOM®

Proven Prevention and Intervention Strategies for Teachers K–8

Allan L. Beane, Ph.D.

free spirit
PUBLISHING®

Library of Congress Cataloging-in-Publication Data
Beane, Allan L., 1950–
  The new bully free classroom : proven prevention and intervention strategies for teachers k–8 / Allan L. Beane.
      p. cm. — (Bully free classroom)
  ISBN 978-1-57542-382-1
  1. School violence—United States—Prevention—Handbooks, manuals, etc. 2. Bullying in schools—United States—Prevention—Handbooks, manuals, etc. 3. Classroom management—United States—Handbooks, manuals, etc. 4. Activity programs in education—United States—Handbooks, manuals, etc. I. Title.
  LB3013.3.B43 2011
  371.5'8—dc23

                                                                                      2011019336

eBook ISBN: 978-1-57542-681-5

Free Spirit Publishing does not have control over or assume responsibility for author or third-party websites and their content. At the time of this book's publication, all facts and figures cited within are the most current available. All telephone numbers, addresses, and website URLs are accurate and active; all publications, organizations, websites, and other resources exist as described in this book; and all have been verified as of June 2011. If you find an error or believe that a resource listed here is not as described, please contact Free Spirit Publishing. Parents, teachers, and other adults: We strongly urge you to monitor children's use of the Internet.

Cover and interior design by Michelle Lee

10 9 8 7 6 5 4 3 2 1
Printed in the United States of America

Free Spirit Publishing Inc.
217 Fifth Avenue North, Suite 200
Minneapolis, MN 55401-1299
(612) 338-2068
help4kids@freespirit.com
www.freespirit.com

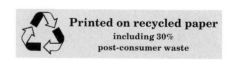
Printed on recycled paper
including 30%
post-consumer waste

As a member of the Green Press Initiative, Free Spirit Publishing is committed to the three Rs: Reduce, Reuse, Recycle. Whenever possible, we print our books on recycled paper containing a minimum of 30% post-consumer waste. At Free Spirit it's our goal to nurture not only children, but nature too!

green press
INITIATIVE

DEDICATION

This book is dedicated to our son, Curtis Allan Beane, who was bullied in seventh grade and high school. It is also dedicated to our daughter, Christy Turner; our son-in-law, Mike; and our grandchildren, Emily Grace Turner, Sarah Gail Turner, Jacob Allan Turner, and Jimmy Andrew Turner. They have been a light in the darkness caused by Curtis's death. I hope this book, and those who use it, will bring light into the darkness of students who are bullied.

ACKNOWLEDGMENTS

I wish to recognize the teachers who, in the initial stages of this book, freely shared their experiences and made suggestions for promoting peer acceptance.

I also want to thank Free Spirit Publishing for believing in this book, and especially Ms. Jessica Thoreson for her help during the writing of the original version. I also wish to thank Free Spirit's Eric Braun for his help, encouragement, writing, editing, and production of this updated edition of the book.

Thank you!

CONTENTS

EMPOWER BYSTANDERS TO BECOME ALLIES

BONUS MATERIAL ON CD-ROM

This Week in School (Early Elementary Reproducible Page)

Bullying Survey (Early Elementary Reproducible Page)

How Can We Respond? (Physical Bullying) (Early Elementary Reproducible Page)

How Can We Respond? (Verbal Bullying) (Early Elementary Reproducible Page)

How Can We Respond? (Social/Relational Bullying) (Early Elementary Reproducible Page)

Together We Can Make School Bully Free (PowerPoint Presentation)

LIST OF REPRODUCIBLE PAGES

PREFACE

Several years ago, the pain of bullying visited our home. When our son, Curtis, was in seventh grade, he was bullied and eventually isolated by several students. My wife and I decided to transfer him to another school system. He found acceptance and a sense of belonging at the new middle school. Then, at age 15, Curtis was in a car accident that changed his life.

Surgeons removed two fingers and one-third of his right hand. He had two other fingers repaired and one rebuilt. When he went back to school, many of his classmates encouraged and supported him. But many were cruel to him, teasing him about his hand. I asked myself, "How can kids be so cruel?" There was a cry from within me for answers. I wanted to know if I could stop cruelty from developing, and I wanted to stop it after it had already developed.

There was also a cry from within my son, and it was deeper and more intense than mine. The bullying had a tremendous impact on his self-esteem, confidence, and emotional health even into his adult years. At the age of 23, he suffered from depression and anxiety. He developed post-traumatic stress from the car wreck and the persistent bullying. He also sought the company of the wrong people. They convinced him to escape his pain by taking an illegal drug, crystal meth. He had a heart problem that no one knew about, and the drug killed him.

That is why I am passionate about preventing and stopping bullying. I understand the pain expressed by children who are bullied and the heartache their families experience. I do not want any student to experience what our son did. I especially do not want any child to take the path he took. I want to stop the pain. I have witnessed the frustration of professionals who seek to prevent and stop bullying. They have a tremendous need for resources designed to help them.

After Curtis's death, my wife, Linda, and I wrote several books, developed numerous other materials and resources, and began presenting at school assembly programs, speaking to parent groups, and training school personnel and others who work with young people. We plan to dedicate the rest of our lives to preventing and stopping bullying.

The Bully Free Classroom, originally published in 1999, was the centerpiece of the Bully Free Program Linda and I developed. It has been widely used over the years in North America and, in translation, abroad. Teachers and schools implement its strategies as part of Bully Free initiatives and in conjunction with other bullying prevention programs. Since the book's initial publication, awareness about bullying has increased dramatically, and research has helped us understand it better. We understand, for example, that witnesses to bullying are as strongly affected by bullying as targets, and we understand that these witnesses have the most power to prevent and end bullying. We know more about relational (or social) bullying. Cyberbullying, which was rarely considered (if at all) in 1999, has become a huge problem.

The New Bully Free Classroom retains the thorough, child-first approach and the effective strategies and activities that made the original book successful. It also includes lots of new material to address the changes that have occurred over the years, including an entirely new chapter on empowering bystanders, several sections on cyberbullying, and an increased focus on relational bullying. I've added a special section addressing on-the-spot responding to bullying (pages 95–99). The "Facts About Bullying" section includes the latest research, and you'll find updated resources throughout the book and in the "Resources" section at the end of the book.

Bullying can be found in every neighborhood, school district, and school. To reduce and prevent it requires a focused effort. Ideally, entire school districts commit to ending bullying, and families and other adults in the community get involved. But even an individual teacher or other adult can make a difference, whether part of a larger effort or not. When adults help kids, bullying *can* be stopped and prevented, or at least significantly reduced.

While it's true that bullying continues to be a problem, I am extremely hopeful. I am hopeful because I have seen firsthand that students can be empowered to reject bullying and cruelty, and because there are dedicated educators like you who are working hard on behalf of our children. Thank you for your efforts.

Allan L. Beane

INTRODUCTION

Since this book was first published in 1999, bullying has been more widely recognized as a serious problem, one that is damaging to the health of children. In fact, the Centers for Disease Control and Prevention has labeled bullying a public health problem. Sensational tragedies caused by bullying (stories involving severe violence and children feeling so hopeless they commit suicide) have gripped the public's attention and set off an alarm.

Much of what we hear about bullying in the media is not representative of the vast majority of bullying that happens in schools—which is less dramatic but far more common—but these stories have helped increase awareness. As a result, adults are more alert for signs of bullying and more willing and able to do something about it. Kids are involved in conversations about bullying that were extremely rare in previous generations, and their improved understanding helps create a climate where bullying is not tolerated. Anti-bullying resources have proliferated. Several states have passed laws mandating that schools have bullying prevention policies, and some encourage or require training of school personnel and a district-wide or school-wide anti-bullying program.

As an educator, you understand the importance of creating school environments that are bully free—environments where all students feel safe, have a sense of belonging and acceptance, and treat others the way they want to be treated. The purpose of *The New Bully Free Classroom* is to help you create this kind of environment in your classroom. This book is most effective as part of a comprehensive school-wide effort to prevent and stop bullying. Anti-bullying efforts work best when every adult and student in your school is involved. Of course, you can make a difference working on your own, too, and that is better than doing nothing.

The New Bully Free Classroom is based on the following philosophy:

- **All children have basically good hearts,** and an effective anti-bullying program should emphasize children's potential for future leadership, affirm their strengths, and encourage them to do good and remarkable things. Therefore, we discourage labeling children as victims or bullies. Some children are mistreated, some children mistreat others, and some children witness mistreatment. Many children fall into two groups or all three groups at different times, and all three groups need help.

- **All children are hurt by bullying,** not just those who are targeted. Those who bully may be hurting just as badly as the kids they bully, and as adults they will face increased vulnerability to various risk factors, including alcoholism and incarceration. The trauma experienced by witnesses to bullying is similar to the trauma experienced by targets. (See pages 5–6 for more information about the effects of bullying.)

- **All children respond differently to bullying.** What may be a mild incident to one child might feel severe to another. While bullying is defined in part by acts that are repeated over time, some children may be hurt so much by a single aggressive event that they are changed for life (see page 4 for a complete definition of bullying). In all cases, what is more important than definitions or labels is the child's experience of the event and the pain the child feels.

- **Witnesses, or bystanders, hold the most important key to ending bullying.** When bystanders encourage or ignore bullying, those who are bullying may feel emboldened to continue—or even escalate—the behavior. When students choose instead to speak out against and report bullying, those who are bullying others realize that their behavior is not acceptable and that it will not be tolerated by peers. Encourage your students to stand up for kids who are targeted with bullying when it is safe to do so and to report all bullying to school staff. Clearly communicate that bullying affects everyone—and that every student can help make school a better place for all.

USING THIS BOOK

The New Bully Free Classroom has four sections. "Create a Positive Classroom" (pages 9–55) features tips, strategies, and techniques designed to change everyone's attitudes and behaviors for the better. "Empower Bystanders to Become Allies" (pages 56–89) focuses on showing all students the power they have to stop and prevent bullying. "Help Targets of Bullying" (pages 90–125) focuses on students who are current or potential targets of bullying. "Help Kids Who Bully" (pages 126–157) addresses kids who have mistreated others. They need your help as much as targets do, and you'll find lots of ideas for turning them around.

Many activities include a variety of options or approaches to try with your students. Throughout this book, "Go Further" suggestions present ways to expand an activity or explore a topic in greater depth. You'll also discover dozens of handouts,

A WORD ABOUT LABELS

Labels such as *bully* and *victim* unfairly typecast students into roles that may shame or humiliate them. Worse, students may unconsciously take on the labels given to them. When talking with and helping students involved in bullying in any role, try not to use these labels. Instead, focus your attention on the behavior or event. Examples for doing this can be found on page 135.

In this book, I have tried to avoid the use of labels as much as possible, although sometimes it is unavoidable. When you see these labels, please keep in mind that they are meant to refer to students *when they are bullying or when they are targeted*. *Bully* may be a role a student played in one or more events, but it is not who the student is. All students are capable of showing positive and negative actions.

I have avoided the term *victim* entirely, because this term implies helplessness. Instead, I talk about students who have been *targeted* by bullying, and occasionally may call these students *targets*.

ready to use and reproducible for your classroom. The included CD-ROM contains all of the book's handouts and a PowerPoint presentation titled "Overview of Bullying: Stop the Pain and Violence." The presentation provides a solid introduction to the problem of bullying and the steps needed to create a bully free atmosphere.

Because this book spans a broad range of grades (K–8), not all activities are appropriate for all classrooms. Some might need "aging up" or "aging down" for your group; specific age levels are not usually assigned, because what students are ready for and capable of doing seldom depends on age alone. To help you adjust activities, some of the reproducible handouts are available on the CD-ROM in younger versions than you will find in the book. (These handouts will be noted.) Some activities are simple and take just a few moments to do; others take more time to introduce, present, and follow through. Most are easy to understand and implement, requiring little or no advance preparation and few or no special materials. You know your students; please feel free to adapt any of these activities or handouts to meet your needs and theirs.

You can read this book from start to finish, or you can dip in anywhere you want to begin. I recommend you start by reading "The Facts About Bullying" (pages 4–8). This will give you a solid understanding of the issue. When you're ready to start working with your students, you may find it most effective to begin with strategies from "Create a Positive Classroom" or "Empower Bystanders to Become Allies." These give everyone a common language and shared understanding of bullying and help set the stage for all students to work together to create a bully free environment.

Throughout this process, it's vital to communicate with parents and caregivers. On page 36, you'll find a letter you can copy or print from the CD-ROM and use to announce that you're using this book and why. Stay in touch with families at various points along the way; you might give them copies of handouts you're using with your students, send brief notes home, or use the phone or email for a quick update. It's especially important to communicate with parents of students who have been involved in bullying.

Whenever you'd like more information, turn to "Resources" at the end of the book (pages 158–173). This section lists and describes books, videos, other materials, organizations, and websites to enhance your teaching and support your efforts to make your classroom bully free.

CREATE AND PURSUE GOALS

The New Bully Free Classroom has a dual emphasis: intervention and prevention. It's not enough to stop the bullying that's already happening; we also need to keep students who aren't yet involved in bullying from starting down that road. To help you stay focused on this dual emphasis, I encourage you to work with your school to establish anti-bullying goals such as the following:

- Send a clear message to students, staff, families, and community members that bullying will not be tolerated.

- Establish and enforce rules and policies focused on bullying.

- Reduce the number of existing bullying situations.

- Create more peaceful and safer schools.

- Promote a sense of belonging and acceptance in all students so they feel connected to their school.

- Educate, involve, and empower students as bystanders to prevent and stop bullying.

- Create a school culture where adults are warm, positive, and trustworthy role models. Adults should be clear authorities as well as caring and respectful in the way they treat students and other adults. Their authority and trustworthiness will be communicated both verbally and nonverbally to students.

- Significantly improve adult supervision on school property, especially in high-risk areas (locker rooms, bathrooms, halls, cafeterias, etc.).

- Restructure the school culture and social environment in a way that adults and students take action and expect immediate intervention, investigation, and confrontation of bullying behavior.

- Provide intervention for children who are bullied and who bully.

I hope this book can help make your classroom a place where all students are free to learn without fear—and you're free to teach without worrying about bullying. I'd love to hear how these strategies and tips work for you; I welcome your comments, letters, stories, and emails. You may contact me in care of my publisher:

Free Spirit Publishing
217 Fifth Avenue North, Suite 200
Minneapolis, MN 55401-1299
help4kids@freespirit.com

Allan L. Beane, Ph.D.

FACTS ABOUT BULLYING

This research-based section provides a broad, general overview of what bullying is, who it affects, and why it is important for adults—including you—to get involved in prevention and intervention. Use it as a resource and inspiration as you work with your students to create a bully free classroom.

WHAT IS BULLYING?

Bullying is a form of aggressive behavior that is intentional, hurtful, and repeated. The person who bullies has more power than the person who is targeted.

Important in this definition are the following criteria that will help you determine if a student is being bullied:

- The mistreatment is *intentional*.

- The mistreatment is *hurtful* (physically or psychologically).

- The mistreatment *occurs more than once*. (Some disagree and say one very hurtful event can be labeled bullying.)

- There is an *imbalance of power* (physical, intellectual, or social). The target has difficulty defending himself or herself.

Within this broad definition are many different types of bullying. **Physical bullying** can mean hitting, slapping, elbowing, shoving, kicking, pinching, or restraining. It can mean flushing someone's head in the toilet, cramming someone into a locker, or attacking someone with spitwads or food. Physical bullying also includes taking, stealing, damaging, or defacing a person's belongings or property.

Verbal bullying includes name-calling; making insulting, racist, or rude remarks; repeated teasing; harassment, threats, and intimidation; and whispering behind someone's back.

Relational (or social) bullying is subtler than other types of bullying. It involves destroying or manipulating relationships (such as turning someone's best friend against him or her). It can mean destroying a person's status within a peer group, destroying others' reputations, humiliating and embarrassing someone, gossiping or spreading malicious rumors or lies, creating hurtful graffiti, excluding someone (social rejection or isolation), and stealing a boyfriend or girlfriend to hurt someone. Displaying negative body language (glaring, casting dirty looks, turning your back to someone), threatening gestures, passing mean notes, and circulating hate petitions (promising to hate someone) are also acts of relational bullying.

Cyberbullying is increasingly prevalent and is addressed in this book in specially focused sections on pages 16–19 and 143–144. It can include spreading gossip, rumors, and lies electronically; sending or posting defamatory or embarrassing photographs and video recordings; sending insulting or threatening email; sending malicious code; sending pornography and other junk email and instant messages (IMs); impersonating someone online to make them look bad; sending or posting cruel jokes electronically; sending or posting malicious gossip electronically; and creating a website designed to humiliate and embarrass someone.

All the different forms of bullying can and often do occur together. All of these behaviors can be interrelated.

HOW BIG A PROBLEM IS BULLYING?

The short answer to this question is "very big." Bullying leads to loneliness, low self-esteem, depression and anxiety disorders, post-traumatic stress, eating disorders, and other long-lasting harmful emotional effects in the adult years. According to one study, being bullied during middle childhood doubled a person's risk of experiencing psychotic symptoms in early adolescence, and experiencing *chronic* bullying increased the risk of having psychotic symptoms by 252 percent (Schreier, et al., 2009).

Bullying creates a stressful and fearful school climate. In 2007, approximately 5 percent of students ages 12–18 reported that they were afraid of attack or harm at school. Seven percent reported that they had avoided a school activity or one or more places in school in the previous six months because of fear of attack or harm (Robers, 2010).

Here are some other facts about the effects of bullying:

- People who bully others or witness bullying have a higher risk of abusing alcohol and other drugs as adolescents and as adults.

- Bullying contributes to poor school attendance. According to the National Association of School Psychologists, 160,000 students per day stay home from school because of bullying (Fried & Fried, 2003).

- Bullying encourages dropping out of school.

- It leads to decreased academic performance.

- It is a root cause of discipline problems for students who bully and students who are bullied.

- Bullying causes some students to engage in self-harm, such as cutting.

- It is often a motivation in school shootings, as students retaliate for bullying.

- Hostile children are more likely to develop diabetes and develop cardiac problems as they age (Elias, 2002).

- Some targets of bullying join a gang, cult, drug group, or hate group to find acceptance and a sense of belonging.

- Students identified as bullies by age eight are six times more likely to be convicted of a crime by age 24 and five times more likely than students who don't bully to end up with serious criminal records by age 30 (Maine Project Against Bullying, 2000). Those who regularly bully in youth often bully in their adult years, too, which hinders their ability to develop and maintain positive relationships. They may grow up to abuse their spouse, children, and coworkers (Beane, 2008).

How often does bullying occur? Estimates vary according to different studies:

- Researchers at Penn State surveyed nearly 12,000 students in grades 5–12, with 22 percent reporting that they were targeted (called names, hit, threatened, or socially excluded) by peers at least twice a month (Davis and Nixon, 2010).

- In the same survey, 48 percent of students reported being regularly (at least twice a month) exposed to relational aggression: rumor-spreading, exclusion, or students working together to be mean to someone. Fifty-four percent of students reported being regularly exposed to verbal abuse: name-calling or threatening comments (Davis and Nixon, 2010).

- In a 2010 survey of more than 2,000 students by Naomi Drew, M.A., 73 percent of students in grades 3–6 in the United States and Canada said that kids are somewhat to very mean to each other; 44 percent said bullying happens often, every day, or all the time; and over 40 percent said they see conflicts happening often or every day (Drew, 2010).

- In a survey of K–12 public school principals, 49 percent said that bullying, name-calling, or harassment of students was a serious problem at their school (GLSEN and Harris Interactive, 2008).

- According to the American Medical Association, 3.7 million kids bully, and more than 3.2 million are targets of "moderate" or "serious" bullying each year (Cohn & Canter, 2003).

While these statistics paint a troubling picture, the problem of bullying is not insurmountable. Research suggests that if teachers, administrators, parents, and students are involved in stopping and preventing bullying, schools can create an atmosphere where making healthy choices is encouraged. An important step is understanding the problem. Read on for more information to help you identify bullying and recognize risk factors.

WHEN AND WHERE DOES BULLYING USUALLY OCCUR?

Bullying occurs in all grades, beginning as early as three to four years of age. It generally peaks in junior high or middle school: three-fourths of junior high and middle school principals say that bullying or harassment is a serious problem at their school, compared to 43 percent of elementary school principals and 45 percent of senior high school principals (GLSEN and Harris Interactive, 2008).

It occurs virtually everywhere: in homes, childcare settings, preschools, elementary schools, middle schools, high schools, neighborhoods, places of worship, city parks, on the trip to and from school, and on the streets.

- It occurs two to three times more often *at* school than on the trip to and from school (Olweus, 2007).

- It is most likely to occur where there is no adult supervision, inadequate adult supervision, poor supervision, a lack of structure, and few or no anti-bullying rules.

- It is more likely to occur where teachers and students accept bullying or are indifferent to it.

- It occurs in large cities and small towns, large schools and small schools—and even one-room schools in other countries (Olweus, 2007).

HOW ARE BOYS AND GIRLS DIFFERENT IN THEIR BULLYING?

Both boys and girls engage in all kinds of bullying. Nevertheless, there are some differences.

- In 2007, 33 percent of female students reported being bullied at school compared to 30 percent of male students (Truman, 2007).

- Boys bully both boys and girls. Girls are more likely to bully other girls, but sometimes they bully boys.

- Boys tend to use more direct behaviors (physical and verbal bullying) than girls do.

- Girls are aggressive, but may use more indirect behaviors to damage relationships.

- More than boys do, girls seek to inflict psychological pain on their targets.

- Boys are just as likely as girls to use social and emotional taunting.

- Girls bully in groups more than boys do.

- Girls often attack targets within a tight networks of friends, which intensifies the hurt.

- Girls are generally better than boys at disguising bullying by behaving well around adults.

See pages 91–93 for guidelines to help you identify students who may potentially bully or be bullied. As you will see, bullying is not often reported to adults, so it is incumbent upon us to be on the lookout for warning signs.

HOW OFTEN DO CHILDREN REPORT BULLYING?

Adults are often unaware of bullying problems, in part because bullied students and bystanders keep it a secret from them. The reasons children keep it secret are varied. They are taught not to "tattle" and think telling someone is wrong. They may have told adults about bullying before, or heard someone else tell adults before, and nothing was done about it, so they see reporting as unhelpful. Many targeted students worry that adults will make the situation worse. Many are embarrassed or feel shame because they feel no one likes them; they feel defective. They may feel shame because they cannot stand up for themselves as they have been taught. Finally, many targeted students do not want to worry their family. They love their family and want to protect them from worry and anxiety.

What else does the research say about the perception of adults in regard to bullying?

- Among students who were bullied regularly, 42 percent told an adult at school. Among those students, only 34 percent reported that the bullying got better after telling; 37 percent reported no change; and 29 percent reported that it got worse (Davis and Nixon, 2010).

- In a survey of students in 14 Massachusetts schools, over 30 percent believed that adults did little or nothing to help with bullying (Mullin-Rindler, 2002).

- Bullied students often feel that adult intervention is infrequent and unhelpful, and fear that telling adults will only bring more harassment from the people who bully them (Cohn & Canter, 2003).

- Almost 25 percent of girls surveyed felt that they did not know three adults they could go to for support if they were bullied (Girl Scout Research Institute, 2003).

- Twenty-five percent of teachers see nothing wrong with bullying or put-downs and consequently intervene in only 4 percent of bullying incidents (Cohn & Canter, 2003).

An anti-bullying program that includes discussions and activities about bullying can help increase the likelihood that children—both targets and witnesses of bullying—will report it.

REFERENCES

Austin, G., J. Huh-Kim, R. Skage, and M. Furlong. 2001–2002 California Student Survey. Jointly sponsored by the California Attorney General's Office, California Department of Education, and Department of Alcohol and Drug Programs. Published by California Attorney General's Office, Billy Lockyer, Attorney General, 2002.

Beane, A. L. *Bullying Prevention for Schools: A Step-by-Step Guide to Implementing a Successful Anti-Bullying Program*. San Francisco: Jossey-Bass, 2009.

Broward County (Florida) Schools. Anti-Bullying Policy. Accessed June 14, 2011, from www.browardschools.com/schools/bullying.htm.

Cohn, A., and A. Canter. "Bullying: Facts for Schools and Parents." Accessed June 14, 2011, from www.nasponline.org/resources/factsheets/bullying_fs.aspx. Bethesda, MD: National Association of School Psychologists, 2003.

Davis, Stan, and Charisse Nixon, Ph.D. "The Youth Voice Project: Victimization and Strategies." Accessed April 1, 2011, from www.youthvoiceproject.com/YVPMarch2010.pdf. Erie, PA: Penn State, 2010.

Drew, Naomi. *No Kidding About Bullying: 125 Ready-to-Use Activities to Help Kids Manage Anger, Resolve Conflicts, Build Empathy, and Get Along* (Minneapolis: Free Spirit Publishing, 2010).

Elias, M. "Kids' Meanness Might Mean Health Risks When They Grow Up." *USA Today*, Sept. 26, 2002, p. D10.

Espelage, D. L., and S. M. Swearer. "Gender Differences in Bullying: Moving Beyond Mean Level Differences." In D. L. Espelage and S. M. Swearer (Eds.), *Bullying in American Schools: A Social-Ecological Perspective on Prevention and Intervention*, pp. 15–35. Mahwah, NJ: Erlbaum, 2004.

Fried, S., and P. Fried. *Bullies, Targets and Witnesses*. New York: Evans, 2003.

Garrett, A. G. *Bullying in American Schools*. Jefferson, NC: McFarlnad, 2003.

Girl Scout Research Institute. *Feeling Safe: What Girls Say*. New York: Girl Scout Research Institute, 2003.

GLSEN and Harris Interactive. *The Principal's Perspective: School Safety, Bullying and Harassment, A Survey of Public School Principals.* New York: GLSEN, 2008.

Janosz, M., I. Archembault, L. S. Pagani, S. Pascal, A. J. S. Morin, and F. Bowen. "Are There Detrimental Effects of Witnessing School Violence in Early Adolescence?" *The Journal of Adolescent Health*, December 2008, pp. 600–608.

Maine Project Against Bullying. "Welcome to Maine Project Against Bullying" [Fact sheet]. Accessed February 28, 2009, from lincoln.midcoast.com/~wps/against/ bullying.html.

Maines, B., and G. Robinson. *The Support Group Method Training Pack.* Thousand Oaks, CA: Sage, 2009.

Miller, T. (Ed.) *School Violence and Primary Prevention.* New York: Springer, 2008.

Mullin-Rindler, N. "Teasing and Bullying: Facts." Wellesley Centers for Women. Wellesley, MA. Accessed February 8, 2009, from www.wcwonline.org/content/ view/1286/299.

Olweus, D. "Bully/Victim Problems Among Schoolchildren: Basic Facts and Effects of a School-Based Intervention Program." In D. J. Pepler and K. H. Rubin (Eds.), *The Development and Treatment of Childhood Aggression*, pp. 411–448. Mahwah, NJ: Erlbaum, 1991.

Olweus, D. "Bullying or Peer Abuse at School: Facts and Intervention." *Current Directions in Psychological Science*, 4(6), pp. 196–200, 1995.

Olweus, D. and S. Limber. *Olweus Bullying Prevention Program: Teacher Guide.* Center City, MN: Hazelden, 2007.

Robers, S., Z. Zhang, J. Truman, and T. D. Snyder. "Indicators of School Crime and Safety: 2010. U.S. Department of Education." U.S. Department of Justice Office of Justice Programs, 2010.

Schreier, A., D. Wolke, K. Thomas, J. Horwood, C. Hollis, D. Gunnell, G. Lewis, A. Thompson, S. Zammit, L. Duffy, G. Salvi, and G. Harrison. "Prospective Study of Peer Victimization in Childhood and Psychotic Symptoms in a Nonclinical Population at Age 12 Years." *Archives of General Psychiatry*, 66(5), pp. 527–536. Accessed April 4, 2011, from archpsyc.ama.assn.org/cgi/content/ abstract/66/5/527.

Schwartz, J. "Violence in the Home Leads to Higher Rates of Childhood Bullying." UPI, via ClariNet. *University of Washington News.* Accessed June 14, 2011, from www.washington.edu/news/archive/26586 from Sept. 12, 2006.

Simmons, R. *Odd Girl Out.* New York: Harcourt, 2002.

Spurling, R. "The Bully-Free School Zone Character Education Program: A Study of the Impact on Five Western North Carolina Middle Schools." Unpublished doctoral dissertation. Johnson City, TN: East Tennessee State University, 2006.

Sullivan, K., M. Cleary, and G. Sullivan. *Bullying in Secondary Schools: What It Looks Like and How to Manage It.* Thousand Oaks, CA: Corwin Press, 2005.

CREATE A POSITIVE CLASSROOM

The tips and strategies in this section will help you create a classroom environment where everyone feels safe, accepted, and appreciated. In a positive classroom, students can learn, teachers can teach, and education—not behavior—is the focus.

These tips and strategies benefit everyone. Here are some good things you can expect to happen along the way:

Your students will learn how to:

- think and talk positively about themselves and others
- notice similarities and appreciate differences
- work together
- treat each other with kindness and respect
- give each other support and encouragement
- respond to bullying in ways that work

You'll discover how to:

- clearly communicate that bullying is not acceptable in your classroom
- reinforce your students' positive behaviors
- get to know and understand your students even better
- treat your students with greater kindness and respect
- model accepting, appropriate behavior in all kinds of situations
- teach your students skills that will help them resolve conflicts, affirm themselves and each other, manage anger, make friends, and be more assertive

EXPOSE THE MYTHS

There are many myths about bullying. The "True or False?" handout (page 37) will expose some of the myths and prompt students to think about what bullying is and how it affects everyone. Answers with brief explanations are given on page 38.

You might read the answers aloud, or have students come up with their own reasons why each statement is a myth. Allow time for discussion. Make copies of the answers to give to students during or after the discussion.

DEFINE BULLYING

Before you can solve (or prevent) a problem, you first have to define it. If you and your students did the "Expose the Myths" activity (above), everyone should have a general idea of what bullying isn't. (It isn't "just teasing," "normal," a "boy thing," etc.) You also want your students to agree on what it is. The process of defining it will help you arrive at a shared understanding and common language about bullying.

You might do this as a class, or divide the class into small groups and give them 10 minutes to work on a definition. Each group can choose one person to write down the group's ideas, and another to read the group's definition aloud when the class reconvenes.

Write students' definitions on the whiteboard or chart paper. Then work together to come up with a class definition of bullying. Here are some concepts you can introduce into the discussion to keep students on track:

- Bullying takes at least two people: a person who bullies and a person who is bullied.

- People often bully to feel strong and superior. They enjoy having power over others.

- People who bully use their power to hurt other people.

Your class definition might use different words but should include the basic elements of this statement:

> Bullying is when a stronger, more powerful person hurts or frightens a smaller or weaker person deliberately (on purpose) and repeatedly (again and again).

See page 4 for more about what bullying is. You might write your class definition on the whiteboard or chart paper and leave it there indefinitely, or have students write the definition in the notebook they use in your class.

BUILD ACCEPTANCE

When students accept each other, they are less likely to bully each other and more likely to defend kids who are targets of bullying. Here are three ways you can build acceptance in your classroom.

ACCEPTANCE STATEMENTS

Work with your class to come up with a list of "acceptance statements" everyone (or most) can agree on. (*Example:* "We are all unique. Our differences make us interesting.") Have students make posters, collages, bulletin boards, or displays illustrating the statements.

ACCEPTANCE PROJECTS

Ask your class to brainstorm ways to help people become more accepting of each other. What do they think everyone should know? How can they get their message across? Through songs? Skits? Stories? Poems? Posters? A school or class blog or website? Announcements over the P.A. system? Articles in the school paper?

Let your students make the important decisions about what types of projects to do. Be available to offer support and advice (and to suggest alternatives to projects that are clearly inappropriate), but try to let your students go wherever their creativity takes them. They might work individually or in small groups.

Go Further

Make a word cloud of your acceptance projects or acceptance statements. Go to a website such as www.wordle.net, type or paste your text into the window, and create your word cloud. Post it on your website, and if you have a Twitter account, use it to link to it.

When the projects are finished, show them off at an open house or parents' night. Invite family members, other teachers, and members of the community and the media to see what your students have accomplished and how they feel about acceptance.

"Our Classroom Is a Place Where . . ."

Distribute copies of the handout "Our Classroom Is a Place Where . . ." (page 39) and discuss each statement. If students agree with the statements, they can sign and date their handouts. Post them around the room to show that your classroom is a place where people accept each other.

Go Further

Send home copies of the handout so students can share them with their families.

When it's time to take down the handouts display, make a poster-size copy of the original handout and hang it on a wall in your classroom. Refer to it often throughout the year. Discuss it with your students, with parents and caregivers at conferences, and with visitors to your classroom.

TALK ABOUT BULLYING

Have a class discussion about bullying. Use the following questions as prompts, or come up with your own.

 IMPORTANT: Tell students not to name names or point fingers. This should be a general discussion, not a time for blaming or accusing.

1. Who can tell me what bullying is?

   If you and your students did the "Define Bullying" activity (page 10), someone can read the class definition.

2. What happens to people who are bullied? How do you think they feel?

3. How do you think people who bully feel?

4. What happens to people who are around bullying? What's it like to see someone get bullied? How does that make you feel?

5. Is there anyone who thinks bullying is a problem in our school? What makes you think that?

6. Is there anyone who thinks bullying is a problem in our classroom? What makes you think that?

7. Who would like to have a bully free classroom?

8. What would it take to make our classroom bully free? What are some ideas for doing this?

Go Further

Write students' ideas on the whiteboard or chart paper. Then have the class vote for the top five. Try their ideas for a week or two. Let students assess their own progress toward making your classroom bully free.

NAME BULLYING BEHAVIORS

What is bullying? Your students probably know the answer(s) to this question. Ask them and list their responses on the whiteboard or chart paper. Your list might include several (or all) of the following. If your students focus mostly on physical bullying (e.g., hitting, kicking), introduce some of the other behaviors listed here (e.g., acting rude, embarrassing people, ignoring people). Students need to understand that bullying encompasses a broad spectrum of behaviors, none of which are "normal" or acceptable.

- act like they rule the world
- act mean
- act rude
- attack people
- boss people around
- brag about being tough
- break people's things
- carry weapons
- cheat
- damage people's things
- embarrass people
- force people to hand over their money
- force people to hand over their possessions
- frighten people
- gossip
- harass people
- haze people
- hit people
- humiliate people
- hurt people's feelings
- ignore people
- insult people
- intimidate people
- kick people
- laugh at people
- leave people out
- lie
- make fun of people
- make obscene gestures
- make people do things they don't want to do
- make people feel helpless
- make people feel inferior
- make people feel invisible
- make people feel uncomfortable
- make racist or sexist comments
- name-call
- pick on or attack people because of their race, religion, gender, family background, culture, etc.
- pick on or attack people because they're different in some way
- push people
- put people down
- refuse to talk to people

GO FURTHER

Turn the list above into a class pledge. Provide an extra-large piece of posterboard or butcher paper, markers, magazines (for cutting out pictures), tape, glue, and scissors. Write across the top in big letters: "As a class, we pledge NOT to . . ." Then let students add words, phrases, illustrations, and pictures to create a colorful poster for your classroom wall—or the hall outside your classroom. They can all sign their names across the bottom. Another option is to use Glogster, a poster-building website (www.glogster.com). Students can scan and upload drawings and type parts of the pledge into word bubbles, boxes, and various other shapes, and they can add other elements, such as graphics, photos, music, and video. All of the elements on their posters can be tweaked in many ways, such as with color and shadow or by tilt, shape, and size, and posters can be shared the same way a blog post can.

- reject people
- say nasty things about people
- say sarcastic things to people
- scare people
- scream
- shove people
- spread rumors
- steal
- swear
- take people's things
- taunt people
- tease people
- tell mean jokes
- threaten people
- touch people in rude or abusive ways
- use physical violence
- use verbal taunts
- write nasty things about people
- yell

SHARE STORIES ABOUT BULLYING

Distribute copies of the handout "Bullying Stories" (page 40). Tell your students that they will use the handouts to write about their own experiences with bullying—as someone who was bullied; as someone who bullied another person; as someone who witnessed a bullying incident and did nothing about it; and as someone who witnessed a bullying incident and either got help or tried to stop it.

Call attention to the "No Names Rule" at the top of the handout. If some students don't understand how they can tell their stories without using names, give examples. ("Someone called me a bad name." "I knocked someone's books off his desk on purpose." "I saw one person trip another, but I didn't say anything." "I told someone to stop pushing my friend.")

Divide the class into small groups (no more than five students each).

IMPORTANT: If you're aware that one student in your classroom has been bullying another, make sure those two students aren't in the same group.

Allow quiet time for students to write their stories. Then allow time for them to share their stories within their groups. Reconvene the class and ask a spokesperson from each group to briefly summarize the stories.

Have a class discussion about the stories. You might ask questions like these:

- Did you hear stories about people getting bullied? How did those stories make you feel?
- Did you hear stories about people bullying others? How did those stories make you feel?
- If you saw or heard someone being bullied, what would you do?
- Did you hear good ways to stop bullying or get help? Are there any ideas you might try if you see or hear someone being bullied in the future?

You might end by saying, "To all of you who saw or heard bullying and did something about it—congratulations! You're bully busters!" For those who didn't, you might add, "You can be a bully buster, too, next time you witness bullying."

TAKE A SURVEY

How much bullying goes on in your classroom, and what kinds? You've probably noticed specific instances, and students might have told you about others. But most bullying goes *unnoticed* and *unreported*.

It goes unnoticed because:

- Bullying is usually done when adults aren't around to see it.
- Bullying is usually done in ways that adults aren't aware of or don't notice (it is done in secret).

It goes unreported because:

- Kids are ashamed of being bullied or afraid of retaliation.

- Kids are worried that adults can't or won't help them, or that adults will blame them.

- Students have reported bullying to adults in the past and no action was taken, or the action didn't help.

- Bystanders—or witnesses—don't want to get involved, or they don't interpret what they're seeing as bullying, but as "teasing" or "normal" or "kids being kids" behavior.

If you want to know what's happening in your classroom, ask your students. One of the best, simplest, and least intimidating ways to do this is by using a survey.

You might use one of the surveys on pages 41–46 (or the early elementary version of the bullying survey included on the CD-ROM). Or invite your students, their parents, and other teachers and staff to help you create a survey. If your school or district is using a bully prevention program, a survey instrument might already exist.

The primary purpose of the surveys is to gather information about the types of experiences your students are having, not to point fingers at specific individuals. If you want a survey to help you identify students who are being bullied, have students write their names on it. Otherwise, keep it anonymous. When you ask students to sign their names, some might be reluctant to admit to certain items. Anonymity might lead to more honest responses.

Depending on your students' age(s) and reading level(s), you might want to read a survey aloud. Some students might need individual assistance in completing the survey.

Give each student as much privacy as possible when completing a survey. Tell students that the survey *isn't* a test (they won't be graded), but it's *like* a test in two important ways: No looking at anyone else's survey, and no talking during the survey.

About "This Week in School" (pages 41–42)

This survey describes things that might happen to a student during a typical week. About half of the things described are pleasant or neutral; about half are unpleasant. This keeps the focus on students' experiences in general, not just bullying.

Introduce the survey with a brief explanation. *Example:*

"This checklist describes things that might or might not happen to you in school. Like: 'This week in school, another student in my class called me names.' Or: 'This week in school, another student in my class said something nice to me.' Read each statement and think about the past week. How often did this happen to you? Never? Once? More than once? Answer by putting a checkmark in that column."

Since the survey asks about "this week," it's best to give it on a Friday. If your students are very young, you might want to ask them what happened to them yesterday or even today; their memories of an entire week might be sketchy or inaccurate.

Use the survey as is or adapt it to meet the needs of your students. If you adapt it, make sure to include a balance of positive, neutral, and negative items. Also make sure to include these six key statements:

4. tried to kick me

8. said they'd beat me up

10. tried to make me give them money

23. tried to hurt me

36. tried to break something of mine

38. tried to hit me

For these six statements:

- Add up the number of times a checkmark was placed under "more than once." Do this separately for each statement. (*Example:* For "4. tried to kick me," three students said "more than once.")

- Divide the score for each statement by the number of surveys completed to get the percentage of student responses. (*Example:* 3 students ÷ 25 in the class = 12%)

- Add all six percentages. (*Example:* 12 + 8 + 12 + 20 + 5 + 10 = 67%)

- Divide this number by six. (*Example:* 67 divided by 6 = 11.16%)

This gives you an idea of how many students in your classroom are being bullied or at risk of being bullied.

You can do the same math for checkmarks placed under "once" for the six key statements. This gives you an idea of the level of aggression in your classroom.

The survey asks students to indicate their sex. You'll probably notice gender differences when you look at the results. The six key statements have a bias toward physical bullying, which seems to be more common among boys. If you want to get a sense of bullying among girls, pay special attention to girls' responses to these six statements:

1. called me names

6. was mean to me because I'm different

34. laughed at me in a way that hurt my feelings

35. said they would tell on me

37. told a lie about me

39. made me feel bad about myself

About the Three "Bullying Surveys" (pages 43–46 and CD-ROM)

On pages 43–44, you'll find a survey for elementary students, and on pages 45–46 you'll find one for middle school students. For very young students, such as kindergartners and first or second graders, an early elementary survey is on the CD-ROM.

You may want to create your own survey, based on these, adapting them to meet the needs of your students. For example, you might want to:

- limit it to questions about bullying in your classroom (skipping those about recess, lunch, the bathroom, and the halls)

- expand it with questions about bullying on the way to and from school (at the bus stop, on the bus, while walking or biking), at school-sponsored events (sporting events, assemblies, fairs, concerts, club meetings), and elsewhere in the school building or on the grounds (in the locker room, between buildings, in the gym)

- add questions about specific types of bullying (teasing, name-calling, pushing, shoving, hitting, kicking, shouting, tripping,

intimidating, ignoring, rejecting, threatening, taking possessions, excluding, swearing, spreading rumors, lying, harassing)

- gather demographic information (race, ethnic background, religion) to try to determine whether a particular group of students is being targeted

When you administer the survey, you may give it to the whole class, use it to interview individual students you suspect are being bullied, or use it to interview small groups of students to get a feeling for what types of bullying and how much bullying goes on in your classroom.

SET RULES

Establish and enforce class rules about bullying and behavior. Rules clearly communicate that bullying is unacceptable and that you expect positive behavior. They also meet students' physical and psychological needs for safety; it's hard for students to learn when they're intimidated, being threatened, and scared, or when they're witnessing intimidating, threatening, and scary behavior.

For rules to be effective, they should be:

- created with student input
- short and simple
- easy to understand
- specific
- agreed upon and accepted by everyone
- enforceable
- enforced consistently and fairly
- communicated to and supported by parents, other teachers, and staff
- reviewed periodically and updated when needed

Note: If your school or district has already established rules about bullying and behavior, share these with your students. If the language seems too complicated, have students put the rules in their own words.

If you're free to make your own class rules, get everyone involved. Have a class discussion or break up into small groups. Ask students to come up with answers to these questions:

- What kind of classroom do you want to have?

- What can everyone do to make this happen?

When students set their own rules (instead of being told to follow rules imposed by adults), they learn to manage their own behaviors. Work together to come up with a list of rules; depending on the age of your students, you might limit the total number to 5 or 10 (the fewer the better). *Examples:*

1. Bullying is not allowed in our classroom.

2. We don't tease, call people names, or put people down.

3. We don't hit, shove, kick, or punch.

4. If we see someone being bullied, we speak up and stop it (if we can) or go for help right away.

5. When we do things as a group, we make sure everyone is included and no one is left out.

6. We make new students feel welcome.

7. We listen respectfully to each other's opinions.

8. We treat each other with kindness and respect.

9. We respect each other's property. (School property, too.)

10. We look for the good in others and value differences.

You might write the rules on a poster titled "Our Class Rules" and have everyone sign their names.

What consequences will students face if they break the rules, and how will you enforce them? This might depend on existing school or district rules; if you have some flexibility, work with your class to determine fair and reasonable consequences.

Post the rules in your classroom where everyone can see them. For a time, you might start each

GO FURTHER

Communicate the rules and consequences in a letter to parents, and share them with other teachers and staff.

day by reading the rules aloud (or having a student read them). Once you feel confident that your students know the rules—and you've seen evidence that they're following them—you can read them weekly. Every month or so, review the rules with your class to see if any changes are needed. Don't hesitate to revise the rules. Tell your class that the rules aren't written in stone and there's always room for improvement.

HELP STUDENTS UNDERSTAND CYBERBULLYING

Cyberbullying is when one or more individuals intentionally and repeatedly sends or posts hurtful, harmful, embarrassing, humiliating, hostile, threatening, or harassing information through email, text messages, instant messages, websites, social networking sites, electronic photographs, or videos. It has become common because it is easy to do (just a few keystrokes), it can be anonymous, and the bullying can be witnessed by many people in a short amount of time. Because of its rapid spread to a wide audience, cyberbullying can lead the target to feel like there is no escape and can be even more devastating and hurtful than other forms of bullying.

Kids who cyberbully are often different from kids who bully in other ways. Whereas kids who bully face-to-face may enjoy the power they feel in getting a reaction out of their targets, many kids who cyberbully may lack the courage or physical strength to be cruel to someone in person. Or they may be motivated by anger or revenge rather than power. Many kids who cyberbully do not realize they are cyberbullying. They may not understand the effect of what they do, or they may forward a mean email or text without thinking much about it. Because of the technology involved, cyberbullying is more common among older kids than younger ones.

Because it's not always clear what cyberbullying is, it is very important for students to learn about it and how to deal with it. To open your discussion, write "What is cyberbullying?" on your whiteboard or chart paper, and ask for answers. Write students' replies on the board without commenting on their accuracy or validity.

Distribute the "What Is Cyberbullying?" worksheet (page 48) and read the definition aloud or ask a student to read it aloud. Examine and discuss this definition in light of the student comments you recorded. Ask students: "Do any parts of this definition surprise you? Which parts? Why?" Have students rewrite the definition in their own words.

Tell your students that cyberbullying comes in a variety of forms, and urge them to think of any examples they may know of from their own lives. Perhaps they were targets of cyberbullying, or perhaps they have cyberbullied someone else, even if they didn't think of it that way at the time. Or they may be aware of cyberbullying that is occurring among other students.

Give students some examples of cyberbullying using the list on pages 4–5 and any others that may be pertinent to your classroom situation. Here are other things that are (or may lead to) cyberbullying. Adjust this list as appropriate for the age of your students.

- **Flaming:** Posting or sending offensive messages over the Internet, most often on an online forum or bulletin board; flaming by more than one person can result in a flame war, or angry online argument

  Example: Members of a sports blog insulting each other personally over their team preferences

- **Harassment:** Repeatedly sending mean, insulting, or threatening messages

  Example: Sending lots of mean emails or text messages to someone to scare the person or force him or her to do something

- **Denigration:** "Dissing" someone online; sending or posting gossip or rumors about a person to damage his or her reputation or friendships

  Example: Creating a "We Hate [person's name]" website where jokes, cartoons, gossip, and rumors about a person are posted

- **Impersonation:** Pretending to be someone else and sending or posting material to get that person in trouble or danger or to damage that person's reputation or friendships

  Example: Getting someone's password and sending emails from his or her account

- **Outing:** Sharing someone's secrets or embarrassing information or images online

  Example: Secretly taking someone's picture (e.g., while they're undressed in the locker room) and posting it on a website or sending it via text message

- **Trickery:** Tricking someone into revealing secrets or embarrassing information, then sharing it online

  Example: Sending someone text messages pretending to be a friend, then forwarding their personal responses to other people with a critical or insulting comment

- **Exclusion:** Intentionally and cruelly excluding someone from an online group

  Example: The leader of a clique pressuring others in the group to "unfriend" someone on Facebook

- **Cyberstalking:** Repeated, intense harassment and denigration that includes threats or creates significant fear

  Examples: Spreading mean rumors about an ex-boyfriend or ex-girlfriend; using technology to repeatedly give unwanted romantic attention

Referring again to the "What Is Cyberbullying?" worksheet, ask students to fill in the blank lines with specific examples of cyberbullying. These examples may be things they have experienced or heard about. Ask for volunteers to share examples they have written. Be sure to let them know they should not use any real names. For example, say, "A person sends tons of texts threatening someone."

Finally, discuss with students the reasons why cyberbullying has become such a big problem:

- it is easy to do

- it can be anonymous

- the bullying can be witnessed by many people in a short period of time

Students and others can work to prevent cyberbullying in much the same ways they can other kinds of bullying: by not going along with it or accepting it, by standing up for those who are bullied, and by reporting cyberbullying to adults. In many states, cyberbullying is against the law, and adults may report it to authorities.

The best defense against cyberbullying is education and prevention, because it can be difficult for schools to discipline students for cyberbullying that takes place off of school grounds or outside of school hours. Some schools have been sued on the grounds of free speech for disciplining children for cyberbullying (and have been on the losing end of the suit). When cyberbullying has occurred, work with the parents involved to alleviate the behavior. Consider adding a provision to your school's discipline policy that reserves the right to discipline actions taken off campus if they are intended to hurt, scare, or otherwise adversely affect a student while in school.

Go Further

Stay up to date on cyberbullying by frequently researching on the Internet. Many excellent books have been written on this topic. Visit the websites listed here to find out more about preventing and stopping cyberbullying.

Anti-Defamation League
adl.org/cyberbullying
Find tips on responding to cyberbullying and staying safe on the Internet. Teachers and administrators can sign up for workshops from A World of Difference Institute, find resources about cyberbullying dangers, and use their free classroom materials and lesson plans on cyberbullying.

Center for Safe and Responsible Internet Use
csriu.org
The Center for Safe and Responsible Internet Use offers professional resources; consulting services to school districts, administrators, and school attorneys; and articles and reports for school professionals. Peruse the site for cyberbullying resources and downloads.

Cyberbullying Research Center
cyberbullying.us
The Cyberbullying Research Center is the publisher of *Bullying Beyond the Schoolyard: Preventing and Responding to Cyberbullying,* and the site is a clearinghouse of information about cyberbullying. Find downloadable PDFs of academic journal articles, research summaries, and fact sheets on such topics as sexting, cyberbullying prevention, self-esteem, and trends in social networking.

CyberTipline
cybertipline.com
Part of the National Center for Missing and Exploited Children, the CyberTipline is a way to report exploitation of children.

National Crime Prevention Council
ncpc.org
Join various campaigns, such as "Cyberbullying: Don't Write It, Don't Forward It" or "Bullying Prevention," which alerts parents to signs that their child may be getting bullied and offers advice on how parents can help their children. The site includes information about what cyberbullying is, why teens take part in it, and how kids can prevent it. Also included are downloadable resources about bullying.

Net Family News

netfamilynews.org

This blog describes its content as "kid-tech news for parents." You'll find up-to-date news on kids' Internet use, anti-bullying legislation, social networking, and more.

SafeKids.com

safekids.com

A blog about online safety, this site offers ideas for dealing with and stopping cyberbullying, preventing sexting, and teaching kids how to be civil online.

Stop Cyberbullying

stopcyberbullying.org

Part of the Wired Safety Group (wiredsaftey.org), this site includes a form you can fill out to report cyberbullying, and each informative Web page can be printed as a Word document or as a PDF for easy dissemination. Join the Stop Cyberbullying campaign and report cyberbullying via Facebook, cell phone, Twitter, or YouTube, and learn about cyberbullying and the law.

WiredSafety

wiredsafety.org

This site contains information about staying safe on the Internet, with tips on Facebook privacy, how to respond to cyberbullying, how to prevent and deal with cyberstalking, and what the law says about it all.

TEACH CYBERBULLYING PREVENTION

Be sure you have done the previous activity, "Help Students Understand Cyberbullying," before you do this one. Make enough copies of the "How to Prevent and Stop Cyberbullying" handout for every student and pass them out. Review the handout together as a class, making sure everyone understands the content. Answer any questions students have. Then put students into groups of three or four and have them look at the examples of cyberbullying they collected on their "What Is Cyberbullying?" handouts. (If you know that certain students are bullying targets of other students, be sure they are not grouped with the students who bully them.) Direct students to take turns reading cyberbullying examples from their sheets and discussing with the group what they could do to stop or prevent them from actually happening.

Give groups about 10 to 15 minutes to do this, then ask for volunteers to tell the class about examples of cyberbullying and the solutions they came up with. Afterward, ask students to take the handout home to their families and discuss it with them.

BUILD AWARENESS ABOUT RELATIONAL BULLYING

Most adults equate bullying with physical and verbal abuse, but social or relational bullying can be just as harmful. What is social bullying? It can be any behavior designed to hurt people by damaging or manipulating their relationships, and it can include subtle to very aggressive behavior. Girls and boys both engage in all forms of bullying, but girls tend to be especially skillful in relational bullying. Girls know that most girls highly value their relationships, which means they are particularly vulnerable to attacks that damage those relationships. When a relationship is damaged or destroyed, it is very hurtful and can leave long-lasting emotional scars. Like other forms of bullying, relational bullying can lead to depression, poor academic performance, loneliness, frustration, anger, eating disorders, overwhelming anxiety, school phobia, and more.

To prevent all forms of bullying, every school in your district should have a school-wide anti-bullying program that addresses all forms of bullying, and everyone in your school must understand that relational bullying is real and not just "girls being girls" or "boys being boys." Students who engage in relational bullying are being mean and hurtful and are breaking school rules. In fact, when they mistreat someone in this way every day, they are engaging in a form of violence. The definition of violence is anything that is hurtful to a person's body, feelings, or things.

Unfortunately, some district-wide anti-bullying polices do not address social bullying. If your school or district does not, talk to the appropriate administrators about it.

When Does Relational Bullying Begin?

Relational bullying has been observed as early as the preschool years. I recall a story a teacher told me about a preschool girl who was sitting at a table with other girls. She said, "Who likes ice cream?" and raised her hand. The other girls raised their hands in unison. She said, "Who likes to watch movies?" and raised her hand. The other girls raised their hands in unison. Then she asked, "Who likes Susan?" and frowned and did not raise her hand. No one in the group raised their hand. Susan was also sitting at the table, saddened and humiliated.

What Does Relational Bullying Look Like?

Relational bullying takes many forms, but they fit into two major categories: *proactive* or *reactive*. When students mistreat others in order to achieve a valued goal, such as raising their status in a clique, their bullying is proactive. When students mistreat someone in retaliation for something, their bullying is reactive. Relational bullying can include social isolation and rejection, manipulation, cyberbullying, intimidation, and spreading rumors and lies. It can be motivated by jealousy, desire for power and control, desire for popularity, desire for acceptance by selected individuals, and even fear of losing something of value.

Relational bullying includes:

- Ignoring someone
- Purposely excluding someone from a group or event
- Convincing peers not to associate with someone
- Gossiping or spreading rumors about someone
- Exposing someone's secrets or telling embarrassing things about someone's private life
- Teasing, taunting, or insulting someone in front of his or her friends
- Manipulating relationships by lying about someone or dividing or building alliances

These acts can be done in person, online (cyberbullying), or through networks of friends.

Increase Awareness

An important step toward reducing relational bullying is simply raising awareness about it in your classroom and in your school. As with cyberbullying (pages 16–19), many students engaging in these behaviors may not think of them as bullying. Discuss relational bullying with your students, and let them know that excluding, humiliating, spreading rumors, and relational aggression are unacceptable. These are acts of bullying, and students can be disciplined under your anti-bullying policy.

After your discussion, have students name as many examples of relational bullying as they can and assign one or a few students to make a poster to hang in the classroom. It may be especially beneficial for students who are engaging in relational bullying to be included in the poster-making project.

Many adults in your building may be unaware of relational bullying as well. Talk to them about the characteristics of this type of bullying, perhaps sharing with them the poster your class made. Urge them to help you observe students, especially students in cliques, when they are in the cafeteria, in gym class, on the playground, in the halls, and elsewhere for clues to which students are group leaders and followers, who comes across as loners, and how they all are interacting.

Go Further

To learn more about relational bullying, specifically among girls, read *Little Girls Can Be Mean: Four Steps to Bully-Proof Girls in the Early Grades* by Michelle Anthony, M.A., Ph.D., and Reyna Lindert, Ph.D. (St. Martin's Griffin, 2010).

As an adult, it's important to model good relational behavior. Don't exclude others and don't gossip or talk badly about others behind their backs. Children will follow your lead.

BE AWARE OF CLIQUES

A *clique* is an exclusive set of people, usually a group that is led mostly by one person who decides who is in and who is out, what is cool and what is not. Generally, members of a clique have to conform by dressing, talking, and acting the same way. Often, members of the clique base their sense of self-worth on what others in the clique think about them, and members of the clique are always in danger of being kicked out or excluded from the group. Membership in a clique generally depends on social status or other factors rather than genuine affection or loyalty to each other. Members of the clique label people outside the clique and often mistreat them.

A clique is not the same as a healthy group of friends. Real friends really like each other and accept each other as they are. Friends don't have to emulate the leader of their group (if they even have a leader), and they generally treat each other with respect. They don't expect each other to conform. They do not dictate who their friends can spend time with.

In short, cliques often lead to relational bullying.

Have a general discussion about cliques with your class, going over the main points from this section, then distribute the "Cliques Survey" handout (page 49) to every student. Go over the instructions together, emphasizing that they should not put their names on the sheet. Give them about five minutes to complete the survey and then collect them. Keep the surveys, as they will help you be aware of cliques in your class and school and be on the alert for relational bullying situations. Let students know that, as with any kind of bullying they witness or are subjected to, they can come to you any time if they want to report a clique or relational bullying. They can do this in person, with a note, or any other way.

COPE WITH CLIQUES

It is also important for you to discuss the do's and don'ts of coping with a clique. Have a class discussion around the question, "If kids in a clique are mistreating you or a friend, what can you do?" Ask for suggestions and record them on the whiteboard or chart paper, discussing each idea as needed. Here are some guidelines:

DON'T:

- threaten them
- make fun of them
- try to embarrass them
- criticize them
- talk about them
- try to earn their favor by impressing them
- retaliate
- let them ruin your day

DO:

- avoid them when you can
- mind your own business and just be yourself (being different from them is okay—in fact, it is probably terrific!)
- like yourself
- be kind to everyone
- talk to yourself in a positive way: "I'm okay. I'm a good person. Plenty of other people like me."
- seek to be friends with others who are good people
- tell an adult if they are hurting you or making you sad

Tell students that it is much more beneficial to a person's health and happiness if he or she has a best friend or one or two good friends than if he or she belongs to a clique. A good friend is:

- Someone you can trust

- Someone who will always defend you

- Someone who will try to stop a rumor about you and tell you about the rumor

- Someone who encourages you to be the best you can be

- Someone who encourages you to do what is right

- Someone who always tries to treat you right

Besides all those great things, good friends also help kids be more bully-proof. Say to your students, *If you have a good friend:*

- You are less likely to be bullied.

- If you *are* bullied, it's less likely that you will be bullied for a long time.

- You are less likely to get as upset about being bullied.

- You are less likely to get angry and take your anger out on others.

For kids who need help making and keeping friends, refer to "Teach Friendship Skills" (page 65), "Get Students Involved in Groups" (page 73), "Teach Students to Affirm Each Other" (page 76), and "Teach Leadership Skills" (page 138).

GO FURTHER

Cliques, Phonies, and Other Baloney by Trevor Romain (Free Spirit Publishing, 1998).

Coping with Cliques by Susan Sprague (Instant Help Books, A Division of New Harbinger Publications, Inc., 2008).

DESIGNATE YOUR CLASSROOM BULLY FREE

If you and your students did the "Talk About Bullying" activity (page 11), chances are they all agreed that they would like to have a bully free classroom (question 7).

Ask if they're willing to designate their classroom as bully free—a place where people accept each other, value each other, and treat each other with kindness and respect. If they are, brainstorm ways to formalize and publicize your class commitment. *Examples:*

1. Make a poster or banner announcing "This Is a Bully Free Classroom." Display it in the hall outside the classroom.*

2. If your class publishes a newsletter or newspaper, devote an issue to the topic of what it means to be a bully free classroom. Invite students to write articles, draw cartoons, or conduct interviews.

3. Write a press release announcing that your classroom has decided to be bully free. Send it to your local media (newspapers, magazines, radio stations, TV stations). They might follow up with a story about your students.

GO FURTHER

Have students visit other classrooms and encourage them to become bully free. They can also meet with the principal, explain what your class is doing, and ask him or her to announce that your whole school is committed to being bully free.

---

*If you'd like, you can order a big, bright "Bully Free Zone" poster. Contact Free Spirit Publishing at 1-800-735-7323 or www.freespirit.com for ordering information.

TEACH ANGER MANAGEMENT SKILLS

What happens to most of us when we're in danger or under stress? We experience the fight-or-flight response. We battle the cause of the danger we perceive or the stress we experience (fight), or we run as fast as we can to get away (flight).

When students are bullied, running away is one option; sometimes it's the *only* option. Your students need to know that fighting is not acceptable except in cases where self-defense is essential.

What can they do instead of fighting or trying to hurt someone back? They can learn and practice other ways to manage their anger.

Distribute copies of the handout "20 Things to Do Instead of Hurting Someone Back" (page 50) and go over it with your students. Explain that this handout gives them 20 different ways to manage their anger. Ask if they know other ways that work, and list their responses on the whiteboard or chart paper.

Go Further

What to Do When Your Temper Flares: A Kid's Guide to Overcoming Problems with Anger by Dawn Heubner (Magination Press, 2007).

How to Take the Grrrr Out of Anger by Elizabeth Verdick and Marjorie Lisovskis (Free Spirit Publishing, 2002).

PROMOTE STRUCTURED ACTIVITIES

Much bullying takes place during unstructured activities, especially recess. Encourage your students to plan ahead for those times and tell you their plans. What will they do during recess? Will they play a game? What kind of game? Who will play? What about the students who won't take part in the game—what will they do? If you're one of the playground supervisors, you can watch to make sure students follow through with their plans. If you're not, you can ask them to report back to you after recess. Try to get them in the habit of deciding in advance how they will spend unstructured time. If they have difficulty making plans, offer suggestions.

Since kids who bully tend to be older, stronger, and more powerful than their targets, you might also explore the possibility of assigning older and younger children to different playground areas. Work out an arrangement with the principal and other teachers.

PROVIDE SUPERVISION

It's believed that some children start bullying because the supervision they get at home is minimal or nonexistent. And kids tend to do their bullying where adults can't observe and intervene. You can't supervise your students at home, but you can—and should—supervise them at school. This may be one of the most effective bully-prevention strategies available to you.

1. Start by considering the level of supervision in your own classroom. Are you able to keep an eye on all (or most) of your students all (or most) of the time? If you're in charge of a large class, this may be difficult or even impossible. How can you bring more adults into your classroom? Arrange for an aide or student teacher. Welcome parent helpers. If local high schools have service learning requirements, find out if students can earn credits for helping out in your classroom.

2. Are you aware of bully problems on the playground, in the lunchroom, or in the hallways? Get together with other teachers and administrators and share what you've heard (or overheard). Increase the number of playground and lunchroom supervisors. Since lockers are common places for bullying, teachers should keep an eye on lockers during class changes.

It's true that spending more time supervising students will increase your workload. But the results are worth it. More supervision equals fewer bullying incidents, especially serious incidents. More positive supervision—where you interact with students, suggest ways they can interact with each other, and model kindness, acceptance, affirmation, and getting along—promotes more positive behavior. Before long, everyone feels safer and more secure, the school climate noticeably improves—and you're spending less time dealing with bully problems.

KEEP GRADES PRIVATE

Most students are concerned about their grades. Those with very high or very low grades are at increased risk of being bullied. For this reason (among others), you should keep grades and test scores private.

- If your students grade their own papers, collect them afterward and record the grades yourself. Don't ask them to call out their results.

- If you have students grade each other's homework assignments and quizzes, reconsider this practice. It probably saves you time, but is it good for your students? Have you noticed any who seem embarrassed or uncomfortable when their papers are being graded by their classmates? Have you noticed students making fun of someone else's papers? Even if you haven't witnessed these behaviors personally, it doesn't mean they're not happening.

- Never discuss a student's grades where other students might overhear.

- Don't post "A" papers or high test scores in your classroom. Celebrate students' achievements in other ways.

USE QUOTATIONS AS TEACHING TOOLS

Collect quotations about friendship, peace, peacemaking, self-esteem, assertiveness, tolerance, understanding, acceptance, kindness, respect, and other topics related to creating a positive environment in your school and classroom. Invite your students to bring in quotations they find.

Begin each day by posting a positive quotation, then ask your students to offer their thoughts on what it means—and how it applies to their own lives. Ask them to keep the quotation in mind throughout the day (you might leave it on the board all day). *Tip:* Quotations also make good journal writing assignments.

Here are several quotations you may want to use to start your collection:

- "If you judge people, you have no time to love them." **Mother Teresa**

- "A friend is a present you give yourself." **Robert Louis Stevenson**

- "We each need to do what we can to help one another no matter how tiny it is. If we do something for peace—each of us—we can all make the difference." **Mairead Corrigan Maguire (1976 Nobel Peace Prize Laureate)**

- "Friendship is the only cement that will ever hold the world together." **Woodrow Wilson**

- "Blessed are we who can laugh at ourselves, for we shall never cease to be amused." **Anonymous**

- "Friendship with oneself is all-important, because without it one cannot be friends with anyone else." **Eleanor Roosevelt**

- "Peace cannot be kept by force. It can only be achieved by understanding." **Albert Einstein**

- "All we are saying is give peace a chance." **John Lennon**

- "The highest result of education is tolerance." **Helen Keller**

SET AND REVIEW WEEKLY GOALS

Start each week with a brief discussion of how everyone can work together to create a positive classroom environment. Set specific goals everyone can agree on and work toward. For ideas, you might review your class rules (see "Set Rules," pages 15–16), acceptance statements (see "Build Acceptance," pages 10–11), or students' ideas for making the classroom bully free (see "Designate Your Classroom Bully Free," page 22). You might ask questions like these:

- What can we do this week so everyone feels safe, accepted, and appreciated?
- What can we do to prevent bullying?
- How will we treat each other?
- How will we expect to be treated?
- What specific actions can help us all have a great week?

As students offer ideas, write them on the whiteboard or chart paper. Try to summarize the ideas into a single, simple statement of goals. Leave it on the board for the entire week.

On Wednesday, review the goals statement with the students. Ask questions like:

- Are we meeting our goals as a class?
- Is there anything we need to work harder on?

On Friday, look back on the week. Ask questions like:

- Did we meet our goals this week?
- In general, how did people treat each other during the week?
- Did we all have a good week? Why or why not?
- What can we do next week to improve?

Invite students' ideas about ways to make your classroom even friendlier, more peaceful, and more accepting. Use those ideas as starters for next week's goal-setting discussion.

Tip: For another approach, see "Assess the Week" (page 30).

ASSIGN RELATED READING

Have students read and report on books about bullying, friendship, conflict, and acceptance.* Discuss them as a class, or have students write original stories featuring characters they encountered in the books. How would these characters handle a fight on the playground? How about a shoving match in the hall? Teasing? Rejection? Hurt feelings? What else? Invite your students to come up with their own suggestions for situations they'd like to portray.

Reading and writing are reasonably non-threatening ways to explore issues of friendship, rejection, prejudice, acceptance, conflict, bullying, and other topics.

TEACH CONFLICT RESOLUTION SKILLS

Conflict between people is normal and inevitable, and not all conflict is harmful or bad. *Destructive* conflict damages relationships, creates bad feelings, and leads to future problems. But *constructive* conflict helps us learn, grow, and change for the better. We see things from other perspectives. We become more open-minded, tolerant, and accepting. We build stronger relationships with the people in our lives.

What makes the difference? How we choose to *manage* the conflicts we experience. It takes (at least) two people to start and sustain a conflict. If both agree to seek a positive resolution, half the battle is won.

Everyone benefits from learning and practicing conflict resolution skills. Kids who tend to bully discover the real power of solving problems without using force or intimidation. Targets are empowered to seek solutions instead of giving up and giving in. Your classroom becomes a place where people are willing to work together.

*See "Books for Children" in "Resources" (pages 161–165) for suggestions. You might also ask your school librarian or the children's librarian at your local public library to point you toward appropriate books.

BULLY FREE **IMPORTANT:** Conflict resolution is a general strategy to build a positive environment and show kids they can resolve issues in a civil, win-win manner. **It is *not* a tool to use in most bullying situations.** Bullying is not a typical conflict, because the balance of power is not even. Students who bully may derive even more power (and enjoyment) from hearing that their targets are afraid or hurt. Instead, bullies need to be held accountable for their actions. Do not use conflict resolution in bullying situations.

Conflict resolution isn't learned (or taught) in a day. For best results, you'll probably want to use a conflict resolution program. Many good ones are available; talk with your principal to find out if your school or district has a preference or has already chosen a program.

Note: Research shows that conflict resolution programs *work*. Students who are not trained in conflict resolution are more likely to withdraw from conflicts or use force in conflict situations. Students who are trained in conflict resolution are more likely to face conflicts, use problem solving to negotiate solutions—and have a more positive attitude toward school in general.*

If you don't yet have access to a conflict resolution program, there's a basic approach you can teach your students right away. Distribute copies of the handout "8 Steps to Conflict Resolution" (page 51). Lead students through it step-by-step. Reinforce it with practice, role plays, skits, or whatever you think will reach your students most effectively.

> ## Go Further
>
> *Training Peer Helpers: Coaching Youth to Communicate, Solve Problems, and Make Decisions* by Barbara B. Varenhorst (Search Institute Press, 2010). Based on Search Institute's 40 Developmental Assets, this handy guide includes 15 peer-training sessions that help prepare students for resolving peer conflicts. Includes a CD-ROM with handouts.

EXPLORE THE LIVES OF FAMOUS PEACEMAKERS

Jane Addams. Amnesty International. Menachem Begin. His Holiness the Dalai Lama of Tibet. Mikhail Gorbachev. The International Committee of the Red Cross. Martin Luther King Jr. Aung San Suu Kyi. Nelson Mandela. Mother Teresa. Barack Obama. Linus Pauling. Yitzhak Rabin. Albert Schweitzer. Rigoberta Menchú Tum. Desmond Tutu. Lech Walesa. Elie Wiesel. Betty Williams. Jody Williams. What do these people and organizations have in common? All are winners of the Nobel Peace Prize, perhaps the world's most revered and prestigious award.

Have students research a Nobel Peace Prize winner or another peacemaker they admire. To share what they learn, they might write brief biographies, present skits, write songs, create collages, or do another activity they choose.

Encourage them to look for answers to this question: "What did this person do that I can do, too?" Help students "translate" their peacemakers' accomplishments into simple, inspiring statements. *Examples:*

- "1998 Nobel Peace Prize winners John Hume and David Trimble worked to find a peaceful solution to the conflict in Northern Ireland. I can be a peer mediator and help my classmates find solutions to their conflicts."

- "1992 Nobel Peace Prize winner Rigoberta Menchú Tum works for human rights. I can learn about the Universal Declaration of Human Rights and tell other people about it."

- "1984 Nobel Peace Prize winner Archbishop Desmond Tutu worked against apartheid in South Africa. I can fight racism, bigotry, and prejudice in my school and community."

---

*SOURCE: *Review of Educational Research* 66:4 (1996), pp. 459–506.

CHANGE SEATING ASSIGNMENTS

If you let students sit wherever they like, it may happen that the shy and lonely kids, bullying targets, or potential targets gravitate toward the outer edges of the class. It also may happen that the aggressive kids or kids who may bully sit toward the back, where their behavior is less likely to be noticed by you.

Take a look at where students are sitting. What do you see? Bring the shy and lonely "outsiders" into the center of the class, where they will have more opportunities to interact with other students. (Don't put them next to each other, or they'll mostly interact only with each other.) Bring the aggressive kids up front, where you can keep a closer eye on them.

Change the seating assignments in your classroom periodically so students can get to know a variety of people.

SAY CHEESE!

Keep a camera close at hand. Routinely take pictures of your students working together, playing together, and interacting with each other in positive ways. Then:

- Post the pictures on your classroom bulletin board, blog, or website. Go ahead and fill it up with lots of pictures over the next several months; don't worry about overcrowding.

    Or . . .

- Display the pictures in an oversize class photo album. Leave it out on a shelf or a corner of your desk so students can look through it often.

When students see themselves in pictures with each other, this gives them a sense of belonging to the group. (This is one reason why coaches take team pictures.) When you keep the pictures together in one place, you send a message of unity and acceptance.

You'll probably notice that your students love looking at the pictures and discussing them with visitors. Don't be surprised if they're a special attraction on parents' night and at open houses.

Go Further

Bring the camera with you on field trips and to school programs. Capture some action shots of students involved in projects, presentations, and sporting events. Schedule a "photo shoot" and encourage students to create their own scenes of classroom harmony and cooperation.

TEACH STUDENTS ABOUT GANGS, HATE GROUPS, AND CULTS

Young people who feel alienated at school, at home, and in their communities are often easy marks for gangs, hate groups, and cults—places where they can find acceptance and gain some sense of having power over other people and their own lives. Learn as much as you can about these groups and, as appropriate, share your knowledge with your students.

Teach students how to respond if they are approached by a member of one of those groups. Say, *You should . . .*

- stay calm and cool
- be confident (stand tall with your head up and shoulders straight and try not to look scared)
- avoid arguing
- politely say "no thanks" to any offers (don't believe you'll be more popular or tougher if you decide to join)
- walk (don't run) to the nearest safe adult, group, or building

Your local police department can provide information about problems specific to your community. Invite an officer to speak to your students and answer any questions they might have about gangs, hate groups, and cults.

TRACK BULLYING ON TV

We already know that students are exposed to a great deal of violence on television. According to the American Psychological Association, research has shown that TV violence negatively affects children in three major ways:

- Children may become less sensitive to the pain and suffering of others.

- They may become more fearful of the world around them and perceive it as a mean and dangerous place.

- They may become more likely to behave aggressively toward others.

Studies have shown that children's television shows contain about 20 violent acts each hour. It's likely that many of your students also watch programs aimed at adult audiences, where the violent content can be frequent, graphic, and realistic.

Bullying is a form of violence against others. Whether physical (hitting, kicking, pushing) or emotional (rejection, put-downs, threats), it can leave those who are bullied feeling powerless and abused.

Tell your students that you want them to track bullying on TV for one week. As they watch their regular programs, they should pay special attention to bullying behaviors. Give each student several copies of the handout "Bullying on TV" (page 52); have more copies available as needed throughout the week. Explain that students should use one handout per program to report on the bullying they see. They should bring each night's handouts to school the next day and give them to you. Review them as they come in to get an overall sense of your students' TV viewing habits and how much bullying they notice.

If you and your students did the "Define Bullying" activity (page 10) and the "Name Bullying Behaviors" activity (pages 12–13), everyone should have a general idea of what these behaviors include. If you didn't do these activities, take a few moments to introduce the main ideas. Make sure everyone understands that bullying encompasses a broad spectrum of behaviors.

At the end of the week, return each student's handouts and have a class discussion about bullying on TV. You might ask questions like these:

- How much bullying did you see on TV? None? A little? A lot?

- What kinds of bullying did you see?

- Which kinds seemed to be most common?

- Experts believe that watching violence on TV is bad for kids. Do you think that watching bullying on TV might be bad for kids, too? Why or why not?

- In general, when bullying happens on TV, do the people who do it get away with it? Do the targets get hurt? Does it seem as if the bullying is the target's fault?

- Now that you've watched for bullying on TV, how do you feel about it? What's your opinion?

GO FURTHER

If students have shows they watch on YouTube or other online sites, have them watch for bullying on these instead.

If students are concerned about the amount of bullying they see on TV, have them write letters to the networks or local affiliates expressing their opinions about specific shows. Find addresses at the library or the networks' websites.

AFFIRM YOUR STUDENTS

Everyone appreciates a compliment. Students especially enjoy knowing that their teacher thinks well of them. Take every opportunity to say something positive to each of your students throughout the day. Make your comments brief, honest, sincere, simple, and *specific. Examples:* "Christopher, I liked the way you helped Maria find her pencil." "Abby, I really appreciate your positive attitude today." "Kai, you did a great job on the reading assignment." Be sure to include all kids equally.

ICE-CREAM CONE BULLETIN BOARD

This is a fun and colorful way to affirm and celebrate your students.

Provide construction paper in several colors (including brown for the cones). Have students create double-scoop ice-cream cones, write their names on the cones, and give them to you. On each scoop, write a positive word or phrase that you think describes that student. Display the cones on a bulletin board or post them around the room.

Here's a list of starter words. You might also ask your students to come up with additional words they would use to describe each other or themselves.

- able to resolve conflicts
- alert
- ambitious
- analytical
- appreciative
- articulate
- assertive
- attentive
- aware
- calm
- careful
- caring
- cautious
- cheerful
- confident
- conscientious
- consistent
- cooperative
- courageous
- courteous
- creative
- dedicated
- dependable
- determined
- dynamic
- eager
- efficient
- empathetic
- energetic
- enthusiastic
- ethical
- fair
- faithful
- focused
- friendly
- fun
- generous
- gentle
- genuine
- giving
- goal setter
- good example
- good follower
- good listener
- good sport
- hardworking
- health-conscious
- healthy
- helpful
- honest
- honorable
- hopeful
- humble
- humorous
- imaginative
- independent
- industrious
- ingenious
- innovative
- inspiring
- intelligent
- interesting
- intuitive
- inventive
- kind
- knowledgeable
- leader
- likable
- likes people
- lively
- logical
- loving
- loyal
- mature
- mediator
- merry
- motivated
- neat
- nice
- obedient
- open-minded
- optimistic
- organized
- patient
- peaceful
- people-oriented
- perceptive
- perseverant
- planner
- pleasant
- polite
- positive
- precise
- problem solver
- professional
- punctual

- quick
- reasonable
- relaxed
- reliable
- reputable
- resilient
- resourceful
- responsible
- safety-conscious
- self-assured
- self-disciplined
- self-starter
- sensible
- sensitive
- service-minded
- sharing
- sincere

- spirited
- stable
- strong
- successful
- tactful
- tender-hearted
- thoughtful
- tolerant
- trusting
- trustworthy
- understanding
- unselfish
- upbeat
- versatile
- willing to compromise
- wise
- witty

ASSESS THE WEEK

According to an old saying, "Before we can decide where we're going, we have to know where we've been." End each week by inviting your students to reflect on the events of that week. Distribute copies of the handout "The Week in Review" (page 54). Tally the results (or have a volunteer do this) and report them on Monday morning. Use the results to set goals or objectives for the coming week.

Tip: For another approach, see "Set and Review Weekly Goals" (page 25).

WEAR "NO BULLYING" BUTTONS

Have students design and make buttons or badges with a "No Bullying" message. They might say "No Bullying!" or "No Bullying Allowed!" or

"Bully Free Classroom!" or whatever students prefer. If you want to make buttons with metal frames and pins, use a button machine. Check to see if your school has one; if it doesn't, contact a button company.* Inexpensive badge holders are available in bookstores or office supply stores.

TEACH POSITIVE SELF-TALK

Positive thinking can be powerful—especially positive thinking about ourselves and our abilities to solve problems, reach goals, cope with hard times, and accomplish what we set out to do. Positive self-talk creates positive beliefs. Positive beliefs lead to positive attitudes and feelings about oneself and others. Positive attitudes and feelings promote positive behaviors.

Successful, capable, competent people tend to be self-affirmers. They don't get carried away ("I'm the greatest!"), but they do give themselves frequent pep talks ("I can do it!").

Many students who are bullied—and even those who aren't—have difficulty with this. It's easy for them to lapse into negative self-talk ("I can't do it" or "Why even try?"), which can set the stage for negative beliefs, attitudes, feelings, and behaviors—and also for failure, which "proves" that their negative self-talk was right.

There are many ways to teach positive self-talk. Here are six you can explore with your students:

1. Have a class discussion about self-talk, both positive and negative. Make sure students know the difference. Give examples or ask them for examples. Explain that positive self-talk *really works.*

2. Hand out copies of "Messages from Me to Me" (page 55), which lists several brief statements students can use in their positive self-talk. Read it aloud or invite students to read individual statements. Suggest that students keep the list and refer to it often.

---

*Badge-A-Minit can get you started with an easy-to-use handpress, sample designs, pinned backs, and instructions. Call 1-800-223-4103 or go to www.badgeaminit.com for more information.

GO FURTHER

Have students pick two or three statements from the list—or come up with their own statements—write them on a 3" x 5" card, and carry the card with them in their pocket or backpack. They can also post the statements as slogans on their blog or use them as wallpaper on their phone, other device, or Twitter page.

3. Have students write brief positive self-talk scripts to keep in their notebooks, at their desks, or on their smart phones. (*Example:* "I know I can do this. I have the ability. If I get stuck, I can ask for help. I can succeed.") When students catch themselves using negative self-talk (or when anyone else catches them), they can read their scripts. The briefer the better; after a few readings, many students will have their scripts memorized. Suggest that they close their eyes and take a few deep breaths before repeating their scripts to themselves.

4. Before starting a new class activity, ask students to close their eyes and silently say one or two positive statements to themselves. Or you might write statements on the whiteboard or chart paper and say them aloud as a class.

5. Divide the class into small groups. Have each group come up with a list of negative self-talk statements, then brainstorm positive self-talk responses. Afterward, the groups can share their lists with the class.

6. Have students complete "Good for You!" certificates (page 53) for themselves, describing their own achievements and accomplishments. See "Teach Students to Affirm Each Other," pages 76–77.

USE HUMOR

Humor is a terrific tool for making everyone feel welcome, accepted, and appreciated. Laughter is good for us *physically* (increasing respiratory activity, oxygen exchange, muscular activity, and heart rate, and stimulating the cardiovascular system and sympathetic nervous system, leading to an overall positive biochemical state) and *mentally* (decreasing stress, lifting spirits, improving moods). Here are six ways to bring humor and laughter into your classroom:

1. Start each day with a joke or two. You might have students bring in their favorite jokes to share. (You may want to have them share it privately with you first, so you can make sure it is appropriate.)

2. For a special treat now and then, show a funny movie.

3. Start a class collection of joke books and cartoon books.

4. Have a "Humor Corner" in your classroom. Stock it with funny books, posters, audiotapes, and other resources.

5. Keep a "Joke Jar" in your classroom. Fill it with brief jokes written on small pieces of paper. Encourage students to contribute their own jokes. (Set a few ground rules first: No hurtful jokes. No biased jokes. No crude or tasteless jokes.) Once a day, you (or a student) can reach into the jar, pull out a joke, and share it with the class.

6. Read humorous stories aloud or give them as reading assignments.

Talk with your class about the difference between laughing *at* someone and laughing *with* someone. Ask questions like these:

- When is it okay to laugh?
- When is it not okay to laugh?

GO FURTHER

When you need more ideas, check out *The Power of Positive Talk: Words to Help Every Child Succeed* by Douglas Bloch with Jon Merritt (Free Spirit Publishing, 2003). This step-by-step guide helps adults instill positive messages and self-esteem in children right from the start. Out of print but worth finding at the library.

- Are there times when laughter can hurt? How can it hurt?

- Are there times when laughter can help? How can it help?

GET STUDENTS INVOLVED IN SERVICE

When students work together to reach a common goal—especially when that goal involves helping others—they experience a sense of unity, personal worth, and belonging. This has a bonding effect on the group as a whole. It also gives students an opportunity to observe and appreciate each other's knowledge and skills.

Research shows that students who participate in service projects feel more connected to their community, develop stronger academic behaviors, and build social confidence and skills—the kind of skills that can help them stand up as allies for targets of bullying.

There are countless ways you and your students can make a difference. Your biggest challenge might be getting your class to choose just one project from among so many possibilities available to you. Here are six suggestions to get started:

1. Ask your principal or school counselor if your school already offers service learning opportunities. If it does, ask your students what they would like to do. (Try the democratic approach and take a vote.)

Go Further

On the Web, check out the National Service-Learning Clearinghouse (www.servicelearning .gov), funded by the Corporation for National and Community Service. This comprehensive information system focuses on all dimensions of service learning, covering kindergarten through higher education and community-based initiatives. You can also write or call: The National Service-Learning Clearinghouse, ETR Associates, 4 Carbonero Way, Scotts Valley, CA 95066; toll-free telephone 1-866-245-SERV (1-866-245-7378).

2. Start a service club in your classroom. Students can begin by identifying an issue they'd like to work on or a problem they'd like to address in your classroom, the whole school, or the school community. (What about a "Stop Bullying" club?)

Go Further

You might want to start a Kids Care Club in your classroom or school. This national organization will provide you with a license to use the Kids Care Club name and logo and send you a Kids Care Start Up Kit including "all the materials you need to turn a group of kids into a force for kindness." For more information, write or call: Kids Care Clubs, 975 Boston Post Road, Darien, CT 06820; toll-free telephone 1-866-269-0510. Or visit their website (www.kidscare.org), where you can print out a membership application.

3. Ask other people in your school or community about ways to serve. Or make this a class assignment and have students gather information. They might contact one or more of the following:

- animal shelters
- arts centers
- children's shelters
- civic groups (*examples:* Elks, Rotary, Kiwanis, Lions Clubs)
- community centers
- congregations
- conservation groups
- food pantries
- homeless shelters
- hospitals
- libraries
- the mayor's office
- residential facilities for people with disabilities
- other schools
- zoos

4. Check your phone book to see if any of these organizations have chapters near you, and ask how your students can serve:

- American National Red Cross
- Boy Scouts of America
- Boys & Girls Clubs of America
- Girl Scouts of the U.S.A.
- Girls, Inc.
- Habitat for Humanity International
- Kids Against Pollution
- Kids for Saving the Earth
- National 4-H Council
- United Way of America
- YMCA of the USA
- Youth Service America

5. Visit your local library or bookstore and look for books about kids and service. *Examples:*

- *The Complete Guide to Service Learning* by Cathryn Berger Kaye (Free Spirit Publishing, 2010). Activities, quotes, ideas, reflections, and resources for guiding service learning in the curricular context.

- *The Kid's Guide to Service Projects* by Barbara A. Lewis (Free Spirit Publishing, 2009). More than 500 service ideas for youth, from simple projects to large-scale initiatives. For ages 10 and up.

- *Teaching Your Kids to Care: How to Discover and Develop the Spirit of Charity in Your Children* by Deborah Spaide (Citadel Press, 1995). Spaide is the founder of Kids Care Clubs. In this practical, inspiring book, she describes 105 projects that develop the charity instinct in children and teens from preschool through high school.

6. Explore the Internet's vast resources on volunteering and service. In addition to the National Service-Learning Clearinghouse (described on page 32), here are four more websites you can visit—and these are just the tip of the iceberg:

- **Nickelodeon's Website for Teachers** (www.nickjr.com/teachers). Stop in to learn about Nickelodeon's ongoing, prosocial campaigns that connect kids to their communities through volunteering.

- **The Points of Light Institute** (www.pointsoflight.org). Founded in May 1990, the Institute is a nonpartisan nonprofit organization devoted to promoting volunteerism. It works in communities throughout the United States through a network of over 500 Volunteer Centers. The website features profiles of "Daily Points of Light"—inspiring true stories about people and organizations helping their communities. Write or call: The Points of Light Institute, 600 Means Street, Suite 210, Atlanta, GA 30318; telephone 404-979-2900.

- **The Prudential Spirit of Community Initiative** (www.prudential.com/ community). Find out about national honorees and finalists—young people actively involved in making their communities better places to live. Download a copy of the booklet "Catch the Spirit! A Student's Guide to Community Service" at www.pueblo. gsa.gov. Or request a free copy by calling 1-888-878-3256.

- **Youth Service America** (www.ysa.org). Through volunteer campaigns, grants, and resources, YSA works to increase opportunities for young people to serve their communities. Stop in to find out more about volunteering, learn the latest news and events in the service field, and more. Or write or call: Youth Service America, 1101 15th Street NW, Suite 200, Washington, DC 20005; telephone 202-296-2992.

MONITOR THE MESSAGES YOU SEND

Children—even very young children—are amazingly perceptive. They know when a student is the "teacher's pet." They can tell when a teacher dislikes a student or doubts the student's abilities to learn and get along with others.

How can you make sure you're sending the right "messages" to your students? Ask other teachers about what has and hasn't worked for them. When you share strategies, experiences, and insights, everyone benefits—you, your colleagues, and students in your school. Meanwhile, consider the following suggestions.

1. Greet each student by name as he or she enters your classroom.

2. Each day, let every student know you care about him or her—in your words, body language, and actions.

3. Make frequent eye contact with every student. Studies have shown that some teachers favor children they perceive as attractive. They make eye contact more often with those students, and they give them more positive attention, reinforcement, affirmations, and feedback. They may call on those students more frequently.

4. Children have a strong need to appear successful in front of their peers and a deep fear of looking foolish or being laughed at. Plan and arrange classroom activities so all of your students can show their strengths, not their weaknesses. *Examples:* Avoid asking poor readers to read aloud to the class. If you know that a particular student has weak math skills, don't insist that he or she work problems on the whiteboard or chart paper.

5. Show interest in every student. This is a powerful motivator and helps all students feel welcome, appreciated, and accepted.

6. Be a good listener. Try to find time each day to really *listen* to each student. Lean forward, paraphrase their comments, and communicate your understanding of what they're saying and feeling.

7. As much as possible, individualize your teaching strategies and assignments. Research indicates that individualized instruction decreases antisocial behaviors in the classroom. It also increases the chances that your students will succeed.

8. Write personal, positive notes and letters to your students throughout the year. Students love getting letters from their teachers. Before the start of the school year, consider sending letters to each of your future students, welcoming them to your class and hinting at some of what they'll be learning throughout the year. This can also help decrease some of their anxiety about the coming year.

9. Even though some students will be smarter, friendlier, better behaved, and more likable than others, make sure they don't become "teacher's pets." Children are sensitive to favoritism and may be jealous of "pets." Jealousy can lead to bullying.

10. Do your best to treat all of your students equally. Avoid giving special privileges to some students and not others. This can create envy and hostility, which in turn can lead to bullying. If a student requires special treatment (for example, because of a medical condition), make sure the rest of the class understands why. (Get the permission of the student and his or her parents first to avoid embarrassment and potential problems.)

11. Remind your students that "equal" doesn't mean "the same." Explain that you'll do your very best to give everyone equal opportunities to learn and grow, but they will learn and grow in different ways.

12. When students see you put your trust in someone, they tend to have more respect for that person—especially if they respect you. Is there someone who seems to be having a hard time in school? Someone who's being picked on, excluded, teased, or bullied? Plan an activity (in class or on a field trip) where you can demonstrate complete trust in that student. When other students see this, they may view the student in a more positive light.

13. It's a real challenge to like every student all the time. Do your best to be accepting, sensitive, and understanding even in difficult situations. Don't hide your feelings, but express them in positive, helpful ways. Give students a chance to respond. *Example:* "I'm disappointed that you didn't finish your math homework. What can we do to keep this from happening again?"

14. We all have biases and prejudices. Some are based on cultural or ethnic background, others on gender, religion, intelligence, or ability level. Examine your own prejudices. How did you come to learn or believe these things? Are they part of your daily life? Are they affecting your teaching? Are they having a negative effect on your students? Be honest with yourself. Make a conscious, deliberate, focused effort to check your prejudices, unlearn them, and get beyond them.

15. Smile, smile, smile. Show your students that you're glad to be their teacher. This may be the most obvious positive message you can send.

16. Think positive thoughts about all of your students. Wish them the best in everything they do. Have high hopes for them. If you're a religious person, you might consider praying for them. A former National Teacher of the Year used to go to school early each day (before the children arrived), sit at a student's desk, and pray for him or her. He believed this made a significant difference in his students' behavior and his own interactions with them.

_____

(Date)

Dear Parent/Caregiver,

As I look back on my school days, I can remember times when kids were bullied. You probably can, too. Bullying has been getting a lot of attention in recent years, but it's hardly a brand-new problem. Bullying has been around forever.

We now know that bullying is serious and can be destructive to the well-being of children. Children who are bullied get hurt and sometimes have long-lasting emotional scars. Kids who bully may grow up to be abusive adults. In rare cases, bullying escalates into violence. And it's not just those directly involved who are affected. Research shows that witnesses to bullying are distracted, intimidated, upset, and hurt just as badly as targets. Bullying in the classroom prevents students from learning and teachers from teaching.

Teachers have a responsibility to do something about bullying. If it's not a problem, we want to make sure it doesn't start. That's called prevention. If it is a problem, we're determined to stop it. That's called intervention.

As your child's teacher, I'm committed to prevention and intervention in my classroom. That's why I've started using a book called _The New Bully Free Classroom_. It's designed to help teachers create a positive environment where everyone feels safe, accepted, and valued.

From time to time, I'll send home materials related to what we're doing in the classroom, and your child might tell you about some of the activities and discussions that are happening in class. If you ever have questions or concerns, I hope you'll contact me personally.

Sincerely,

_____

(Name)

_____

(Telephone and Email)

TRUE OR FALSE?

	TRUE	FALSE
1. Bullying is just teasing.		
2. Some people deserve to be bullied.		
3. Only boys bully.		
4. People who report or complain about bullying are babies.		
5. Bullying is a normal part of growing up.		
6. Bullying will stop if you ignore it.		
7. Everyone who bullies has low self-esteem. That's why they pick on other people.		
8. It's tattling to tell an adult when you're being bullied.		
9. The best way to deal with being bullied is by fighting or trying to get even.		
10. People who are bullied might hurt for a while, but they'll get over it.		

ANSWERS TO TRUE OR FALSE?

1. **Bullying is just teasing. FALSE**
Bullying is much more than teasing. While many bullies tease, others use violence, intimidation, and other serious tactics. Sometimes teasing can be fun, but bullying always hurts.

2. **Some people deserve to be bullied. FALSE**
No one ever deserves to be bullied. No one "asks for it." Often, people who are "different" in some way get teased. Being different is not a reason to be bullied.

3. **Only boys bully. FALSE**
Girls bully, too.

4. **People who report or complain about bullying are babies. FALSE**
People who report or complain about bullying are standing up for their or someone else's right not to be bullied. They're more grown up than the people who bully.

5. **Bullying is a normal part of growing up. FALSE**
Getting teased, picked on, pushed around, threatened, harassed, insulted, hurt, and abused is not normal. People who think it is normal are less likely to say or do anything about it, which gives those who do it the green light to keep bullying.

6. **Bullying will stop if you ignore it. TRUE AND FALSE**
Some kids might stop bullying and go away. But others will get angry and keep bullying until they get a reaction. That's what they want.

7. **Everyone who bullies has low self-esteem. That's why they pick on other people. FALSE**
Some people who bully have high self-esteem. They feel good about themselves, and picking on other people makes them feel even better. Most of the time, bullying isn't about high or low self-esteem. It's about having power over other people.

8. **It's tattling to tell an adult when you're being bullied. FALSE**
It's smart to tell an adult who can help you do something about the bullying. It's also smart to tell an adult if you see or hear about someone else being bullied.

9. **The best way to deal with being bullied is by fighting or trying to get even. FALSE**
If you fight with someone who bullies you, you might get hurt (and hurt someone else). Plus, you might get into trouble for fighting. If you try to get even, you're acting the same as the person who bullied you. And the person might come after you again to get even with you. Either way only makes things worse.

10. **People who are bullied might hurt for a while, but they'll get over it. FALSE**
Bullying hurts for a long time. Some kids drop out of school because of bullying. Some become so sad, desperate, afraid, and hopeless that they commit suicide. Many adults can remember times when they were bullied as children. People don't "get over" being bullied.

OUR CLASSROOM IS A PLACE WHERE . . .

We don't all have to be the same.

We don't all have to think the same.

We don't all have to act the same.

We don't all have to talk the same.

We don't all have to dress the same.

We don't all have to believe the same things.

We have the right to be ourselves.

We like it that people are different.

We know that our differences
make us interesting and unique.

We honor different ways of being, acting, and
believing—even when we don't agree with them.

We do our best to solve problems peacefully.

We speak up if we see others being treated unfairly.

We treat each other the way we'd like to be treated.

We treat each other with respect.

BULLYING STORIES

Use the spaces below to write about experiences from your life.
Follow the NO NAMES RULE: Don't use anybody's name.

Describe a time when someone's words or behavior hurt you.	Describe a time when you saw or heard about bullying but didn't do anything about it.
Describe a time when you said or did something to hurt another person.	Describe a time when you saw or heard about bullying and either got help or tried to stop it.

THIS WEEK IN SCHOOL

Read each statement and think about the past week. Put a check mark in the column that describes how often that happened to you during the week. When you're through with the checklist, give it to the teacher.

Today's date: _____

Check this box if you're a boy ☐   Check this box if you're a girl ☐

THIS WEEK IN SCHOOL, ANOTHER STUDENT IN MY CLASS:	NEVER	ONCE	MORE THAN ONCE
1. called me names			
2. said something nice to me			
3. said something rude or mean about my family			
4. tried to kick me			
5. made fun of my appearance			
6. gave me a present			
7. said they'd beat me up			
8. invited me to join them			
9. tried to make me give them money			
10. tried to scare me			
11. loaned me something I wanted to borrow			
12. was mean about something I did			
13. sent me a mean text message			
14. told me a joke			
15. told me a lie			
16. got other kids to gang up on me			

CONTINUED →

THIS WEEK IN SCHOOL, ANOTHER STUDENT IN MY CLASS:	NEVER	ONCE	MORE THAN ONCE
17. tried to make me hurt someone else			
18. smiled at me			
19. helped me carry something			
20. tried to hurt me			
21. helped me with my schoolwork			
22. made me do something I didn't want to do			
23. complimented me			
24. took something away from me			
25. shared something with me			
26. said something rude or mean about the color of my skin			
27. shouted at me			
28. played a game with me			
29. talked with me about things I like			
30. laughed at me in a way that hurt my feelings			
31. said they would tell on me			
32. tried to break something of mine			
33. told a lie about me			
34. tried to hit me			
35. made me feel bad about myself			
36. made me feel good about myself			

BULLYING SURVEY: ELEMENTARY

Do not write your name anywhere on this survey.

Circle the best answer.					
Ⓐ ALMOST NEVER Ⓑ A LITTLE Ⓒ SOMETIMES Ⓓ A LOT Ⓔ ALMOST ALWAYS					
1. I see other students hit, pinched, kicked, tripped, pushed, or grabbed.	A	B	C	D	E
2. I am hit, pinched, kicked, tripped, pushed, or grabbed.	A	B	C	D	E
3. I see other students ignored or rejected.	A	B	C	D	E
4. I am ignored or rejected.	A	B	C	D	E
5. Hurtful and mean notes are written about other students.	A	B	C	D	E
6. Sometimes students are called names, teased, or made fun of.	A	B	C	D	E
7. I see things damaged or stolen from other students.	A	B	C	D	E
8. Things are damaged or stolen from me.	A	B	C	D	E
9. I see other students bullied in other ways.	A	B	C	D	E
10. I am bullied in other ways.	A	B	C	D	E
11. I am bullied in the classroom.	A	B	C	D	E
12. I am bullied in the hall.	A	B	C	D	E
13. I am bullied in the lunchroom.	A	B	C	D	E
14. I am bullied on the playground.	A	B	C	D	E
15. I am bullied on the bus or while waiting for the bus.	A	B	C	D	E
16. I am bullied while walking to or from school.	A	B	C	D	E
17. Most students try to help other students who are bullied.	A	B	C	D	E
18. When students see someone bullied, most of them join in, laugh, or cheer it on.	A	B	C	D	E
19. I feel safe at school.	A	B	C	D	E
20. I feel safe at home.	A	B	C	D	E
21. If I were bullied, I would tell an adult at school.	A	B	C	D	E

CONTINUED →

Circle the best answer.

(A) ALMOST NEVER   (B) A LITTLE   (C) SOMETIMES   (D) A LOT   (E) ALMOST ALWAYS

22. If I heard about or saw someone bullied, I would tell an adult at school.	A B C D E
23. If I were mistreated by other students, my friends would help me.	A B C D E
24. Adults at school try to stop bullying when they know about it.	A B C D E
25. There are some adults at school who bully students.	A B C D E
26. My teacher(s) has classroom rules against bullying.	A B C D E
27. I know the punishment for bullying.	A B C D E

BULLYING SURVEY: MIDDLE SCHOOL

Do not write your name anywhere on this questionnaire.

Use the scale below and respond to each item by circling the appropriate letter. (A) ALMOST NEVER (B) A LITTLE (C) SOMETIMES (D) A LOT (E) ALMOST ALWAYS	
1. I see other students hit, pinched, kicked, tripped, pushed, elbowed, touched, or grabbed in a hurtful or embarrassing way.	A B C D E
2. I am hit, pinched, kicked, tripped, pushed, elbowed, touched, or grabbed in a hurtful or embarrassing way.	A B C D E
3. I see other students ignored, rejected, lied about, have rumors told about them, or have hurtful and mean notes written about them.	A B C D E
4. I am ignored, rejected, lied about, have rumors told about me, or have hurtful and mean notes written about me.	A B C D E
5. I see other students called names, teased, made fun of for the way they look or dress, or put down in a hurtful way.	A B C D E
6. I am called names, teased, made fun of for the way I look or dress, or put down in a hurtful way.	A B C D E
7. I see other students forced to do things they don't want to do.	A B C D E
8. I am forced to do things I don't want to do.	A B C D E
9. I see other students' things damaged or stolen from them.	A B C D E
10. I have had things damaged or stolen from me.	A B C D E
11. I see other students bullied in other ways.	A B C D E
12. I am bullied in other ways.	A B C D E
13. I am bullied in the classroom.	A B C D E
14. I am bullied while walking to or from school.	A B C D E
15. I am bullied while riding on or waiting for the bus.	A B C D E
16. I am bullied in the lunchroom.	A B C D E
17. I am bullied in the gym or locker room.	A B C D E
18. I am bullied in the bathroom.	A B C D E
19. I am bullied in other places in the school.	A B C D E
20. I am bullied by one student.	A B C D E

Use the scale below and respond to each item by circling the appropriate letter.

(A) ALMOST NEVER　**(B)** A LITTLE　**(C)** SOMETIMES　**(D)** A LOT　**(E)** ALMOST ALWAYS

21. I am bullied by more than one student.		A B C D E
22. Most students try to help other students who are being bullied.		A B C D E
23. When students see someone bullied, most of them ignore it.		A B C D E
24. When students see someone bullied, most of them join in, laugh, or cheer it on.		A B C D E
25. I feel safe at school.		A B C D E
26. I feel safe at home.		A B C D E
27. I feel unhappy at school because I am being bullied.		A B C D E
28. I feel lonely at school because no one likes me.		A B C D E
29. I feel upset because I see students being bullied.		A B C D E
30. I feel afraid because I am bullied.		A B C D E
31. I sometimes stay home because of bullying at school.		A B C D E
32. If I were bullied, I would tell an adult at school.		A B C D E
33. If I heard about or saw someone being bullied at school, I would tell an adult at school.		A B C D E
34. If I were bullied at school, I would tell an adult at home.		A B C D E
35. If I were mistreated by other students, my friends would help me.		A B C D E
36. I am able to make friends at school.		A B C D E
37. If an adult at school saw bullying, he/she would try to stop the bullying.		A B C D E
38. My principal and/or assistant principal try to stop students from bullying.		A B C D E
39. Some adults at school bully students.		A B C D E
40. My teachers have classroom rules against bullying.		A B C D E
41. The punishment for breaking classroom rules about bullying is clear.		A B C D E
42. Some adults at school talk to us about bullying.		A B C D E

WHAT IS CYBERBULLYING?

Name: _____ Date: _____

Instructions: Read the following definition of cyberbullying and rewrite it below in your own words.

Cyberbullying is when someone uses computers, cell phones, or other technology to scare, threaten, embarrass, or hurt someone. It can be done with email, text messages, instant messages, websites, social networking sites, electronic photographs, and so on.

_____

_____

_____

What does cyberbullying look like? Write down examples of cyberbullying:

_____

_____

_____

_____

_____

_____

_____

_____

_____

Cyberbullying is when someone uses computers, cell phones, or other technology to scare, threaten, embarrass, or hurt someone. It can be done with email, text messages, instant messages, websites, social networking sites, electronic photographs, and so on. Here are some guidelines for preventing and stopping it.

- Behave online the same way you would behave in real life. Remember that the Golden Rule also applies when using technology: Treat others the way you want to be treated.

- If friends are cyberbullying, tell them to stop.

- Refuse to pass along mean or bullying messages.

- Refuse to participate in mean or bullying websites or Facebook pages.

- Don't respond to mean or threatening messages sent to you or anyone else. Don't retaliate.

- Report to an adult any threatening or harassing messages you receive.

- Don't open messages or attachments from unfamiliar senders.

- Don't give your email address or cell phone number to people you don't know well.

- Ask an adult to help you block messages from people who cyberbully.

- If bullying comes from a personal account, ask an adult to report it to the person's email account provider, which is usually the word after the @ symbol.

- Change your cell phone number or email address if bullying continues to be a problem.

- Exit a chat room, forum, or message board if someone is bullying. Write down the individual's screen name and report it to an adult.

- Do not delete threatening messages. It is important to maintain a record of the threats. If necessary, ask an adult to install a monitoring software program on your computer, such as Spectorsoft. This software collects and preserves electronic evidence.

- Ask your parents to consider taking legal action. Sometimes, threatening to close the cyberbully's Internet service provider or instant messaging account is enough to make the bullying stop.

CLIQUES SURVEY

Read the following statements, and for each one place a check in the column for "Always," "Sometimes," or "Never."

	Always	Sometimes	Never
1. My friends are mean to me.			
2. My friends are mean to kids not in our group.			
3. My group of friends has a leader.			
4. There are some kids my friends will not let into our group.			
5. One or more of my friends spread rumors about other people.			
6. There is a group of kids I'd like to be friends with, but they won't let me join them.			
7. I belong to more than one group of friends.			
8. All my friends dress pretty much the same.			
9. Some of my friends keep secrets from each other.			
10. One or more of my friends has been hurt (emotionally or physically) by other friends in our group.			
11. My feelings have been hurt by one or more of my friends.			
12. I am afraid to go against my friends' ways or opinions.			

20 THINGS TO DO INSTEAD OF HURTING SOMEONE BACK

When someone hurts you, it's normal to feel angry. You might even want to get back at the person by hurting him or her. But you can choose not to do that. You can do one (or more) of these things instead.

1. STOP and THINK. Don't do anything right away. Consider your options. Think about what might happen if you try to hurt the other person.

2. Know that what you do is up to you. You can decide. You are in charge of your actions.

3. Tell yourself, "It's okay to feel angry. It's not okay to hurt someone else. Even if that person hurt me first."

4. Tell the person, "Stop that! I don't like that!"

5. Keep your hands to yourself. Make fists and put them in your pockets.

6. Keep your feet to yourself. Jump or dance or stomp.

7. Walk away or run away.

8. Tell the person how you feel. Use an "I-message." *Example:* "I feel angry when you hit me because it hurts. I want you to stop hitting me."

9. Take a deep breath, then blow it out. Blow your angry feelings out of your body.

10. Find an adult. Tell the adult what happened and how you feel.

11. Count slowly from 1 to 10. Count backward from 10 to 1. Keep counting until you feel your anger getting smaller.

12. Think cool thoughts. Imagine that you're sitting on an iceberg. Cool down your hot, angry feelings.

13. Think happy thoughts. Think of something you like to do. Imagine yourself doing it.

14. Treat the other person with kindness and respect. It won't be easy, but give it a try. This will totally surprise the other person, and it might end the conflict between you.

15. Draw an angry picture.

16. Sing an angry song. Or sing any song as loudly as you can.

17. Remember that getting back at someone never makes conflict better. It only makes it worse.

18. Take a time-out. Go somewhere until you feel better.

19. Find another person to be with.

20. Know that you can do it. You can choose not to hurt someone else. It's up to you.

Adapted from *A Leader's Guide to We Can Get Along* by Lauren Murphy Payne, Claudia Rohling, and Pamela Espeland (Free Spirit Publishing Inc, 1997).

From *The New Bully Free Classroom®* by Allan L. Beane, copyright © 2011. Free Spirit Publishing Inc., Minneapolis, MN; 800-735-7323; www.freespirit.com.

8 STEPS TO CONFLICT RESOLUTION

1. **COOL DOWN.** Don't try to resolve a conflict when you're angry (or the other person is angry). Take a time-out or agree to meet again in 24 hours.

2. **DESCRIBE THE CONFLICT.** Each person should talk about the conflict in his or her own words. No put-downs allowed! *Important:* Although each person may have a different view of the conflict and use different words to describe it, neither account is "right" or "wrong."

3. **DESCRIBE WHAT CAUSED THE CONFLICT.** What specific events led up to the conflict? What happened first? Next? Did the conflict start out as a minor disagreement or difference of opinion? What happened to turn it into a conflict? *Important:* Don't label the conflict either person's "fault."

4. **DESCRIBE THE FEELINGS RAISED BY THE CONFLICT.** Again, each person should use his or her own words. Honesty is important. No blaming allowed!

5. **LISTEN CAREFULLY AND RESPECTFULLY WHILE THE OTHER PERSON IS TALKING.** Try to understand his or her point of view. Don't interrupt. It might help to "reflect" the other person's perceptions and feelings by repeating them back. *Examples:* "You didn't like it when I called you a name." "Your feelings are hurt." "You thought you should have first choice about what game to play at recess." "You're sad because you feel left out."

6. **BRAINSTORM SOLUTIONS TO THE CONFLICT.** Follow the three basic rules of brainstorming:

   - Everyone tries to come up with as many ideas as they can.

   - All ideas are okay.

   - Nobody makes fun of anyone else's ideas.

   Be creative. Affirm each other's ideas. Be open to new ideas. Make a list of brainstormed ideas so you're sure to remember them all. Then choose one solution to try. Be willing to negotiate and compromise.

7. **TRY YOUR SOLUTION.** See how it works. Give it your best efforts. Be patient.

8. **IF ONE SOLUTION DOESN'T GET RESULTS, TRY ANOTHER.** Keep trying. Brainstorm more solutions if you need to.

If you can't resolve the conflict no matter how hard you try, agree to disagree. Sometimes that's the best you can do. Meanwhile, realize that the conflict doesn't have to end your relationship. People can get along even when they disagree.

BULLYING ON TV

Today's date: _____

Your name: _____

Name of the show you watched: _____

What channel was it on? What network (or website)? _____

Did you notice any bullying?   **YES**   **NO**

If yes, describe what happened: _____

_____

_____

How was the person who was bullied affected? _____

_____

_____

What did the target do about the bullying? _____

_____

_____

What, if anything, happened to the person who bullied? _____

_____

_____

Did it seem that:

The target deserved to be bullied?   **YES**   **NO**

The bullying was the target's fault?   **YES**   **NO**

GOOD FOR YOU!

_____ did something special.
(Student's name)

Here's what _____ did:
(Student's name)

Today's date: _____

Your name: _____

THE WEEK IN REVIEW

Today's date: _____

Your name (if you want to give it): _____

Think back on the past week in this classroom. Read each statement, then check the column that best describes how you feel about your week.

THIS WEEK IN SCHOOL:	ALL OF THE TIME	MOST OF THE TIME	SOME OF THE TIME	NEVER
1. I was respected as a person.				
2. I treated others with respect.				
3. I was treated fairly.				
4. I treated others fairly.				
5. People helped me when I needed help.				
6. I helped others.				
7. We cared for each other.				
8. We worked hard to make our classroom a positive place to be.				
9. I felt like I belonged.				
10. I helped others feel like they belonged.				
11. I was encouraged to do my best.				
12. I encouraged others to do their best.				
13. We worked together to solve problems.				
14. We cooperated with each other.				
15. I felt accepted.				
16. I helped others feel accepted.				

MESSAGES FROM ME TO ME

"I'm a good person."

"I deserve to be treated with kindness and respect."

"I'm special and unique."

"I'm creative and talented."

"I can set goals and reach them."

"I can solve problems."

"I can ask other people for help."

"I have a right to be imperfect."

"I have a right to make mistakes."

"Everyone makes mistakes."

"I can learn from my mistakes."

"I'm valuable and worthwhile . . . just the way I am."

"I can get through this."

"I'm learning and growing."

"I'm not alone."

"I'm okay."

"I'm strong and capable."

"Even if I don't feel so great right now, I'll feel better soon."

"I can be patient with myself."

"I can manage."

"I can cope."

"I can do this."

"I can succeed."

"I can try again."

"I can expect the best of myself."

"I'm brave and courageous."

"I believe in myself."

"I'm not afraid."

EMPOWER BYSTANDERS
TO BECOME ALLIES

Research has shown that bystanders have a great potential power to reduce or end bullying. According to the award-winning website bullying.org, when peers intervene on behalf of a bullying target, the bullying stops within 10 seconds 57 percent of the time. When an entire school—students and adults—works together to create a positive environment, bullying can be reduced significantly.

Students who stand united against bullying and who know how to safely intervene when they see someone being bullied are no longer bystanders, but *empowered bystanders* or *allies*. But in order to become allies, students need to know that adults desire and value their efforts to be a voice of kindness, acceptance, and courage. When students are able to confidently stand up for bullied students, they often find it rewarding. They know it is not right to bully others, and when they do what they know is right, it helps them feel good about themselves.

Like the material in "Create a Positive Classroom," the tips and strategies in this section benefit everyone. Here are some good things you can expect to happen along the way:

Your students will learn how to:

- understand what it means to be empowered bystanders or allies
- understand ways students can be allies
- provide emotional support to students who are bullied
- define *empathy* and understand its importance
- show they understand how someone feels and that they care
- discuss feelings associated with being bullied
- discuss feelings associated with seeing someone bullied
- break the code of silence and report bullying incidents
- differentiate between reporting and "ratting," "tattling," or "snitching"
- describe the rewards associated with being allies
- build empathy and realize that other people have feelings, wants, and needs that are just as real and valid as their own

You'll discover how to:

- identify potential allies in your classroom
- mobilize the masses—witnesses and bystanders—to become bully busters
- help students accept their differences
- reduce or eliminate common barriers to bystanders becoming allies
- model and reinforce ally behavior
- create an atmosphere in which students believe that bullying is not okay

HELP BYSTANDERS UNDERSTAND THEIR ROLE

Have a class discussion about how bullying affects everyone: bullied students, students who bully, and students who witness bullying. Focus particular attention on the effect on witnesses, asking students to recall a time they saw someone bullied. How did they feel? What did they do? What else could they have done? (Ask students to avoid using anyone's name; keep the stories general.) As students share their stories, you may want to take mental notes of situations you need to remember.

Explain that *bystanders* are students who witness bullying and do nothing to help the target. Some may laugh or encourage the bullying. *Allies* are students who take action to stop bullying when they witness it.

Ask students, "Why is it important for bystanders such as yourselves to speak out against bullying and support those who are bullied?" Refer back to your discussion of how it feels to be bullied and to see someone bullied. Bullying can cause fear, pain, discomfort, and anger in everyone, not just the target. When students act as allies, they help everyone feel more secure and they make their school safer.

Next, ask your students, "How do you think a bullied student would feel if you helped him or her?" Then ask, "How would *you* feel if you helped a student who was bullied?" Hopefully, many of them will say they would feel good about themselves.

As a group, brainstorm ways students can act as allies. Ask, "What can you do when you see someone bullied?" List responses on the board, chart paper, or electronic whiteboard. If students need help, you might suggest a couple answers, such as:

- Don't laugh.
- Tell the student who is bullying to stop it.
- Ask the bullied student to walk away with you and your friends.
- Ask the bullied student to sit with you or play with you.

Distribute the "If I Want to Stop Bullying, I Can . . ." handout (page 78) and discuss each item as a group. Give students a few minutes to add any ideas they have on the blank lines—ideas you discussed as a group or ones they come up with on their own. Consider having them work in groups. Ask them to take the handout home and discuss it with their parents.

Finally, brainstorm a few bullying scenarios and ask for volunteers to act out brief role plays of some of the situations. Be sure each scenario has a bystander who is faced with the opportunity to act as an ally. It can be instructive to play out several different endings, including negative and positive endings. For example, if students are role-playing a scene in which one student threatens another in an unsupervised hallway, consider having students play out the scene with the bystander:

- walking away
- laughing
- standing up for the target

Also be sure to role-play scenarios in which the bullying is reported to adults. This is one of the most important things a bystander can do. Have a class discussion about which adults students can count on to help them.

HELP BYSTANDERS DEVELOP EMPATHY

Empathy is the ability to identify with and understand another person's feelings, situation, motives, and concerns—to put ourselves in someone else's place or, as the saying goes, "in someone else's shoes." This is one of the most important traits we develop—and the sooner, the better.

Empathy is basic to positive relationships with friends, peers, family members, and everyone else we encounter throughout our lives. Research has shown that children are born with a predisposition toward empathy. However, if it isn't encouraged and supported, it doesn't grow.

It's not enough for students to empathize with people they have things in common with. That's easy. They also need to empathize with people who are very different from them—in their needs, experiences, points of view, life circumstances, beliefs, ethnic and cultural backgrounds, talents, abilities, accomplishments, and so on. They need to be able to think about how other people feel—and, eventually, how other people might feel or would feel in response to specific events and circumstances. When bystanders can feel empathy for targets of bullying, they are much more likely to act as allies for the targets.

Ask students, "How can we know how someone feels?" Some desired answers are:

- Listen to what they say.
- Look at their face and body.
- Ask them how they feel.
- Watch how the person acts.

There are many ways you can build empathy in your students. Here are several ideas you can try.

Ask Questions

During lessons, group work, and other times, ask questions that draw students' attention away from themselves and toward the feelings, needs, and concerns of others. *Examples:*

How would you feel if . . .

- you were the new kid in school?
- you were the most popular student? The least popular student?
- someone made fun of you or called you names?
- you came to school every day without eating breakfast?
- your parents were divorced?
- someone picked on you all the time?
- you didn't have a home or a safe place to live?
- walking down the street was dangerous?
- you were the smallest kid in class?
- you were the biggest kid in class?
- you couldn't speak English very well?
- you had a hard time reading?
- you used a wheelchair?
- you wore glasses?
- you couldn't hear well or at all?
- you had an illness and felt sick much of the time?

Go Further

Teaching Tolerance is a national education project dedicated to helping teachers foster equity, respect, and understanding in the classroom and beyond. Free and low-cost resources—including video and text teaching kits, posters, books, and *Teaching Tolerance* magazine—are available to educators at all levels. Write or call: Southern Poverty Law Center, 400 Washington Avenue, Montgomery, AL 36104; telephone 334-956-8200. On the Web, go to: www.teachingtolerance.org.

These and other questions might be topics for class discussions or journal writing (see "Weekly Journaling," page 68). You can also distribute the "I Feel . . ." handout (page 79) and have students fill it out. When they are finished, review each sentence with the group and ask for volunteers to share their answers.

TAKE FIELD TRIPS

Expose students to people whose lives are different from their own. You might form a relationship with a class of students from another school and exchange visits. Also consider visiting a juvenile home, an assisted-living facility, a children's hospital, a senior citizens' home, or a homeless shelter. When appropriate, you and your students might build relationships (with frequent visits) or start an email pen-pal exchange. Or you might volunteer as a class to help at one of the places you visit. Plan volunteer experiences carefully. Check with your principal about procedures, and be sure to get permission from students' parents.

LEAD AN IMAGINATION EXERCISE

Have students sit comfortably and quietly in their chairs (or on the floor—you'll need cushions or a rug) with their eyes closed. Ask them to imagine that another person is sitting directly across from them. This should be someone they don't know very well, or someone they have neutral or negative feelings about. Then guide them with questions and suggestions like these:

- Picture the person in your mind. Is it a man or a woman? A boy or a girl? What color hair does the person have? What color eyes? What is he or she wearing? How is he or she looking at you?

- Say to yourself, "[The person's name] is a human being. So am I. This is something we have in common."

- Ask yourself [pause between each question to allow time for students to think about it]:

  - What do I really know about this person? Where does my knowledge come from—my own experience with him or her?

things other people have said? rumors? gossip? my own prejudices or biases?

- What might be important to this person?

- What is something this person might like? What is something this person might not like?

- What are this person's needs? What does he or she want out of life?

- What are some reasons this person acts the way he or she does?

- What problems might this person have?

- What might this person be struggling with?

- What might this person be afraid of?

- What might this person wish he or she could do?

End by asking, "Were you able to see the world through the other person's eyes? How did that feel? What did you discover about the person—and about yourself?"

HELP STUDENTS DEVELOP A FEELINGS VOCABULARY

It's easier to empathize with feelings we can name. There are many ways you can help your students develop a feelings vocabulary. Here are some starter ideas:

- Invite students to name their feelings. When they enter your room, say, "Hello, [name]! How are you feeling today?"

- Make a large "pockets poster" for your room. Tape or staple several pockets to a piece of posterboard. Label each pocket with a feeling. (*Examples:* happy, sad, excited, worried, tired, wide awake, confused, anxious, contented.) Cut strips of paper (such as construction paper) and write one student's name on each strip. When students arrive in your classroom, each puts his or her name strip in the pocket that best describes how he or she is feeling. (This also gives you a general idea of the "mood" your class is in.)

- Use books, videos, and posters to explore feelings and ways to express them.

- Ask students to draw a picture or write a brief story about caring about someone.

- Play a "What Am I Feeling?" game. Pair students and have them sit across from each other. As one student imagines feeling a certain way and shows it in his or her body language and facial expression, the other student tries to identify and name the feeling.

- Distribute copies of the handout "50 Words and Phrases That Describe Feelings" (page 80). Practice the words with your students. Make sure they understand what each one means. Invite them to use the words in class discussions, writing assignments, and reports. You might also include them in spelling lessons.

Share Feelings with a Partner

This activity is for younger students (kindergarten or first grade, most likely). Make one paper heart for every two students and cut each heart in half in a unique pattern, so that each half matches up only with its other half. (You may want to laminate them so you can use them again.) Mix up the halves in a box and distribute them to students (or let them draw their own). Direct students to find the student with the half that matches theirs. When they find each other, tell partners to share with each other what they feel when someone is hurt or frightened by someone.

Discuss Feelings Caused by Bullying

Prepare a large poster board, chart paper, or interactive whiteboard with the title Feelings Caused by Bullying and the following words written on it:

- angry
- fearful
- sad
- embarrassed
- nervous
- concerned

You may want to add other words that describe how people may feel when they witness bullying or are bullied. Go through the words with your class and discuss what each one means. Then read the following bullying scenarios, pausing after each one to ask students to tell you which word on the poster describes the feelings they would have in that situation. (*Note*: When they use a word, you may want to place an adhesive bandage, or Band-Aid, over the word.)

- *Situation*: A boy near you at circle time or the morning meeting keeps poking a girl next to him.

- *Situation*: You are in line at lunch and a girl who bullies you every day cuts in line in front of you.

- *Situation*: A girl in your class (who often calls other students names) calls you a mean name.

- *Situation*: You are playing with two friends when another student, whom your friends don't like, tries to join in. Your friends say he can't play and tell him to go away.

Ask students to think of other words that describe feelings caused by bullying and list them on the poster. Give each student an adhesive bandage and ask them to wear it on their wrist as a reminder that bullying hurts.

Go Further

Good-Bye Bully Machine by Debbie Fox and Allan L. Beane, Ph.D. (Free Spirit Publishing, 2009). Ages 9–12.

What's the Difference? Plays About Tolerance by Catherine Gourley (Crabtree Publishing Company, 2010). Ages 9–12.

Hey Little Ant by Philip M. Hoose (Tricycle Press, 1998). Ages 4–8.

TEACH BYSTANDERS SKILLS

It's best to do this activity after you've done "Help Bystanders Understand Their Role" (page 57) and "Help Bystanders Develop Empathy" (page 58). Open a class discussion about the power of one person to be a positive influence in the lives of others by telling a personal anecdote about such an experience in your own life. Perhaps someone encouraged you when you needed it, stuck up for you, or helped you accomplish something difficult. Similarly, you may tell a story about a time you had the opportunity to do so for someone else. Was it an easy choice to help the other person? What might have happened if you didn't? How did you feel after you did it? Emphasize that these situations are important opportunities for people to step up and be heroes to someone else.

Next, ask for volunteers to share how someone has had a positive influence on their lives.

Remind students of your earlier discussions about empathy and bystanders and allies. When someone is being bullied, any witness to the bullying has an opportunity to do the right thing.

ALLY SKILLS

What exactly can students do to empower themselves against bullying? What are the specific ally skills they need? Discuss with students the following steps to follow when they witness a bullying situation:

1. **Trust your instincts.** If you see a situation that you think might be bullying, it probably is. Listen to your gut to determine if there is a real problem. (If needed, review the definition of bullying on page 10.) Ask the person being targeted, "Do you need help?"

2. **Decide to be an ally.** Maybe nobody else is doing anything about the situation. Maybe it would be easy to walk away or avoid getting involved. Think: This is your opportunity to make a difference in someone's life, and to make your school safer. Decide to do something.

3. **Determine if the situation is dangerous.** Is more than one person bullying? Are there weapons involved? Do the kids seem especially angry or dangerous? Again, trust your instincts, and if the situation seems dangerous, skip directly to Step 8. If someone could get hurt, report it to an adult *immediately*.

4. **Assertively tell the person who is bullying to stop.** Use a strong voice and make eye contact with the person. Stand up tall and don't look afraid. Then tell the target to join you and get away with you.

5. **Form a group.** If the bullying does not stop, get some friends. You may want to do this in any case. Being in a group helps you and your friends feel safer and braver, and it will make it harder for the person to keep bullying. As a group, assertively tell the person to stop.

6. **Walk away with the target.** Take your group with you. People who bully want an audience, and when you walk away, you are not only getting the target to safety but also removing the audience.

7. **Give support and empathy.** Say to the person who was bullied: "I'm sorry that happened to you. You didn't deserve it. I hope it never happens again." Invite the person to join you at recess or lunch.

8. **Report the incident.** Tell a teacher or other adult what happened. Be specific about what happened, where it happened, and when.

Consider having students make posters with the eight steps, using students' own words. You might include student stories as examples and plenty of suggested dialogue.

OVERCOMING BARRIERS TO BEING AN ALLY

Even though we may know it's the right thing to do, it isn't always easy to stand up to bullying. Ask your students: "What are some reasons (barriers) that would keep you from helping a bullied student?"

List student responses on the board, chart paper, or electronic whiteboard. Expect answers such as:

- I'm afraid I will be bullied.

- I'm afraid the student who bullies will not want to be my friend.

- I'm afraid of getting in a fight.

- I don't want people to think I'm a nerd (goody-goody, teacher's pet, etc.).

How can students overcome these barriers? As a class, brainstorm solutions and record answers on your interactive whiteboard or chart paper. Discuss each idea. Here are some guidelines:

- If you are afraid of being bullied or fighting: Always think about safety. You don't want to get hurt. The best thing to do is to surround yourself with friends who will support you. Ask them to join you and indicate their support and agreement with you. Students only bully those they can have power over and hurt. If you act confident and stand up for someone, you look powerful and are much less likely to be bullied. Be assertive when a student tries to bully you, and report it to an adult.

- If you are afraid you'll lose a friend, or if you're afraid of what people will think of you, remember that true friends will not abandon you because you stand up against bullying. Look for supportive friends. You may be surprised when you stand up to bullying how many friends will side with you. They may have wanted to do the same thing but were afraid. These friends are likely to look up to you.

Distribute the "Ally Reflection Sheet" handout (page 81) and ask students to complete it. Give them about 10 minutes to do so, then ask for volunteers to share their answers. Collect the reflection sheets.

PROVIDE BYSTANDERS OPPORTUNITIES TO PRACTICE SKILLS

For this activity you'll need to make copies of the four "How Can We Respond?" handouts (pages 82–85, or on the CD-ROM for early elementary versions), and the number of copies needed is based on your class's total number of students, divided by four. (For example, if you have 28 students, you will need to make seven copies of each handout.)

Divide the class into four groups of students (try not to group a student with students he or she bullies) and give the students in each group one type of handout: One group gets the physical bullying handout, one gets the verbal bullying handout, another gets the social bullying handout, and the last group gets the cyberbullying handout. Each handout has the same general instructions; go over them as a class to make sure all students understand what they will do, then let your groups get to work discussing their role play. As students prepare for role-playing, circulate in the room and answer questions and provide suggestions as needed. You might remind them about the ally skills they learned previously (page 61). Consider having each group select a facilitator to help keep them focused and record ideas.

Go Further

- Have students research young people who have acted as allies to those in need or were heroes to other kids. Consider sources such as Kids Are Heroes (www.kidsareheroes.org) and the Compassionate Action Institute's Kid Heroes page (www.pleasebekind.com/heroes.html).

- Ask students to research famous people who stood up against some of the world's historical atrocities.

- Encourage students to watch for examples of empowered bystanders in the media and have them share what they observed.

- Ask students to write their own "As an Empowered Bystander, I . . ."

If you have time, consider having groups come up with at least two endings to their scenarios, or having groups switch sheets so different groups act out different types of bullying situations. You may also consider letting students invent totally new scenes rather than using the ones on the handouts, depending on their skill and interest levels.

Give the groups about 10 minutes to prepare, then have each group role-play its assigned situation. After each role play, have a short class discussion about the response to bullying in the scene, offering different or additional solutions to the bullying situations if needed.

Go Further

Take digital photos of the role plays and post them on a class blog or website dedicated to stopping bullying or chronicling your class's efforts. Have a student from each group summarize the scene the group acted out and ask for people to suggest other resolutions to the conflicts in the comments section. If you have a Twitter account, you can post a link to the blog and ask teachers from other schools—even from other countries—to have their students read the posts and comment.

MOBILIZE BYSTANDERS

According to Denver psychologist (and bullying expert) Carla Garrity, "You can outnumber the bullies if you teach the silent majority to stand up."

Most students do not bully and are not bullied. They are witnesses or bystanders—kids who might not know what to do and might be afraid to get involved. In some cases, they're "lieutenants" or "henchmen" for someone who bullies, offering support for the kid bullying and sharing a bit of his or her power without actually doing the bullying.

Most students want to help when someone is bullied, but they are afraid or they don't know what to do. If you can "mobilize the masses" to take action against bullying, you'll significantly reduce the bullying that occurs in your classroom and school.

OFFER SPECIFIC SUGGESTIONS

Students can make a difference simply by the way they react when they witness bullying incidents. Share these suggestions with your students, and ask if they have ideas of their own.

If you want to stop bullying, you can:

- refuse to join in
- refuse to watch
- speak out ("Don't treat him that way. It's not nice." "Stop hitting her." "Don't use those words." "Don't call him that name." "I'm going to tell the teacher right now.")
- report any bullying you know about or see
- stand up for the person being bullied and gather around him or her, or invite the person to join your group (there's safety in numbers)
- be a friend to the person being bullied
- make an effort to include students who are normally left out or rejected
- distract the person bullying so he or she stops the bullying behavior

Role-play various ways to react to bullying incidents.

HAVE STUDENTS SIGN A CLASS PLEDGE

Make a copy of the "Class Pledge" (page 86). Introduce it by saying that *everyone* can help your classroom become and stay bully free. Read the pledge aloud, then pass it around for everyone to sign. Post it in a prominent place in your classroom. Or turn the pledge into a large poster and invite students to decorate it and sign it.

BREAK THE CODE OF SILENCE

Research has shown that students are reluctant to tell adults about bullying. They don't believe it will help and fear it will make things worse. Often, they're right.

Adults may not act on what they learn. They may not keep the confidence of young people who tell. And if they don't know much about bullying, they may give poor advice—such as "fight back" or "solve your own problems." A code of silence exists, especially as students move toward middle school, when the unspoken rule becomes "don't tell on other kids." Meanwhile, the kids who bully make it known that anyone who reports their behavior will be their next target.

You can and should break this code of silence. Here are some ways to do so:

- "Share Stories About Bullying" (page 13)

- "Take a Survey" (page 13)

- "Respond Effectively to Reports of Bullying" (page 65)

- "Learn More About Your Students" (page 68)

- "Use a Notes-to-the-Teacher Box" (page 69).

As you encourage students to come forward with their bullying stories, make sure they know the difference between "reporting" and "tattling," "ratting," or "snitching." Tattling, ratting, or snitching is when one student tells on another for the purpose of getting the other student in trouble. Reporting is when one student tells on another for the purpose of protecting someone else or himself. When your students fully understand this, reporting will become less of a social taboo and more of a positive, acceptable action.

If a student comes to you to report bullying he or she has witnessed:

1. Listen carefully.* Ask questions to clarify the details. Who was involved? What happened? When? Where? Were there any other witnesses? Take notes.

2. If the student requests confidentiality, respect his or her wishes.

3. Thank the student for talking with you.

If a student comes to you to "just talk" and you suspect that he or she has witnessed or has been or is being bullied:

1. Be patient. Don't expect all the details to come pouring out immediately. The student may be reluctant to give specifics out of embarrassment or shame.

2. At first, don't question the student too closely. Avoid questions that imply he or she might have done something wrong or "deserved" the bullying in any way.

BULLY FREE **IMPORTANT:** Some targets provoke bullying—by pestering, teasing, fighting back (even though they always lose), and coming back for more. But this doesn't mean they deserve to be bullied.

3. Approach the topic gently and indirectly. Give the student the option to talk about it or not.

4. If the student still skirts the issue, let him or her know that you're willing to listen anytime he or she wants to talk. Leave the door open for future conversations.

5. Once the student begins talking about the incident (or several incidents), don't be surprised if it's like a dam breaking. Let the student talk. Just listen. Try not to interrupt with suggestions or opinions. This might be the first time the student has told anyone about the bullying.

6. Be sympathetic, but don't overreact. The student will probably be emotional; it's your job to stay calm. On the other hand, don't trivialize what the student tells you. What sounds like simple teasing to you might be terrifying to him or her.

7. Let the student know that you believe what he or she is telling you.

8. Ask the student if he or she has any ideas for changing the situation.

---

*See "Be a Good Listener" (page 99).

IMPORTANT: This boosts self-confidence and self-esteem; you're letting the student know that you think he or she is capable of coming up with solutions to the problem. But even if the student has ideas, don't stop here. Bullying is not just another peer conflict. It's *always* a power imbalance. Adult intervention is required.

9. Ask the student if he or she wants your help. Chances are the answer will be yes, otherwise the student wouldn't have come to you. But sometimes what a student needs most at the moment is an adult who will listen respectfully and believe what he or she says.

10. Offer specific suggestions. (You'll find several throughout this section of the book. See also "Explore Ways to Deal with Bullying" on page 94.)

IMPORTANT: If you're not sure what to say or suggest, promise the student that you'll get back to him or her. Then seek advice from someone with experience in this area, such as another teacher, your principal, or the school counselor.

11. Redouble your efforts to create a positive classroom where bullying is not tolerated.

12. If at any time the student mentions, threatens, or alludes to suicide, take this very seriously. *Get professional help immediately.*

Whether your reporter is a witness or a target, be sure to follow through. Make it very clear that when someone tells you about a bullying incident, you *will* take action and you *won't* just "let it go."

RESPOND EFFECTIVELY TO REPORTS OF BULLYING

Much (even most) bullying occurs where adults can't see it and intervene. Kids who bully don't want adult audiences. You need to rely on students for information about bullying you don't witness personally. How can you encourage them to come forward? You might want to post these suggestions in your classroom:

- If you *see* someone being bullied, tell the teacher.
- If you *know* that someone is being bullied, tell the teacher.
- If you *think* that someone might be bullied, tell the teacher.
- If you *do nothing* about bullying, you're saying that bullying is okay with you.
- We have the power to stop and prevent bullying in our classroom, but we have to work together!

Give students several options for telling you about bullying. If they're comfortable doing this, they can tell you face-to-face—before or after school, in private (especially if they fear reprisals from the person bullying them). They can write about bullying in their journals (see "Weekly Journaling," page 68). Or they can write you a note (see "Use a Notes-to-the-Teacher Box," page 69).

No matter how much you encourage your students to keep you informed about bullying in your classroom, *reporting will stop* if you don't respond quickly and effectively. Your students need to trust that if they risk telling you about bullying, you'll do something about it. Anything less compromises or destroys that trust. See "On-the-Spot Responding," pages 95–99.

Your school or district might already have procedures in place for intervening with bullying and responding to reports of bullying. If so, follow these procedures. You'll find additional tips and suggestions in the "Help Targets of Bullying" and "Help Those Who Bully" sections of this book.

TEACH FRIENDSHIP SKILLS

Some kids bully because they don't have friends, feel lonely, and seek attention by bullying. Some kids are bullied because they're isolated and easier to pick on. All students—those who bully, those who are bullied, and those who witness it—can benefit from learning and practicing friendship skills. Here are two activities you can try with your students.

FRIENDSHIP TIPS

Distribute copies of the handout "12 Tips for Making and Keeping Friends" (page 87). Read and discuss each tip in turn. During the discussion, you might ask students to give examples from their own experience of how they have used these friendship skills. You might also comment on times when you've seen students use these skills with each other.

Tell students: *Part of being a friend is sticking up for each other. That's also a benefit of having friends.*

GO FURTHER

Challenge your students to choose one friendship tip to work on during the next week. Then, at the end of a week's time, ask them to report on their progress. They might do this orally or in writing.

FRIENDSHIP BOOSTERS AND BUSTERS

Ask your students, "What makes someone a good friend?" Invite them to think about their own friends and what they like most about them. Write their ideas on the whiteboard or chart paper under the heading "Friendship Boosters." *Examples:*

- A good friend is always there for you.
- A good friend is someone who listens.
- A good friend is someone who likes you for who you are.
- A good friend is someone you can trust.
- A good friend is someone who trusts you.
- A good friend is honest.
- A good friend encourages you to do and be your best.
- A good friend is someone who understands you.
- A good friend is someone who shares with you.
- A good friend respects your property.
- A good friend respects your rights.
- A good friend is fair.
- A good friend is someone who sticks up for you.
- A good friend doesn't try to get you to do things you shouldn't do.

Next, ask your students, "What kinds of things can hurt a friendship or keep people from making friends?" Write their ideas on the whiteboard or chart paper under the heading "Friendship Busters." *Examples:*

- bragging
- name-calling
- being bossy
- teasing
- making fun of others
- acting conceited
- lying
- spreading rumors
- stealing
- being rude
- being sarcastic
- ignoring people
- making people feel left out
- cheating
- hitting
- being mean
- embarrassing people
- trying to get people to do things they don't want to do or shouldn't do

If you and your students did the "Name Bullying Behaviors" activity (page 12), someone will probably notice the similarities between these "Friendship Busters" and bullying behaviors. If not, point it out. You might ask questions like these:

- Can acting like a bully ruin a friendship?
- Can acting like a bully get in the way of making friends?

WELCOME NEW STUDENTS

New students are more likely to be accepted if they join your class at the start of the school year. If a new student arrives during the year, make a special effort to welcome him or her.

A day or two before the new student is scheduled to arrive, alert your class. If you have any information about the new student (has the family recently moved from another town, city, or state? Does the student have any special talents, interests, abilities, or needs?), share it with the class. (You may want to get permission from the family before sharing certain information; use your judgment.) Ask questions like these:

- How would you feel if you were new in our school? If you were new in our class?

- How would you want us to treat you?

- What would make you glad to be in our class?

- What can we do to make [student's name] feel welcome?

Brainstorm ideas with your class. Here are a few starter ideas:

- Create a colorful "Welcome [Student's Name]!" banner to hang in your room.

- Make greeting to cards to give the new student.

- For the first week or two, ask for volunteers to be the new student's "buddy"—showing him or her around, making introductions, sitting with him or her at lunch, and so on. *Tip:* Change buddies every day or every other day. Make sure that buddies come from different groups within the class.

- Create a "welcome kit" to give to the new student. Include a student handbook, a map of the school, a class directory (see the next activity), a school calendar, a map of your town or city, information about school clubs and activities (with contact names and telephone numbers), a special treat of some kind (a candy bar, a coupon for an ice-cream cone at a local business), and anything else you and your students can think of that might be useful and fun.

EXPLORE EXPECTATIONS

Sometimes people behave in ways we expect them to behave. We communicate our expectations—in words, actions, and body language—and other people respond in kind. Similarly, how we treat others is often based on our expectations. Does this mean that changing our expectations can change someone else's behavior—or our own behavior? It's worth exploring.

As a class, talk about the power of expectations. You might ask questions like these:

- Where do our expectations come from? Our own experiences? Things other people have told us? Or a combination of the two?

- Do you think expectations can influence our behavior? Why or why not?

- If you expect that someone will treat you with kindness and respect, how do you act toward that person?

- If you expect that someone will be mean or rude to you, how do you act toward that person?

- If someone has high or positive expectations of you, how do you know? How does that make you feel?

- If someone has low or negative expectations of you, how do you know? How does that make you feel?

- Do you think that changing your expectations of another person might change the way you treat him or her?

- Do you think that changing your expectations of another person might change the way he or she treats you?

- If kids consistently act as allies to kids who are bullied, how do you think people's expectations will change over time?

You might illustrate these concepts with examples from your own experiences. Or use examples like these:

- "[Student's name], imagine that each day when you come to class, I expect that you will interrupt me, tease people sitting near you, and refuse to do your schoolwork. How will I treat you? How will you act then?"

- "[Student's name], imagine that each day when you come to class, I expect that you will be polite, helpful, and ready to work. How will I treat you? How will you act then?"

Suggest that students try this activity:

1. Think of someone you don't usually get along with. How do you expect him or her to treat you? How do you communicate your expectations?

2. Try changing your expectations for a few days or a week. See if that makes a difference in how the person treats you—and how you treat him or her.

If your students are keeping journals (see the next activity), you might ask them to record their thoughts and experiences.

Summarize by asking the class:

- What might happen if we all came to school each day expecting the worst from each other? How would we treat each other? How would we act? What kind of classroom would we have?

- What might happen if we all came to school each day expecting the best from each other? How would we treat each other? How would we act? What kind of classroom would we have?

- What if we all expected our classroom to be bully free every day? Would we work to make it that way? To keep it that way?

- What if we expected each other to stick up for each other—to act as allies when needed?

LEARN MORE ABOUT YOUR STUDENTS

The more you know about your students, the better you can meet their learning needs—and their needs to belong, feel accepted, and get along with each other. This all contributes to an environment in which students feel they belong, will treat each other kindly, and will be more willing to stick up for each other in bullying situations.

You're probably doing many things already to get to know your students better: greeting them by name when they enter your classroom, communicating with them one-on-one, asking about their days and weeks, listening when they come to you with a problem, concern, or exciting news. Here are two more ideas you may want to try.

WEEKLY JOURNALING

Reading your students' journal entries can give you insight into their actions and help you understand the problems they face each day. Commenting on their entries—with brief, encouraging notes, never criticisms—can strengthen your relationship and improve two-way communication.

If possible, provide your students with spiral-bound notebooks or small blank journaling books. Then introduce the activity by saying something like this:

"Each week, I'll give you a topic to write about in your journal. I'll ask you to write about your thoughts or feelings, something you care about, or something important to you. My only request is that you write at least one paragraph. Otherwise, your entries can be as long or as short as you want. I'll collect the journals and keep them between journaling times. I'll be reading your journals as a way to get to know you better. I'll also be writing back to you with my own thoughts and responses. Your journals will never be graded or criticized. Think of this as another way for us to communicate with each other."

Here's a short list of sample topics to start with. Create your own topics based on what you learn about your students and what you'd like to know.

- a time when I felt happy
- a time when I felt sad
- a time when I felt proud
- a time when I felt scared
- the last time I helped someone
- the last time I got into trouble
- my definition of a friend
- my definition of caring
- my greatest achievement
- my hopes for the future

Consider keeping your own journal and sharing your entries with your class as you see fit.

My Favorites

Distribute copies of the handout "My Favorites" (page 88). When students complete them, you can either collect the handouts to review privately, invite students to tell the class about some of their favorite things, or post the handouts around the room and give students time to read them. *Tip:* Tell your students ahead of time which option you'll choose, in case they prefer to keep their responses private.

If the handouts are shared, consider having a class discussion about them. Ask questions like:

- Did you discover that you have things in common? What things?
- Were there any surprises?
- Did you learn anything new? What did you learn?
- Are there things that everyone likes?
- Are there things that no one likes?

Go Further

Have students create a poster or bulletin board listing and/or illustrating things they have in common.

USE A NOTES-TO-THE-TEACHER BOX

Put a "Notes-to-the-Teacher Box" on the corner of your desk. It might be large or small, decorated or plain. (You could ask your students to decorate it.) It should have a lid with a slit in the top. Make sure it is secured and in a place where no one can tamper with it.

To explain the purpose of the box, you might say:

"Here's another way for you to communicate with me. If there's anything you want to tell me about—a problem you're having at school, a classroom issue, an exciting event, or anything at all you'd like me to know—just write me a note and drop it in the box. I'm the only person who will open the box and read the notes inside, and I'll check the messages at the end of each day.

"You don't have to sign your name if you don't want to, but I hope you will. I can only reply to you personally if you sign your name.

"You can also use the box to tell me about bullying in our classroom. You can write about bullying that happens to you, or bullying you witness personally. If you've been bullying someone else and you want to stop, you can write about that, too."

Then be sure to follow through. Check the box daily. Respond appropriately to the notes your students write. If students have special concerns, arrange to meet with them privately.

If notes reveal that some of your students are being bullied or are bullying others, try the suggestions in the "Help Targets of Bullying" and "Help Those Who Bully" sections of this book.

 IMPORTANT: If a student uses the box to disclose abuse or another serious problem, follow your school's reporting procedures. Help your student get the support and assistance he or she needs.

HELP STUDENTS ACCEPT THEIR DIFFERENCES

If you and your students did the "Build Acceptance" activity (page 10), students learned ways to accept each other. Kids also need to know how to accept themselves. Bystanders who have strong self-esteem are more likely to act as allies when they see other kids being bullied. Any student who can accept himself or herself is more likely to feel empathy for targets as well.

Self-esteem also helps targets and potential targets, of course. Most bullying targets are "different" from the majority in one or more ways. Kids who are looking for someone to bully zero in on differences and make them the focus of their attacks. Kids are bullied for being too tall, too short, too thin, or too heavy; for having a physical disability or learning difference; for belonging to ethnic, racial, cultural, or religious groups that aren't the "norm"; for having special needs . . . for almost any reason that sets them apart.

How can you help students accept themselves? Here are several ideas to try. Ask other teachers and experts (e.g., your school counselor, local spokespersons) for more suggestions.

- Model acceptance and affirmation by learning as much as you can about your students' differences. Invite them to educate you.

- When assigning projects and reports, allow students to research their differences. A student who wears glasses might report on the history of eyeglasses . . . and identify famous people in history who have worn them. A student with a chronic illness might contact a national organization, learn about other people who have his or her illness, and share their stories. All students can report on their heritage. Encourage students to identify reasons to be proud of their differences, and/or positive ways to cope with their differences.

- Help students identify role models who share their differences. (For example, Whoopi Goldberg, Albert Einstein, Thomas Edison, former U.S. president George H.W. Bush, Keira Knightley, and race car driver Jackie Stewart all have something in common: dyslexia.)

- Ask your librarian or media specialist to recommend books and other resources related to your students' differences. Incorporate them into lessons and displays. Differences may include racial or ethnic differences, physical differences, learning differences, or disabilities. You could also focus on multiple intelligences or the different skills and abilities your students have.

- Overweight students are often picked on and rejected, especially if they lack social skills. You might want to contact the National Association to Advance Fat Acceptance (NAAFA) for information about its Kids' Project. A nonprofit human rights organization, NAAFA has been working since 1969 to eliminate discrimination based on body size. Write or call: NAAFA, PO Box 4662, Foster City, CA 94404; telephone 916-558-6880. On the Web, go to www.naafa.org.

- Are there local support groups for people with disabilities and other differences? Find out and get in touch with them. You might invite a speaker to visit your class or school.

- Make it a privilege for students to help other students with something they are good at, such as tutoring or coaching a sport.

- As a class or a school, raise funds to buy a piece of equipment or other resources to help students with special needs.

- Help students talk more openly about their differences. A willingness to talk indicates a positive attitude and acceptance, which serves as an example for others. Students who are embarrassed or ashamed of their differences can become targets for bullying.

- Help students develop a sense of humor. Kids who can laugh at themselves are better able to cope with teasing. Humor can also defuse potentially volatile situations.

REWARD COOPERATION

Often, when we plan group activities for our students, we focus on the *product*—the paper, project, or other end result we expect them to accomplish. Another equally important (perhaps more important) aspect of group activities is teaching students how to cooperate as they work toward a common goal.

Plan some group activities that stress this as the main purpose. *Examples:*

- a craft project designed so each student can make a contribution

- an anti-bullying classroom campaign, complete with posters, slogans, songs, and skits

- friendship role plays

- kind-word crosswords or search-a-word puzzles

- new games for the rest of the class to play

Emphasize the value of effort over results. Establish checkpoints along the way during which students can report on how well they're working together, whether they're enjoying the process, and what they're learning from each other.

Sit in with each group, observe, and comment on what you see. Compliment students for their willingness to get along and value each other's unique abilities.

This type of group activity offers several rewards. It encourages unity and acceptance and discourages perfectionism. It invites students to take risks and explore new interests without fear of rejection. It gives them opportunities to acquire new skills and reveal hidden strengths, which boosts their standing among their peers. When students cooperate, everybody wins.

ENCOURAGE RANDOM ACTS OF KINDNESS

Random acts of kindness are proven, powerful ways to create a more positive environment anywhere—in the classroom, at home, and in the community. Here are five activities you can do with your students to promote kindness and help them form the habit of doing nice things for others "just because."

CLASS DISCUSSION

Talk about kindness as a class. You might ask questions like these:

- When was the last time someone did something really nice for you? What did the person do? How did it make you feel?

- Did the person have a reason for acting that way? Did he or she expect something from you in return? Or was the person kind "just because"?

- Have you ever done something nice for another person without being asked, and without expecting anything in return? What did you do? How did you feel? How do you think the other person felt?

- What if everyone in this class made the effort to be kind to each other? What would our class be like? Is this something we should try? How can we start?

Ask students to offer suggestions. List them on the whiteboard or chart paper. Have them vote on one or more to try for the rest of the week.

GO FURTHER

Read aloud from *Kids' Random Acts of Kindness* (Conari Press, 1994). In this wonderful book, kids from around the world tell their own stories of sudden, impetuous acts of kindness. Also available and just as inspiring are *Random Acts of Kindness* and *More Random Acts of Kindness* (Conari, 2002 and 1994).

KINDNESS BOX

Take a box with a lid (a large shoe box works well) and cut a slit in the top. Label it the "Kindness Box" and decorate it (or have students decorate it), then put it on a shelf or a corner of your desk.

Invite students to write brief notes about acts of kindness they do or witness and drop them in the box. Once a week, once a day, or whenever you choose, dip into the box, pull out a note, and read it aloud to the class. Thank your students for their kindness to each other.

KINDNESS PALS

Write your students' names on slips of paper, put the slips in a hat or box, and have students draw names. (Anyone who draws his or her own name should draw again.) Explain that by the end of the week, everyone should commit at least one act of kindness for the person whose name they drew. If you think your students might need ideas, brainstorm some as a class and write them on the whiteboard or chart paper to serve as reminders.

At the end of the week, invite students to tell the class what they did. After each student reveals his or her act of kindness, lead the class in applause.

If your students are keeping journals (see page 110), ask them to write about their acts of kindness. When you read their entries, be sure to leave a positive comment or two congratulating them on their efforts.

KINDNESS REPORTER

Select one student each week to serve as a "kindness reporter." He or she will watch for acts of kindness and briefly describe them in a notebook. (*Tip:* Kids might enjoy using a special notebook or steno pad provided for this purpose.) At the end of the week, have the reporter share the good news with the class.

BIG BOOK OF KINDNESS

Ask your students to watch for and collect stories about kindness. They might write brief descriptions of stories they see on television or in movies, or bring in stories from newspapers or magazines. Or they might write stories about kindness they experience in their own lives—at home, at school, in their neighborhoods, in clubs or organizations they belong to, and so on.

As students gather their stories, have them paste or write them on large sheets of paper. They can decorate them with drawings, photos, collages, or whatever they choose. Punch holes along the edges and bind the sheets together with pieces of string or yarn. Add cardboard covers with decorations and the title "Our Big Book of Kindness." Keep the book available so students can look through it and add to it often.

Another option is to collect these stories on a class "Kindness Blog."

TEACH ASSERTIVENESS SKILLS

Some students don't know what to do or how to react when they're bullied or when they see others bullied. In general, kids who bully tend to be aggressive—they behave as if their rights matter more than anyone else's rights. Targets tend to be passive—they behave as if other people's rights matter more than theirs. Between these two extremes lies *assertiveness*. Assertive people respect their own rights *and* other people's rights. Assertiveness is an important trait for targets to adopt, and is a useful skill for bystanders who want to be empowered to act as allies. It is not easy to stand up against bullying, and assertiveness skills can help.

Most of us could benefit from assertiveness training. Here are some tips and strategies for teaching your students to be more assertive. Practice them with your students and offer coaching where needed. Students who are naturally shy and withdrawn, and those who have been (or are) bullying targets, will need extra help learning and using assertiveness skills.

KNOW YOUR RIGHTS

Ask your students, "Do you have any rights? Do you know what they are?" As they offer ideas, write them on the whiteboard or chart paper. Make sure these rights appear somewhere on the list:

1. We have the right to think for ourselves.
2. We have the right to have and express our opinions, views, and beliefs.
3. We have the right to make decisions about our lives.
4. We have the right to say no.
5. We have the right to say yes.
6. We have the right to stand up to people who tease us, criticize us, or put us down.
7. We have the right to have and express our feelings.
8. We have the right to respond when someone violates our rights.

GO FURTHER
Have students create and illustrate a "Student Bill of Rights" poster for the classroom.

WATCH YOUR BODY LANGUAGE

Sometimes body language speaks more loudly than words. Kids who slouch, mumble, fidget, avoid looking people in the eye, back off, and appear frightened and worried are more likely to be targeted than those whose body language expresses confidence and positive self-esteem. It's not right or fair—those kids don't deserve to be bullied any more than other kids—but it's true.

Teach students how to look assertive. Practice with role plays, skits, and face-to-face discussions. Here are the five basics of assertive body language:

1. Stand up straight. Stand with your feet shoulder width apart so you feel balanced and stable.

2. Keep your head up.

3. Keep your shoulders straight. Don't hunch.

4. Look people in the eye. Not over their heads, not at the ground—right in the eye. Try not to appear hurt.

5. Don't back off when you're talking to someone. Move closer—but not too close. Keep a comfortable distance between you (at least arm's length).

When you look assertive, you're more likely to *feel* assertive, and other people are more likely to treat you with respect.

Pair assertive body language with assertive words spoken in a firm, confident, calm, determined voice. Don't mumble or whine—but don't shout, either. Then say what you mean and mean what you say.

USE THE ASSERT FORMULA

Distribute copies of the handout "The ASSERT Formula" (page 89) and lead students through it. Have them practice the formula in skits and role plays.

 IMPORTANT: Some kids who bully enjoy hearing that they've hurt people, so it's best in many cases to skip the "Effect on Me" step.

GIVE BYSTANDERS ASSERTIVENESS STRATEGIES

Here are some assertiveness techniques specifically for bystanders. Review these with your class and practice example dialogues. All bystanders can be allies to bullied students. After initially using any of these techniques, allies should walk away with the targeted student.

- **Make assertive statements on behalf of the target.** Say, "Stop it!" or "This is a waste of [target's name] time and my time."

- **Fogging.** Admit that you also have the characteristic the person is using to tease someone: "You know, I need to lose weight, too. Big deal."

- **Broken record.** Repeat "What did you say?" "That's your opinion," or "So?" each time the bullying student insults or teases the target.

- **Confront the student** concerning his or her spreading rumors and lies about someone. Refuse to spread the lies and demand that the rumors stop.

- **Expose the ignorance of bullying statements** about someone with a disability or medical problem. Reveal the facts.

- **Give permission to tease.** Say, "Well, it's okay to say what you want. It doesn't bother [target] and it doesn't bother me."

GET STUDENTS INVOLVED IN GROUPS

Students who are bullied have plenty of experience feeling isolated, excluded, rejected, and afraid. They need experience feeling welcome, safe, and accepted.

> **GO FURTHER**
> Check out assertiveness training programs and opportunities at local community and youth organizations. Arrange for a trainer to visit your class and demonstrate ways to be assertive.

Consider starting a counseling group (see "Provide Counseling," page 136) for *any* students who need help making friends and practicing social skills—not just bullying targets. Other types of groups are valuable, too. Try to mix kids who are targeted with kids who are already allies to bullied kids or who are likely to act as allies. Once students begin to build relationships in these groups, they may be more likely to stick up for each other. Here are some types of groups to consider:

- a peer support group
- a new student orientation group
- a cooperative learning group
- a special interest group or club

For students who aren't ready to integrate with their peers during unstructured times (such as recess), consider starting a club that meets at those times. Meetings can be structured around specific topics (how to make friends, how to stand up to bullying), or students can learn and practice social skills. Some of the meetings should be set aside for fun and play.

This type of club also provides an alternative for students who are new to the school and not yet comfortable or confident on the playground. The club you form should provide a well-supervised environment that allows and encourages friendships to develop. Once they do, students may be less reluctant to go outside and play.

You can also suggest that students get involved with groups, clubs, and youth-serving organizations in your community. For starter ideas, see page 108. Parents can also arrange these opportunities for their children; you could raise the topic during a parent-teacher conference. The goals of any group involvement should be to develop the student's peer support network, self-confidence, and social skills.

PROMOTE TEAMWORK

Students who participate in group activities are more likely to have positive feelings about other people. They develop fewer biases and prejudices—or rethink the biases or prejudices they already have.

Talk as a class about the attitudes, skills, and abilities people need in order to work well in groups. Ask your students to think about what makes a good team member and a good team. Write their ideas on the whiteboard or chart paper. If they have difficulty coming up with ideas, start by offering one or more of these:

Good team members . . .

- accept each other as equals
- support the group's goals
- respect the group's rules
- participate in discussions
- listen to each other during discussions
- disagree without being disagreeable
- express their needs and feelings honestly
- do their fair share of the work
- have a positive attitude
- suggest solutions to problems

Good teams . . .

- set clear goals and agree to reach them together
- set clear rules and agree to follow them
- resolve any disagreements fairly and peacefully
- identify the strengths of individual team members, then use those strengths to benefit the team as a whole
- compromise when there's a conflict
- share the responsibilities equally among the team members

Ask your class:

- Do you think our class is a good team? Why or why not?
- What could we do to work more efficiently as a team? Does anyone have specific ideas we can try?

WORK TOGETHER TO SOLVE A PROBLEM

When you and your students work together to solve a problem outside the classroom—when you face a common "enemy" as a group—you naturally grow closer to each other in the process. This builds unity, acceptance, and the satisfaction of joining forces for a good cause.

Ask your students to brainstorm problems they'd like to address. These might be problems in your school, your community, or the world. (*Examples:* pollution, smoking, drugs, cruelty to animals, homelessness, hunger.) Write their ideas on the whiteboard or chart paper. Afterward, have students choose one problem to work on. You could either ask for a show of hands or prepare secret ballots so students can vote for their top choices.

Once you've identified a problem, find ways for your students to take action and make a difference. For ideas, see "Get Students Involved in Service" (page 32).

SET UP A PEACE PLACE

Set aside a corner of your classroom as the "Peace Place." Tell students they can go there when they need to resolve a conflict, talk with another student about a problem they're having, or just spend some quiet time when they're feeling upset, frustrated, or overwhelmed. This can be a good place for ally relationships to be built.

Furnish your Peace Place with a small table or desk, two or three chairs (or cushions or beanbags), peaceful posters (nature scenes, animals, people), and a music system (CD or MP3 player) with quiet music or nature sounds. Start and build a small library of appropriate books—on friendship, conflict resolution, peacefulness, and related topics—and keep them on a bookshelf in your Peace Place.

As a class, develop a set of short, simple rules for the Peace Place. Have students make and decorate a poster listing the rules. *Examples:*

1. If you're having a problem with another student, ask him or her to go to the Peace Place with you and talk it over.

2. If another student asks you to go to the Peace Place, say yes.

3. When you're in the Peace Place, use gentle, respectful words.

4. Take turns talking and listening.

5. Be a good listener. Pay attention to what the other person says. Don't interrupt.

6. If you can't solve the problem on your own, ask the teacher for help.

7. The Peace Place is special. Keep it neat and clean.

TEACH STUDENTS TO AFFIRM THEMSELVES

Provide students with small blank books or notebooks (or put these on your list of school supplies to send home to parents at the start of the school year). Have students label their books "What's Good About Me" and use them to list and describe their positive characteristics. Get them started by asking questions like these:

- What do you like about yourself?

- What are you good at? What are you best at?

- What are your positive characteristics?

- What good things would you like other people to know about you?

- What makes you proud of yourself?

You might also refer to the list of starter words in "Affirm Your Students" (page 29).

If your students are comfortable with it, allow other people (students, teachers, other school personnel, visiting parents, aides) to add their own comments to students' books. To ensure that comments are positive, set two rules: (1) Everyone must sign his or her comment(s). (2) No one may write in another person's book without his or her permission. This will help students build relationships and feel like allies.

Every so often, you might want to ask a student if it's okay to read aloud from his or her book. If it is, choose a few comments to share with the class. This encourages students to recognize and acknowledge each other's positive characteristics and notice similarities.

It's likely that these books will become cherished possessions—something your students will treasure for many years. For more ways to help children learn to affirm themselves, see "Teach Positive Self-Talk" (page 30).

TEACH STUDENTS TO AFFIRM EACH OTHER

When students affirm each other, everyone feels accepted, appreciated, and valued. Here are six approaches you can try with your students.

AFFIRMATIONS BOX

Take a box with a lid (a large shoe box works well) and cut a slit in the top. Label it the "Affirmations Box," decorate it (or have students decorate it), and put it on a shelf or a corner of your desk.

Invite students to write positive statements about each other whenever they would like and to drop them in the box. Once a week, once a day, or whenever you choose, dip into the box, pull out a statement or two, and read it aloud to the class.

This is a powerful way to encourage students to notice and appreciate each other's positive qualities. It helps them see qualities they might have overlooked and discover similarities.

AFFIRMATIONS CARDS

Write each student's name on a 3" x 5" card. Hand out the cards randomly (just make sure no one gets his or her own name). Then have each student write something positive about the student named on the card. *Examples:* "Sara is a terrific soccer player." "Ren is always willing to help." "Zach tells the best jokes." "Ashley has a great smile." Explain that you need students to take this seriously, because you (or they) will be reading their statements aloud. Ask students to sign their statements. (Anyone who's tempted to write something negative will think twice if his or her signature is on the card.)

Give the class a few minutes to write their statements. Collect them and quickly review them to make sure all statements are positive. Then hand them back to the appropriate students and invite volunteers to read their statements aloud. If a student isn't comfortable doing this in front of the class, you can offer to read his or her statement. Either way, everyone should enjoy the experience.

Do this several times during the school year—once a week or once a month.

GO FURTHER
Take individual photos of your students and display them on a bulletin board along with their positive statements. Teachers who have done this report that students visit the bulletin board often, reading the statements and pointing out similar positive comments.

AFFIRMATIONS CIRCLES

Divide the class into two groups. (If you have an uneven number of students, join this activity yourself.) Have one group form a circle facing inward. Have the other group form a circle around the first group. Each student in the outer circle should stand directly behind a student in the inner circle.

On your cue, each student in the outer circle should put a hand on the shoulder of the student in front of him or her, then whisper a positive, encouraging statement in that student's ear. The statement should be brief, honest, sincere, and simple. *Examples:* "I like the way you draw." "Thanks for helping me study for the math test." "I see you got your hair cut. It looks great." "I think you're the friendliest person in the class." "I'm glad you're my friend."

Next, have the students in the outer circle move one person to the left (or the right) and do it again (hand on the shoulder, positive statement). Keep going until the outer circle has moved all the way around the inner circle. Then have the circles switch places—the outer circle becomes the inner circle, and students who have been giving positive statements now have the chance to receive them.

Afterward, talk about the activity. Ask: "How did it feel to *say* something positive to another person? How did it feel to *hear* someone make a positive, encouraging statement about you?"

Thumbs Up

When one student makes a negative "thumbs-down" comment about another, immediately ask him or her to make two positive "thumbs-up" comments about that person. If the student has difficulty doing this (or won't do it), ask the class to make the positive comments. *Tip:* If you did the "Ice-Cream Cone Bulletin Board" activity (page 29), you can have one student read what you wrote about the student who was the target of the "thumbs-down."

Encourage your students to use a "thumbs-up" sign in class, on the playground, in the lunchroom, in the halls, and elsewhere to show their approval and support for each other.

Applause! Applause!

Invite your students to show their approval of a classmate's performance, good deed, or other positive action in a time-honored way: with applause. Encourage them to applaud vigorously and often.

You might say, "We applaud—or clap—for people to let them know we like something they're doing or something they've done. We enjoy it when people clap for us, and they enjoy it when we clap for them." Ask students to suggest times when they might applaud each other.

Have a brief practice session and set some ground rules so students don't get carried away. For example, they should stop clapping on a signal from you—perhaps when you raise your hand. You might create an "Applause!" sign or banner for your classroom. Point to the sign or banner to remind students to applaud when it's appropriate.

Good for You! Certificates

Once a week or twice a month, ask students to celebrate each other's achievements and accomplishments by completing "Good for You!" certificates (page 53). Explain that the achievements and accomplishments can be large or small, and they don't necessarily have to happen in the classroom or even be school-related.

Keep several copies of the certificate on hand. Post completed certificates around the classroom for a few days, then allow the honored students to take them down and bring them home to share with their families. *Tip:* Make sure all students are recognized often, not just the same few students. Fill out certificates yourself for students whose achievements and accomplishments might otherwise go unnoticed.

IF I WANT TO STOP BULLYING, I CAN . . .

Refuse to join in.

Refuse to stand guard or watch for adults.

Refuse to laugh.

Ask the target to walk away with me and my friends.

Report the bullying to an adult.

Stick up for the bullied student by saying:

Stop it!

Leave him alone.

Don't treat him that way!

Bullying isn't allowed in our school.

Stop hitting her!

Don't call him that name!

Stop picking on her!

I'm reporting this to the teacher.

I can also:

_____

_____

_____

I FEEL . . .

Name: _____ Date: _____

Instructions: **Complete the following sentences.**

When I see someone cry, I feel _____

_____

When I see someone afraid, I feel _____

_____

When I see someone laughing, I feel _____

_____

When I hear someone tell a joke, I feel _____

_____

When I see someone yelling, I feel _____

_____

When I hear someone called a mean name, I feel _____

_____

When I see someone share, I feel _____

_____

When I see people play together, I feel _____

_____

When I see someone left out, I feel _____

_____

When I see people fighting, I feel _____

_____

When I see someone stick up for another student, I feel _____

_____

When I tell the teacher about someone being mean to someone, I feel _____

_____

When I tell the teacher that someone is being mean to me, I feel _____

_____

50 WORDS AND PHRASES THAT DESCRIBE FEELINGS

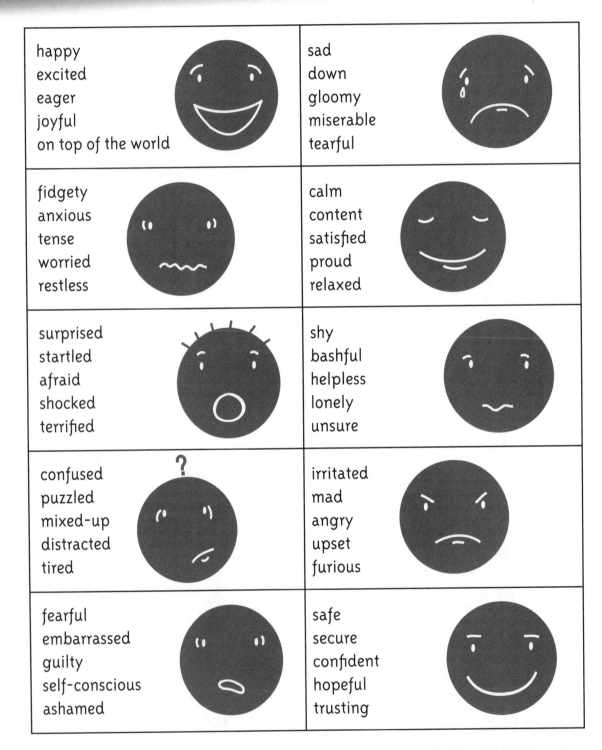

happy excited eager joyful on top of the world	sad down gloomy miserable tearful
fidgety anxious tense worried restless	calm content satisfied proud relaxed
surprised startled afraid shocked terrified	shy bashful helpless lonely unsure
confused puzzled mixed-up distracted tired	irritated mad angry upset furious
fearful embarrassed guilty self-conscious ashamed	safe secure confident hopeful trusting

Adapted from *A Leader's Guide to We Can Get Along* by Lauren Murphy Payne, Claudia Rohling, and Pamela Espeland (Free Spirit Publishing Inc, 1997).

ALLY REFLECTION SHEET

Name: _____ **Date:** _____

Today you learned about being an ally. What does that mean?

_____

_____

_____

What are some skills you learned?

_____

_____

_____

_____

_____

_____

What are some things you plan to do differently because of this lesson?

_____

_____

_____

_____

_____

_____

_____

_____

_____

_____

Read the short bullying stories below, discuss them as a group, and choose one. How can you end this story in a positive way? Decide how you will end the story, then prepare to act it out in front of your class. Here are some guidelines to help you get started:

- Determine what roles your group members will play and what each person will say and do. Besides the people bullying and being bullied, be sure you have followers (people who encourage the bullying) and bystanders.

- Do not use the names of real people. The story should be totally made up.

- You may add content to make the event seem real, such as made-up background information, a name for the school, and grade levels for all the individuals involved.

- When you perform your scene, you may need to prepare the class by telling them important information, such as the location of the scene (for example, hallway, locker room, playground), and background information, such as the fact that this is not an isolated event (the bullying has happened before).

Bullying Situation: Scott has been picking on Andrew a lot the last couple weeks. Andrew is walking toward the bus when Scott knocks his books out of his hands and laughs. When Andrew squats down to pick them up, Luis knees him in the shoulder and knocks him over. Scott and Luis stand there laughing over Andrew. Other students look at each other with concern, but so far nobody has done anything.

Bullying Situation: Oscar thinks it's hilarious to pinch Dawn, and he does it every chance he gets. Today in the hall between classes, he corners her and pinches her over and over, laughing as he does it. The hall is full of kids walking by. Dawn looks embarrassed and upset.

Read the short bullying stories below, discuss them as a group, and choose one. How can you end this story in a positive way? Decide how you will end the story, then prepare to act it out in front of your class. Here are some guidelines to help you get started:

- Determine what roles your group members will play and what each person will say and do. Besides the people bullying and being bullied, be sure you have followers (people who encourage the bullying) and bystanders.

- Do not use the names of real people. The story should be totally made up.

- You may add content to make the event seem real, such as made-up background information, a name for the school, and grade levels for all the individuals involved.

- When you perform your scene, you may need to prepare the class by telling them important information, such as the location of the scene (for example, hallway, locker room, playground), and background information, such as the fact that this is not an isolated event (the bullying has happened before).

Bullying Situation: Lauren says she caught Victor picking his nose, and she has been making fun of him for more than a week. At lunch, she points at him and calls out "Victor the Picker! Victor the Picker! You're so gross, Victor the Picker!" Other kids are laughing and start calling him the same name, and nobody will sit by him.

Bullying Situation: Jackson is known for being mean to lots of kids, and lately he's been targeting Bennett by calling him really mean names. In class, the teacher calls on Bennett to answer a question, and while everyone's attention is on him, Jackson makes a crude comment about him. The whole class hears, and many kids laugh.

HOW CAN WE RESPOND?
SOCIAL/RELATIONAL BULLYING

Read the short bullying stories below, discuss them as a group, and choose one. How can you end this story in a positive way? Decide how you will end the story, then prepare to act it out in front of your class. Here are some guidelines to help you get started:

- Determine what roles your group members will play and what each person will say and do. Besides the people bullying and being bullied, be sure you have followers (people who encourage the bullying) and bystanders.

- Do not use the names of real people. The story should be totally made up.

- You may add content to make the event seem real, such as made-up background information, a name for the school, and grade levels for all the individuals involved.

- When you perform your scene, you may need to prepare the class by telling them important information, such as the location of the scene (for example, hallway, locker room, playground), and background information, such as the fact that this is not an isolated event (the bullying has happened before).

Bullying Situation: Cathy, Chantal, Jane, and Jo Beth have been good friends all year, but last week Cathy started teasing Jo Beth for wearing clothes that are out-of-date and too big for her, and lately the other girls have joined in. When Jo Beth comes to sit with them in the media center, Cathy takes the book of poetry Jo Beth has in her hands and says, "I can't believe you actually read this stuff. You're so weird! Go sit somewhere else." The other girls agree, and Jo Beth slowly gets up and sits at a different table to read her book.

Bullying Situation: Katie and Jon used to be best friends, but they had a fight. Since then, Katie has been spreading false rumors about Jon, saying that he often pees his pants. Now kids are starting to avoid Jon. At recess, Eric spits water from the drinking fountain onto Jon's pants, and everyone laughs at Jon and says he peed his pants. Katie is there, too.

Read the short bullying stories below, discuss them as a group, and choose one. How can you end this story in a positive way? Decide how you will end the story, then prepare to act it out in front of your class. Here are some guidelines to help you get started:

- Determine what roles your group members will play and what each person will say and do. Besides the people bullying and being bullied, be sure you have followers (people who encourage the bullying) and bystanders.

- Do not use the names of real people. The story should be totally made up.

- You may add content to make the event seem real, such as made-up background information, a name for the school, and grade levels for all the individuals involved.

- When you perform your scene, you may need to prepare the class by telling them important information, such as the location of the scene (for example, hallway, locker room, playground), and background information, such as the fact that this is not an isolated event (the bullying has happened before).

Bullying Situation: Seth creates a "We Hate Dena" website, asking other kids to sign on and promise to kick Dena in the butt every time they see her. Dena has been kicked in the butt many times this week, and today at recess she sees two kids looking at the website on a portable device. When the kids notice her looking at the site, they close the page, but it's too late. Dena is humiliated.

Bullying Situation: Rick and Jorge used to be good friends, but they had a fight. In the locker room after gym class one day, Rick took his phone out of his gym bag and took a picture of Jorge in the shower. He sent the picture to several friends, who forwarded it to more friends, and Rick even posted the photo on Facebook. Jorge confronts Rick in the hallway at school, and the two begin arguing loudly.

CLASS PLEDGE

1. We won't bully others.

2. We will help students who are being bullied.

3. We will include students who are left out.

4. We will report any bullying we know about or see.

Signed:

12 TIPS FOR MAKING AND KEEPING FRIENDS

1. **Reach out.** Don't always wait for someone else to make the first move. A simple "hi" and a smile go a long way.

2. **Get involved.** Join clubs that interest you. Take special classes inside or outside of school. Be a volunteer.

3. **Let people know you're interested in them.** Don't just talk about yourself; ask questions about them.

4. **Be a good listener.** Look at people while they're talking to you. Pay attention to what they say.

5. **Risk telling people about yourself.** When it feels right, let them in on your interests, your talents, and what's important to you. *But . . .*

6. **Don't be a show-off.** Not everyone you meet will have your abilities and interests. (On the other hand, you shouldn't have to hide them—which you won't, once you find friends who like and appreciate you.)

7. **Be honest.** Tell the truth about yourself, what you believe in, and what you stand for. When asked for your opinion, be sincere. Friends appreciate truthfulness in each other. *But . . .*

8. **Be kind.** There are times when being tactful is more important than being totally honest. The truth doesn't have to hurt.

9. **Don't just use your friends as sounding boards for your problems.** Include them in the good times, too.

10. **Do your share of the work.** That's right—work. Any relationship takes effort. Don't always depend on your friends to make the plans and carry all the weight.

11. **Be accepting.** Not all of your friends have to think and act like you do. (Wouldn't it be boring if they did?)

12. **Learn to recognize the so-called friends you can do without.** Some people get so lonely that they put up with anyone—including friends who aren't really friends at all.

MY FAVORITES

Your name: _____ **Today's date:** _____

My favorite TV show _____

My favorite place to go _____

My favorite thing to do in my free time _____

The thing I like *most* about school _____

The thing I like *least* about school _____

My favorite athlete/sports personality _____

My favorite radio station _____

My favorite food _____

My favorite place to eat _____

I like people who . . . _____

I don't like it when people . . . _____

My favorite magazine _____

My favorite book _____

My favorite movie _____

My favorite website _____

The job I'd like to have when I grow up _____

My favorite game _____

My favorite video game _____

My greatest hope _____

My biggest worry _____

If I could go anywhere in the world, I'd go to . . . _____

My favorite type of music _____

My favorite singer/group/musician _____

My favorite actor/actress _____

The person I admire most _____

My favorite time of the day _____

THE ASSERT FORMULA

A stands for **ATTENTION.** Before you can talk about and try to solve a problem you're having with someone else, you need to get his or her attention. *Example:* "Sean, I need to talk to you about something. Is now a good time?"

S stands for **SOON, SIMPLE, AND SHORT.** Speak up as soon as you realize that your rights have been violated. Look the person in the eye and keep your comments brief and to the point. *Example:* "It's about something that happened in the hall today."

S stands for **SPECIFIC BEHAVIOR.** What did the person do to violate your rights? Focus on the behavior, not the person. Be as specific as you can. *Example:* "I didn't like it when you pushed me against my locker, I dropped my books, and you kicked them across the hall."

E stands for **EFFECT ON ME.** Share the feelings you experienced as a result of the person's behavior. *Example:* "It was embarrassing, plus I was late for class. I had to wait for the hall to clear before I could pick up my books."

R stands for **RESPONSE.** Wait for a response from the other person. He or she might try to brush you off with "What's the big deal?" or "Don't be a baby" or "Can't you take a joke?" or "So what?" Don't let it bother you. At least it's a response. On the other hand, the person might apologize.

T stands for **TERMS.** Suggest a solution to the problem. *Example:* "I want you to stop bothering me in the hall. If you don't, I'll report you to the teacher."

Tips: The ASSERT Formula may feel strange and awkward at first. It isn't foolproof, and it won't always work. In some situations—for example, bullying that involves physical violence—it might make things worse. And some kids love getting any kind of response, even an assertive response. If your being assertive seems to anger or provoke the person who is bullying you, walk away or run away.

Adapted from *Fighting Invisible Tigers: Stress Management for Teens,* copyright © 2008 by Earl Hipp, Free Spirit Publishing Inc.

HELP TARGETS
OF BULLYING

If you were bullied as a child, you can probably remember how you felt. You may recall the specifics of each incident—the people, places, words, insults, frustration, pain, anger, and powerlessness.

The good news: Your students don't have to endure the bullying you put up with when you were their age. We know more about bullying now than we did even when this book first came out in 1999, and we know more about how to prevent it and stop it. We know more about how to help targets of bullying—and why we should and must help them.

The "Create a Positive Classroom" and the "Empower Bystanders to Become Allies" sections of this book include many tips and strategies that can benefit targets and potential targets. *Examples:*

- "Teach Anger Management Skills" (page 23)
- "Teach Conflict Resolution Skills" (page 25)
- "Teach Positive Self-Talk" (page 30)
- "Teach Friendship Skills" (page 65)
- "Use a Notes-to-the-Teacher Box" (page 69)
- "Teach Assertiveness Skills" (page 72)
- "Teach Students to Affirm Themselves" (page 75)

"Help Targets of Bullying" also has plenty of activities and ideas you can use with all of your students. But most of the material here focuses on students who desperately need adults to understand and care about what they're going through, and to do something about it.

As you try these ideas with your class, individual students, and small groups, and as you share them with other teachers and staff, here are some good outcomes you can expect to see:

Your students will learn how to:
- stick up for themselves and each other
- feel stronger, more confident, and better about themselves
- strengthen their bully resistance skills
- build their social skills
- plan ahead to avoid potential problems
- use humor and other "power skills" to disarm kids who bully them

You'll discover how to:

- identify targets or potential targets

- encourage students to report bullying

- act quickly and effectively when you learn of a bullying incident

- communicate with parents and get them involved in making your classroom bully free

- equalize the power between those who bully and those who are bullied

- protect yourself

BE ALERT

Most bullying takes place where you (and other adults) can't see it or hear it. Kids who bully need an audience of peers to establish their power over the target, but the last thing they want is an audience of adults who have power over them and can make them stop.

Pay attention to interactions between your students. Are there some who seem fearful, withdrawn, lonely, and shy? Are there others who seem especially aggressive, need to "win" all the time, seek excessive attention, and are always pushing school boundaries or class rules? How do they get along with each other? What happens when they're seated beside each other, or are assigned to the same groups and expected to work together? Be watchful and alert.

Talk with lunchroom supervisors, hall monitors, playground supervisors, gym teachers, and other adults who spend time with your students. Ask for their insights and input into relationships between your students. What have they seen? What have they heard? Learn as much as you can. It may be that bullying has gone on behind your back (even under your nose) and you simply haven't noticed it. If so, you're not alone.

IDENTIFY TARGETS OR POTENTIAL TARGETS

You may know that some students in your classroom are targets of bullying—because you've witnessed bullying events personally, other students have reported them to you, or the targets themselves have come forward.

But most bullying goes unnoticed and unreported. How can you identify targets or potential targets? You can watch for specific behaviors—and you can seek input from students' parents.

Experts have determined that bullying targets usually fit into one of two broad categories: passive (or submissive) targets and provocative targets. No one student will have all these characteristics, but this list can be a guide to help you identify potential targets in your classroom and school.

PASSIVE OR SUBMISSIVE TARGETS

- They are generally quiet, cautious, sensitive, and perhaps easily moved to tears.

- They may be insecure and have little self-confidence (negative self-esteem), perhaps as the result of bullying.

- If boys, they are usually physically weaker than their classmates, particularly those who bully, and they do not like to fight.

- They are likely to have few or no friends, perhaps as a result of bullying.

- They may be afraid of getting hurt or hurting themselves.

- They may find it easier to associate with adults than with peers.

Provocative Targets

Only 15 to 20 percent of victims are of this type.

- Compared to passive or submissive targets, provocative targets are likely to be bullied more often and by more peers.

- They may have a short temper and may try to fight back if bullied, but usually without success.

- They may be restless, clumsy, immature, unfocused, or generally perceived as awkward. Some are hyperactive; they may be fidgety, impulsive, or restless and have difficulty concentrating.

- They may have reading and writing problems.

- They may be disliked by adults because of their often irritating behavior.

- They may try to bully weaker students and therefore may be both victims and bullies.

- Some are popular, and some are not. Their popularity may decrease in higher grades, but it rarely reaches the lowest popularity levels.

Look for Warning Signs

For any student you suspect might be a target or potential target, complete the "Warning Signs" checklist (pages 114–115).

IMPORTANT: These forms should be kept confidential. You may want to share them with other adults—teachers, your principal, the school counselor, the student's parents—but they should never be accessible to students.

Get Parents' Input

If a student shows some or many of the warning signs, contact the parents. Arrange a face-to-face meeting at school.

No parent wants to hear that his or her child might be a target or potential target of bullying, so you'll need to offer a lot of reassurance along the way. You might start by emphasizing your commitment to making your classroom bully free. Share information about school-wide efforts to reduce and eliminate bullying. Then tell the parents that you've noticed some behaviors at school that may indicate their child is being bullied or could be a potential target of bullying. Give examples. Explain that targets of bullying often exhibit other behaviors that don't show up at school, and you need their help identifying those behaviors.

Ask if they have noticed any of the following in their child:

- Frequently ill*

- Frequently complains of headache, stomachache, pains, and so on*

- Has sudden changes in behavior (e.g., bedwetting, nail-biting, tics, problems sleeping, loss of appetite, depression, crying, nightmares, stammering, stuttering)*

- Anxious, fearful, moody, sad; refuses to say what's wrong

- Doesn't want to go to school, refuses to go to school, starts skipping school

- Changes walking route to school, wants to change buses, begs to be driven to school (refuses to walk or ride bus)

- Comes home from school with scratches, bruises, damage to clothes or belongings, etc. that don't have obvious explanations; makes improbable excuses

- Possessions (books, money, clothing, etc.) are often "lost," damaged, or destroyed

- Frequently asks for extra money (for lunch, school supplies)

- Carries or wants to carry "protection" (e.g., guns, knives, forks, box openers) to school

---

*Ask the parents if their child has been seen by a doctor recently; if not, suggest that they make an appointment. A doctor can determine if these symptoms and behaviors might have other causes. A doctor can also gently question a child to learn if he or she is being bullied.

- Sudden loss of interest in homework, school-work, academic performance

- Has few or no friends; is rarely invited to parties or other social events

- Seems happy/normal on weekends but not during the week; seems preoccupied/tense on Sundays before school

- Obsesses about his or her height, weight, appearance, clothes, etc.

- Has started bullying other children/siblings; is aggressive, rebellious, unreasonable

- Talks about or attempts to run away from home

- Talks about or attempts suicide*

Keep a written record of your meeting and any relevant information the parents share with you. Thank the parents for coming in and talking with you. Tell them that you'll communicate with them often about their child's behavior and progress, and about your efforts to make sure the bullying stops (or never starts). Then be sure to follow through.

TALK WITH OTHER TEACHERS AND STAFF

If you think that a student is being bullied or might be at risk, share your concerns with other teachers or staff members.

If the student spends part of the day in another classroom, talk with that teacher. How is the student treated by other kids in the class? Has the teacher noticed any sudden changes in the student's behavior? (See "Identify Targets or Potential Targets," page 91.) Has the student said anything about feeling worried, anxious, or afraid to be in school?

Talk to a playground supervisor or hall monitor to find out how the student is treated at recess or during class breaks. If the student rides the bus to and from school, talk to the bus driver. Cafeteria and maintenance workers and other staff often have lots of contact with kids, so they are important adults to talk with.

Other adults may be aware of events in the student's life that could indicate a bullying situation. You might also discover that problems you've noticed are not isolated incidents. If so, find out more and follow through.

EXAMINE YOUR OWN BELIEFS

To help students gain the strength and skills to stop being targets of bullying, to help those who bully change their behavior, and to reduce or eliminate bullying in your classroom, you need to believe that bullying is a problem that can be identified, addressed, and resolved.

Since you're reading this book, chances are you're already convinced. But many adults (including teachers) have lingering misconceptions about bullying. It's worth taking the time to do a reality check on your own beliefs. Following are four examples of erroneous thinking about bullying and the people involved in bullying. See also "Expose the Myths" (page 10).

"Bullying isn't a problem in my classroom or in our school."

Some teachers and administrators make this claim. In fact: Bullying in schools is a worldwide problem. Numerous research studies indicate that bullying exists wherever formal schooling environments exist. See "Facts About Bullying" on pages 4–8.

"It's best to let students solve their own problems, without adult interference. This is how they learn to get along in the world."

Many adults tell children not to "tattle" about bullying. In a normal peer conflict (e.g., sharing toys, deciding who goes first in a game, arguing about rules or privileges), kids should be allowed and encouraged to figure out and try their own solutions.

However, bullying is not a normal peer conflict. Here are two reasons why:

1. In a normal peer conflict, both parties are emotionally involved. Both experience painful or uncomfortable emotions; they're hurt,

---

*If parents report this behavior, urge them to seek professional help *immediately*. Follow the guidelines established by your school or district.

upset, angry, frustrated, disappointed, or outraged. In a bullying situation, it's usually only the targeted child who feels emotional pain. In contrast, the bully might feel satisfied, excited, or nothing at all (flat affect).

2. In a normal peer conflict, both parties have some power—sometimes equal power, which is why arguments, disagreements, and differences of opinion can seem to last forever. In a bullying situation, there's *always* a power imbalance. One student has all or most of the power; the target has little or none.

For these reasons, adult intervention with bullying is necessary. This is not "interference." It's helping young people with a problem they aren't equipped to solve on their own.

"I've heard that bullying starts in the elementary school years, peaks in the middle school years, and declines during the high school years. That sounds almost like 'growing pains.' Maybe bullying is just a normal, unavoidable part of life."

Bullying does seem to follow this very general pattern, although many adults experience bullying in their relationships and in the workplace. We get over our "growing pains," but the effects of being bullied (and of bullying others) can last a lifetime.

For targets, feelings of low self-esteem, isolation, powerlessness, and depression can continue into adulthood. The psychological harm they suffer as children can interfere with their social, emotional, and academic development. They may develop health problems due to the prolonged stress of being bullied. Some targeted children drop out of school; some commit suicide.

What about those who bully? A longitudinal study by psychologist E. Eron at the University of Michigan found that kids who bully continue bullying throughout their lives. There are more court convictions, more cases of alcoholism, and more personality disorders among adults who bullied as children than among the general population. Adults who bullied use more mental health services and have difficulty maintaining relationships.

"I was bullied at school, and I survived. Bullying builds character."

If you were bullied at school, you probably have very clear memories of what happened and how you felt about it. Maybe you even have nightmares related to bullying you experienced as a child. Why would you wish this on any of your students? And what kind of "character" does bullying build? If bullying is allowed to continue, children learn that might is right, bullies get their way, aggression is best—and adults can't be counted on to help.

EXPLORE WAYS TO DEAL WITH BULLYING

"What should you do when someone bullies you?" Many students don't know the answer to this question. Of course, there isn't just one right answer; it depends on the specific situation. But certain responses are generally more effective than others.

The "What Should You Do?" handout (page 116) invites students to consider several possible responses to bullying. Answers with brief explanations are given on pages 117–118.

You might read the answers aloud, and/or have students come up with their own reasons why each response would or wouldn't work. Allow time for discussion. Make copies of the answers to give to students during or after the discussion.

Note: Answers are presented as "best answers" because each real-life situation is different. At the end of this activity and discussion, students should understand that: (1) there's more than one way to respond to bullying, (2) some responses can make things better, and (3) some responses can make things worse.

IMPORTANT: Tell students that in some situations—when they're being bullied by a gang, when they're in real danger of getting beat up or worse, when there's any chance that a weapon might be present—the best response is always to get away as fast as they can and tell an adult.

ON-THE-SPOT RESPONDING

As a member of your school's professional team, it's your responsibility to intervene immediately when you observe any inappropriate behavior, whether it's physical, verbal, social, or via technology. While it is important to file reports on bullying incidents, not all mistreatment or inappropriate behavior can be labeled bullying. In cases where it is not repeated or for other reasons it isn't bullying, hold students accountable for their actions and deal with it as necessary—perhaps simply with a warning.

When you see a student being bullied, intervene by using the following steps and report the incident as specified in your school's anti-bullying policy. When you intervene effectively, you accomplish four important goals:

1. You put a stop to that particular bullying incident.

2. You make it clear that you won't tolerate bullying.

3. You change students' expectations of what will happen when they mistreat someone.

4. You encourage other targets and witnesses to tell you about bullying you don't witness personally.

The plan described here is only for on-the-spot responses to bullying and short-term follow-up. It assumes that your school has a larger bullying response policy that includes anti-bullying prevention measures, prosocial approaches, and other positive programming strategies to help the student who bullies others. This plan is meant to protect and instruct the people involved in specific bullying incidents at the time they happen. Be sure to consult your school's discipline policies and procedures prior to using the following strategies.

These steps may not be appropriate for all situations. Some bullying events may involve students who are violent and may even threaten adults around them. Use your judgment based on your observations, professional knowledge, and experience with the individuals involved.

GENERAL RESPONSIBILITIES

- Respond immediately and consistently to bullying.

- Investigate all rumors and reports of bullying.

- Follow established school discipline plans, policies, and procedures.

- Don't do anything that further isolates or stigmatizes the targeted student. Don't blame the student, and don't joke around about the bullying.

- Maintain open communication lines with bullied students, students who bully, their followers, any bystanders, and parents.

RESPONSE STEPS

The on-the-spot response steps are summarized using the acronym SCAT ASAP:

Stop the bullying and take control
Confront the bullying student
Apply consequences
Teachable moment

Area supervision
Safety plan for target
Appropriate paperwork
Parents called if necessary

IMPORTANT: Throughout this process, keep written records of conversations, actions taken, follow-through, and so on. You'll want these for reference and also to include in the students' files.

Stop the Bullying and Take Control

If you witness bullying, immediately intervene and put a stop to it. Many times when students misbehave, they don't expect anything to happen. Therefore, your first step is to gain control of the situation and let students know that you are in charge.

- Don't shout from a distance unless injuries are a possibility.

- With a *firm*, *calm*, and *matter-of-fact* voice, make "I need you to" statements:

- Say to the kid who bullied, "I need you to take two steps back" or "I need you to sit down."

  - Say to the bystanders, "I need you to step back and stay here."

  - Say to the target, "I need you to stay here."

- Step between the target and the person bullying to block their eye contact with each other.

- Obtain and maintain nonthreatening eye contact with the kid who bullied.

- Explain that your role and the role of all students is to make sure everyone is treated right and feels safe in the school.

- Let students know that what you saw was inappropriate and violates school rules. Tell them you may file a report.

- Don't touch, threaten, or plead with the person who bullied, and don't tell the person you are upset because of the way he or she is acting.

- If this person is disrespectful and challenges your power, address the student by name, and say:

  - Who do you believe is in charge here?

  - What do you think would happen if someone decided to disobey me? (If the student doesn't know the possible consequences, tell him.)

  - It looks like you have a choice to make.

- If the student continues his or her power play, direct everyone to leave the scene and tell them you wish to talk to them later. Call for help from the nearest adult or whomever you are required to contact (or send a student to get the adult).

Confront the Bullying Student

If the bullying continues, command the student who is doing it to stop, and call the student by name. Do not *ask* the student to stop ("James, will you please stop calling Susan names?"). You may specify the behavior you desire by making an "I need you to" statement. *Example*: "James, I

need you to sit down and obey the rules." Do not ask the target or person bullying to explain what happened in front of other students. This is not the time to sort out the facts.

If the bullying stops, compliment the student for stopping. If the bullying doesn't stop, state again that the mistreatment of others violates school rules and there may be consequences for this behavior. Make sure the student knows how serious the behavior is, but avoid lecturing, because that may provide the attention that some kids who bully crave.

If the student who bullied is very resistant, do not respond aggressively. An aggressive response could prompt an increase in the behavior and perhaps aggression toward you. If the student's response to your question is a question, do not answer, but ask the student your next question. It's best to ask the following questions:

- What is the rule about calling someone hurtful names?

- What could be a consequence for disobeying that rule?

- Why do you think that rule is important?

Say again to the student, "It looks like you have a decision to make." If you feel it is appropriate, tell him or her that you and other adults in the school will be watching to make sure he or she treats others right.

Apply Consequences

If possible, immediately apply consequences or make sure consequences are applied as soon as possible. Apply progressively more severe consequences for repeated incidents. Consequences will depend on the behavior and the number of times you have seen the student mistreat someone. As much as possible, the consequences should be fair, logical, and connected to the offense. Of course, some consequences can be applied only by your principal and/or the central office.

Do not ask the student to apologize in the heat of the moment. Give everyone time to cool down. It is usually not effective to ask for a verbal apology. Do not ask students to meet and "work it out." This can re-traumatize the bullied student and generally doesn't help. Refer to the "Help Those Who Bully" section for more ideas about how to support a student whom you caught misbehaving. The important things are to make the student accountable for her or his actions and to support the student to make changes.

Note: Your school's anti-bullying policy may require you to notify the families of the students involved in the incident.

Teachable Moment

Ask the bystanders to stay so they can hear you provide support for the target. Tell the target that you're glad to know about the bullying and that you will not tolerate bullying of any kind. Say that the student does not deserve to be treated that way, and you will try to help him or her stay safe. Give the student hope by saying that you are confident the bullying can be stopped. Make arrangements to meet later and develop a plan to help the student. Make sure the bystanders and target understand the importance of reporting mistreatment to an adult.

Note: Don't go overboard with emotional support, because it can be embarrassing for the targeted student. Even though it is a good idea to use the incident as a teachable moment, in some cases, it may be best to provide all or some of the emotional support in private. Use your judgment and knowledge of the student.

Speak to the bystanders before they leave the area. At this time, do not ask anyone to describe what happened. Instead, let them know you saw their response to the bullying. If they tried to help the target, compliment them, even if they were not successful. If their response was inappropriate, explain what they could have done differently and say that the next time they see someone bullied they should respond in a more active and prosocial manner. It may be that they weren't sure what do to or that they were fearful.

If you have discussed ally skills (page 61), remind them of what they've learned. In short:

- Don't laugh.

- Don't join in.

- Don't cheer.

- Don't gather around.

- Don't ignore it. Try to help the victim.

- Don't stand guard and watch for adults.

Explain the importance of telling an adult when they or someone else is mistreated. Reporting is not tattling or ratting on someone. It's what a good person should do. Tell them they have a responsibility to keep the school peaceful and safe. It's not just the responsibility of the adults.

You may want to go over the assertiveness skills on pages 72–73, especially the assertiveness skills for bystanders.

Area Supervision

If required, stick around. Remain in the area until you are certain things have cooled down.

Safety Plan for Target

Meet with the targeted student as soon as possible after the event to determine the extent of the mistreatment and to develop a safety plan. Always start by asking targeted students what they think needs to be done to keep them safe until the bullying situation is investigated. Make sure students understand they are not expected to deal with bullying alone. Bullying is not just the problem of targeted students. It's your problem, the problem of other adults in the school, and the problem of students' families.

Here are some guidelines for establishing the safety plan. Some of these strategies will need to be adjusted or used or not used depending on when and where the bullying is occurring.

- Ask targeted students to select an adult to report to every day regarding how they were treated.

- Tell them not to retaliate. Retaliation usually makes bullying worse and last longer. It also increases the risk of getting seriously hurt or hurting the bully and getting into trouble with the school or the law (or both).

- Tell them to try to stay calm and cool if they are bullied again—don't act upset. Students who bully want to upset their targets. The following techniques may help targeted students stay calm:

  - Imagine being surrounded by a magical, bully free shield.

◆ Keep an object in a pocket, bag, or purse—like a smooth rock—that they can rub when fearful, upset, or angry. This will help remind them to think before saying or doing something that causes more problems.

▪ Direct them not to walk alone or go to unsupervised areas in the school alone, if possible.

▪ Tell them to try to avoid the student who has been bullying them and avoid places where the student is known to hang out or where there is not much adult supervision. If the targets cannot avoid the person bullying them, then they should at least try to keep their distance.

▪ Advise students to mix up their routines by using different hallways and stairwells.

▪ Tell targeted students to use their best judgment and follow their instincts. For example, if someone wants their bag and they think they will be harmed, they should give up the bag and walk away with confidence, acting as if the incident didn't hurt them. They should then report the incident to a trusted adult. Safety is more important than possessions.

▪ Ask them to give you a secret visible signal when they are being mistreated.

▪ Advise targeted students to walk over to an adult and start a conversation with him or her or walk into a crowd when the person who bullies them approaches.

▪ Explain that a forceful, assertive yell can be effective if they yell exactly what they want the other student to stop doing. However, they should be careful not to yell in a way that expresses hurt or helplessness. For example, "Stop hitting me!" tells the bully what to stop doing, whereas "Leave me alone!" makes the target sound like a victim.

Your part of the safety plan may involve several of the following steps. As always, use your judgment about what is appropriate.

▪ Increase and improve supervision of targets and those who bully them.

▪ Surround targeted students with other students you know will not bully them.

▪ Assign older students to be a "helper" or "buddy" to targeted students and supervise their interactions.

▪ Remind targeted students' teachers that it is not wise to leave their classrooms unsupervised.

▪ Consider creating a *No Contact Contract* (in-school restraining order) with students who bully.

▪ Ask bullying students to sit near the teacher's desk for a few days or permanently. Separate them from followers who encourage the bullying.

▪ Require bullying students to be the last ones to leave the classroom between classes and after school.

▪ If students are bullied while walking to or from school or while riding the bus, make arrangements for them to be accompanied by a family member or to carpool to school until the situation can be dealt with by the school and director of transportation.

▪ If students are bullied on the bus and they get off at the same stop as someone who bullies them, ask that the driver let the targeted students off the bus first, giving them time to reach home before letting the bully off.

Appropriate Paperwork

Complete the appropriate bullying situation report form as required by your school and send copies to the appropriate school personnel. Let the teachers of all students involved know what you have observed. Ask them to increase their supervision of their interactions and to note what students are saying about them. Tell them that you want to hear *good* news about the students' behavior, not just bad news.

Parents Called If Necessary

If the behavior warrants, and if it is determined appropriate by your school, contact the families of the target and the student who bullies, or require the students to do so. In some cases, it may be best *not* to notify the parents or guardians of the student who bullies, especially when parents are known to be abusive. Before calling the family, discuss the situation with the appropriate school personnel. When the family is contacted, tell the adults you talk to that additional information will be gathered and that they will be contacted soon to discuss the situation.

Some bullying situations may require a meeting with the target's family and a separate meeting with the family of the student who bullied the target. It is usually not wise to have both families in the same meeting. Prior to each meeting, gather information about the situation. Have other incidents occurred? Have intervention and prevention strategies been previously implemented? What have you done to keep the targeted student safe? You will also want to discuss plans for the meeting with the appropriate school personnel. Seek their guidance. It may be necessary for more than one school official to be present at the meeting: for example, a counselor, school psychologist, or assistant principal.

At the meeting, present the school's view of the problem and the need for intervention. Discuss the strategies that have already been implemented and whether these have been effective. Be sure to allow time for parents or caregivers to voice their concerns and for answering their questions.

Provide the parents or caregivers with a plan they can implement at home. The plan may include resources and activities to meet the needs of their child and to help stop and prevent the bullying. At the end of the meeting, let the family know you will keep them informed, and ask them to keep you informed as well.

> If you learn about bullying secondhand—for example, a student tells you about it, you receive a report in your "Notes-to-the-Teacher" box (see page 69), you read about it in a student's journal (see page 110), or you learn about it in some other way—you still need to take immediate action. Modify these steps as needed, and be sure that students know you are acting on the issue.

Continue to communicate with your colleagues and the parents until the situation is clearly resolved.

WHAT IF THE STUDENTS ARE FIGHTING?

Follow these suggestions from the Crisis Prevention Institute on how to break up a fight:*

- *Get assistance.* Intervening alone is dangerous.

- *Remove the audience.* Onlookers fuel the fire. The intensity of an altercation often parallels the intensity of the bystanders. Remove them as quickly as possible.

- *Avoid stepping between the combatants.* This puts you in a vulnerable position and the combatants' aggression can quickly shift to you.

- *Always try verbal intervention first.* Often one or both combatants are waiting for someone to arrive and stop the fight. Avoid the temptation to immediately revert to physical intervention.

- *Use a distraction.* A distraction (e.g., loud noise, flickering of lights) can be enough to break the intensity of the aggression long enough to give you an edge.

- *Separate the combatants.* As soon as possible, break visual contact between the combatants. As long as they can see one another, their hostility will likely continue.

BE A GOOD LISTENER

If a student comes to you to report a bullying incident—as a witness or a target—the first and most important thing you should do is *listen*.

It's estimated that we spend about 70 percent of our waking hours communicating (reading, writing, speaking, listening), and most of that time goes to listening. Yet we receive little or no training on *how* to listen. In school, we learn how to read, write, and speak . . . but not how to listen. We assume that listening "comes naturally."

---

*Copyright © 1994 by the Crisis Prevention Institute, Inc. Used with permission.

There's an old saying: "We were born with one mouth and two ears because listening is twice as hard as talking." Here's how to be a good listener.

DO:

1. **Pay attention and be quiet.** Listening means not talking!

2. **Use attentive body language.** Face the speaker squarely, lean slightly toward him or her, and keep your arms and legs uncrossed.

3. **Make and maintain eye contact.** This allows you to pick up on the speaker's body language and facial expressions—important clues to how he or she is feeling.

4. **Be patient.** Allow time for the speaker to say what's on his or her mind. Especially if the speaker is embarrassed or uncomfortable, this might take a while. Also, people generally think faster than they speak. And students might not have the vocabulary or life experience needed to find precisely the right words.

5. **Ask for clarification if you need it.** Confirm the accuracy of what you're hearing. *Examples:* "I'm not sure I understand. Could you go over that again?" "Could you repeat that please?" "Can you tell me more about that?"

6. **Empathize.** Try to put yourself in the speaker's place to see his or her point of view.

7. **Ask questions to encourage the speaker and show that you're listening.** *Best:* Open-ended questions. *Worst:* Questions that require simple yes or no answers.

8. **Reflect the speaker's words and feelings from time to time.** *Examples:* "It sounds like you felt hurt when Marcy ignored you at recess." "I hear you saying you're angry because of how George treated you." Reflecting (also called mirroring) is simply paraphrasing what the speaker has said—objectively, without interpretation, emotion, or embellishment.

9. **Mirror the speaker's feelings in your own face.** If the speaker looks sad, hurt, or angry, you should, too.

10. **At points along the way, summarize what you're hearing the speaker say.** Check with the speaker to make sure you've got it right. *Example:* "You're saying that Zach pushed you against your locker, and you dropped your books and papers on the floor, and then Zach stepped on your math book."

11. **Use encouraging body language.** Nod your head, smile, lean a little closer to the speaker (but not too close).

12. **Use brief interjections to indicate that you're listening.** *Examples:* "I see." "Go on." "Tell me more." "Uh-huh." "Really." "Hmmmm." "What then?" "So. . . ."

13. **Really concentrate on what the speaker is saying.** Stay focused on his or her words.

14. **Invite the speaker to name his or her feelings.** *Examples:* "When Marcus called you a bad name, how did you feel?" "When Su-Lin made fun of you in front of the others, how did you feel?"

If you listen intently, you should feel somewhat tired afterward. That's because listening is *active*, not passive.

DON'T:

1. **Talk.** This is not the time to offer your advice or opinions. Wait until *after* the speaker has finished talking or asks for your input.

2. **Interrupt.** You don't like being interrupted when you're talking. Interruptions are rude and disrespectful.

3. **Doodle.** You'll probably want to take notes, however. Tell the speaker why—because you want to keep the facts straight and have a written record of your conversation.

4. **Tap your pen or pencil, shuffle papers, wiggle your foot, look at your watch, yawn, etc.** These behaviors indicate boredom.

5. **Argue with, criticize, or blame the speaker.** This puts him or her on the defensive.

6. **Mentally argue with the speaker or judge what he or she is saying.** This takes your focus off the speaker's words.

7. **Evaluate or challenge what the speaker is saying.** Just listen.

8. **Interrogate the speaker.** Ask questions for clarification, or to encourage the speaker to tell you more. Make sure your questions don't imply that you doubt what the speaker is saying.

9. **Allow distractions.** Turn off your computer, and don't answer your cell phone (or even have it out). If someone else approaches you and the speaker, politely but firmly say, "I'm listening to [student's name] right now. I'll have time for you when we're finished here."

10. **Think ahead to what you're going to say when the speaker stops talking.** This is called "rehearsing," and it takes your focus off the speaker.

11. **Let your mind wander.** Sometimes a speaker's words can trigger our own thoughts, memories, and associations. If you feel this happening, change your body position and use one of the "Do's" listed on page 100. This should get you back on track.

12. **Mentally compare what the speaker is saying with what you've heard from other students.** If you're gathering information about a bullying incident or series of incidents, take notes and compare your notes later.

Tip: Consider sharing some or all of these do's and don'ts with your students. Knowing how to listen is a social skill that builds friendships.

SEND A CLEAR MESSAGE

When you talk with a student who has been (or is being) bullied, you may find that the student blames himself or herself for being in the wrong place at the wrong time, provoking the bullying, doing something to attract the other student's attention, or somehow "asking for it." Make it very clear that bullying is *never* caused by the person who is bullied. Tell the student:

- It's not your fault that you're being bullied.
- You didn't ask for it.
- You don't deserve it.
- You didn't do anything to cause it.
- Bullying isn't normal. It isn't okay.
- You don't have to face this on your own. I will help you. Other people will help you, too.

You might write these sentences on a card, sign it, and give it to the student. Or you might ask the student to repeat these sentences after you:

- "It's not my fault that I'm being bullied."
- "I didn't ask for it."
- "I don't deserve it."
- "I didn't do anything to cause it."
- "Bullying isn't normal. It isn't okay."
- "I don't have to face this on my own. My teacher will help me. Other people will help me, too."

Strong, positive statements like these can help students start feeling better about themselves—a bit more powerful and less like victims.*

PROVIDE COUNSELING

Being bullied is a very traumatic experience. If at all possible, bullied children should have access to some type of counseling—by a school psychologist, guidance counselor, or another trained adult. Peer counseling can also help.

See if your school can start a group for targeted students—a place where they can interact with others, build their social and friendship-making skills, and practice getting along. Group meetings can be structured and focus on specific topics (e.g., avoiding fights, avoiding kids who bully, coping with stress, being assertive), or they can be less structured (students can talk freely about issues that are important to them).

---

*See also "Teach Positive Self-Talk" (page 30) and "Teach Students to Affirm Themselves" (page 75).

EMPOWER PARENTS

As you work to make your classroom bully free, get students' parents involved and keep them informed. Parents can be your allies—and can also clue you in to bullying situations you might not be aware of.

Tell parents about your efforts to prevent and intervene with bullying in your classroom. You might do this at parent-teacher conferences, on parents' night, during open houses, and in notes you send home with students.

As early as possible during the school year, give parents copies of "Keeping Kids Bully Free: Tips for Parents" (pages 119–121).

IMPORTANT: It's best to give this to parents in person. If this isn't possible, attach a brief cover letter introducing the handout and explaining why you're sending it home: because you believe *all* parents can benefit from this information. Otherwise you might alarm parents unnecessarily. If "Keeping Kids Bully Free" arrives out of the blue, a parent's first thought might be, "Oh no! This must mean that *my* child is being bullied!" Preparation and explanation can prevent unnecessary worry and misunderstandings.

ENCOURAGE A POSITIVE ATTITUDE

All students—especially those who have been or are being bullied—can benefit from facing life with a positive attitude. Encourage your students to look for what's good in their lives. This might be as simple as a sunrise, warm gloves on a cold day, or a puppy's wagging tail. Help them see that no matter how bad things might seem at the moment, something good is waiting just around the corner.

Use stories of hope and courage to inspire students to feel optimistic and reach for the stars. Ask your school librarian or the children's librarian at your local public library to point you toward appropriate books, or consider the following examples.

- *A Child's Garden* by Michael Foreman (Candlewick, 2009). Ages 4–8.
- *Champions: Stories of Ten Remarkable Athletes* by Bill Littlefield (Little, Brown, 1993). Ages 9–12.
- *Kids with Courage: True Stories About Young People Making a Difference* by Barbara A. Lewis (Free Spirit Publishing, 1992). Young adult.
- *Real Kids, Real Stories, Real Change* by Garth Sundem (Free Spirit Publishing, 2010). Ages 9–13.

BUILD STUDENTS' SELF-ESTEEM

Most people who are bullied have low self-esteem. Here are six ways you can build self-esteem in *all* of your students.*

STAR CHARTS

Create a separate chart for each student. Whenever he or she does something positive or helpful, write it on the chart and decorate it with a star. Or create charts listing specific positive/helpful behaviors you want to encourage in your classroom.

FEEL-GOOD POSTERS

Create a poster for each student (or have students create their own posters). Put a photograph of the student at the center. Surround it with positive comments about the student. Display the posters in the classroom; they'll be especially noticed and appreciated on parents' night and at open houses.

FEEL-GOOD LISTS

Have students write "My Feel-Good List" at the top of a sheet of paper and draw a vertical line down the middle. Have them label the left side "Things I Like About Myself" and the right side "Things My Teacher Likes About Me." Have them list 10 things they like about themselves in the left column and turn them in to you. After

---

*See also "Affirm Your Students" (page 29), "Teach Students to Affirm Themselves" (page 75), "Teach Students to Affirm Each Other" (page 76), and "Teach Positive Self-Talk" (page 30). There are many books and resources available on helping students build self-esteem, develop self-confidence, and form a positive self-concept. Several are listed in "Resources" at the end of this book.

you complete the second column for each student, pass them back. They can share their lists or keep them private—whatever they prefer.

Tip: If any students have difficulty completing their columns, offer help. Make simple suggestions. *Examples:* "Everyone has talents, and so do you. What are some of your talents? What are you good at? What do you do best?" They can also take their lists home and ask their parents and siblings for help.

Tell students that whenever they feel down or sad, they can look at their lists and feel better about themselves.

SELF-ESTEEM BOOSTERS

Ask students, "What are specific things you can do to feel good about yourself?" Write students' ideas on the whiteboard or chart paper. If they have difficulty getting started or run out of ideas too soon, you might suggest some of the following:

- use positive self-talk (see "Teach Positive Self-Talk," page 30)
- learn a new skill
- develop/strengthen a skill you already have
- start a new hobby
- join a club or group that interests you
- earn money from doing a job or chore
- volunteer to help someone (see "Get Students Involved in Service," page 32)
- read a book
- get involved in a cause you care about
- take a class in self-defense
- exercise every day
- make a new friend
- be more assertive (see "Teach Assertiveness Skills," page 72)
- get more sleep

Once you've written a list of ideas on the board, have students read it over (or you can read it aloud to the class) and choose three to five ideas they might like to try. Have them write the ideas in a notebook or on a sheet of paper. Encourage

them to try the ideas as soon as possible; offer to help them find resources, get in touch with groups or organizations, and so on. Wait a few days (or a week), then ask students to report on their progress.

CHOICES

Whenever possible, give students opportunities to make choices—all kinds of choices. They might decide where to sit, how to arrange their desks, what types of projects to work on (e.g., written reports, oral reports, art projects). Even if their choices aren't always successful, find something positive about them to recognize. If you must comment on a poor choice (with the goal of helping students make better choices next time), do it privately, not publicly.

THEY'RE THE TEACHERS

Set aside time to learn with and from your students. Let them tell you about their interests, demonstrate their skills, talents, and abilities, and show off a little. Give them opportunities to do things better than you; students delight in this, and it gives them a major self-esteem boost.

TEACH POSITIVE VISUALIZATION

Let your students in on the secret of "mind over matter." It's a fact that many successful athletes have improved their performance with positive visualization—mentally "seeing" themselves succeed. *Examples:* golfer Tiger Woods, champion boxer Muhammad Ali, basketball player Michael Jordan, and olympic swimmer Michael Phelps.

In a famous experiment, an Australian basketball team divided into three groups. All three wanted to be able to make more free-throw baskets.

- Group 1 practiced taking foul shots for 30 minutes every day. After 20 days, they noticed a 24 percent improvement.
- Group 2 did nothing. They noticed a 0 percent improvement.

■ Group 3 practiced mentally. These players didn't actually shoot baskets. Instead, they imagined themselves shooting baskets. They noticed a 23 percent improvement—nearly as great as Group 1, who practiced for 30 minutes every day.

Learn about positive visualization and mental imagery. Teach your students how to use it—especially those who are or have been targets of bullying, or who lack friends, social skills, and self-esteem.

Example: Teach students to see/imagine themselves getting along with others. With practice, they'll project an attitude of confidence and acceptance, which will improve their chances of fitting in. *Tip:* The more details they can imagine, the better. Can they picture themselves walking into a room? Smiling at people? Saying hello? Can they see people smiling back at them? What do they look like? What are they wearing? What are they saying? How does it feel to be in a group of smiling, welcoming people?

Go Further

Read *Self-Esteem* (revised edition) by Matthew McKay, Ph.D., and Patrick Fanning (New Harbinger Publications, 2000). This step-by-step program for building self-esteem includes a detailed description of how to use visualization for self-acceptance.

PLAY A "POSITIVE SELF-TALK" GAME

Write a series of put-downs or nasty names on individual slips of paper. Or invite your students to do this, but be sure to read the names before you use them to make sure they're not *too* nasty (or obscene, personal, specific, racist, etc.).

Drop the slips into a hat. Invite one student to draw a slip out of the hat and give it to you. Write the put-down or name on the whiteboard or chart paper.

Tell the class they have your permission to call the student that name (or use the put-down) *just for now* because you're going to play a game. Be sure to choose a student who can handle this, and get the student's permission first.

Have the class form two lines with enough space between them for you and the student to walk comfortably. As you and the student walk through the group, the other students call him or her the name (or use the put-down). Meanwhile, you whisper positive comments in the student's ear. *Examples:* "You're not like that." "You can stay calm." "Don't believe what they say." "You're more mature than they are."

Next, the student walks back through the group alone, using positive self-talk ("I'm not like that," "I can stay calm," and so on).

Repeat this game with the other students. Afterward, talk about how they felt when you whispered positive comments to them, and when they used positive self-talk.

For more tips on helping students develop this powerful skill, see "Teach Positive Self-Talk" (page 30).

SEE YOUR CLASSROOM THROUGH YOUR STUDENTS' EYES

Students who are bullied often say that adults "never noticed" the way they were treated. Try seeing your classroom (and yourself) through your students' eyes.

Watch how students interact. Listen to how they talk to each other. If you were a child, would you be comfortable in your classroom? Would you feel safe, welcome, accepted, and free to learn? Is this a place where you could be and do your best without feeling threatened, intimidated, or excluded? Would you feel as if the teacher were approachable—as if the teacher would really listen if you reported a problem or asked for help?

Try being a student for an hour (or a day). Have your students teach the lessons and manage the class. You might learn a great deal about how they see you.

SHARE TIPS FOR STAYING BULLY FREE

Make several copies of "Ways to Stay Bully Free" (page 122). Cut along the dotted lines and give one card to each student. (*Tips:* Make copies on heavy paper or thin cardboard. Laminate them for durability.) Spend class time discussing the ideas listed on the cards. Students can keep the cards in their pockets or backpacks and review them whenever they need ideas or reminders.

Go Further

Get a classroom copy of *Bullies Are a Pain in the Brain*, written and illustrated by Trevor Romain (Free Spirit Publishing, 1997). With wit and humor, this little book teaches children ages 8 to 13 ways to become bully-proof.

TRY THE METHOD OF SHARED CONCERN

The Method of Shared Concern is a nonpunitive, counseling-based intervention model that was developed by Swedish psychologist Anatol Pikas in the 1980s. It has since been used successfully in many parts of the world.

It involves conducting structured interviews with individuals who have bullied, during which they are asked to take responsibility for their actions and commit to more responsible behavior. Interviews are also done with targets and then with groups that comprise both students who have bullied and students who have been bullied.

This method is not designed to teach children how to make friends, or to reveal detailed facts about the bullying situation. It is designed to change the situation by getting children to change their behavior.

Shared Concern seems to be most effective with children age nine and older, but it has also been used with younger children. It involves a three-stage interviewing and meeting process:*

1. individual interviews with each child

2. follow-up interviews with each child

3. a group meeting

PRELIMINARIES

1. Determine that a bullying situation exists—that one or more children are being bullied by another child or group, and that this has been going on for a period of time.

2. Get reliable information about who is involved, and identify the ringleader of the bullying.

3. Talk to the teachers of the students who bully and who are bullied. Schedule interviews with the children. Ask the teachers not to alert the children that they will be interviewed. They should simply send the children to the interviews as scheduled.

 IMPORTANT: Plan to conduct all of the interviews in sequence, without a break, so the children involved don't have the opportunity to talk to each other between interviews.

4. Arrange to do the interviews in a room where you'll have privacy and won't be interrupted. It's best if there are no windows. If windows can't be avoided, the child being interviewed should sit with his or her back to the window.

5. Know and understand your role. Throughout the interviews, you will be a nonjudgmental facilitator who encourages children to consider their own behaviors and the consequences of their behaviors, then suggest alternate behaviors. *Notes:* Young children may find it difficult to come up with ideas; you may need to offer suggestions. Girls seem to have a hard time finding a middle ground between "friends" and "enemies." You may need to explain that they're not being asked to make the other children their "best friends."

---

*The procedure and guidelines described here are adapted from *Tackling Bullying in Your School*, edited by Sonia Sharp and Peter K. Smith (London: Routledge, 1994), pp. 79–88. Used with permission.

INITIAL INTERVIEWS (7–10 MINUTES EACH)

Interview the ringleader first, then the rest of the kids who are part of the bullying group (if there is one), then the children who are being bullied. See the guidelines and sample scripts on pages 123 and 124.

IMPORTANT: The interviews must be nonconfrontational. Students should appear relaxed when they return to class.

Each interview should end with the child agreeing to try his or her own suggestion(s) during the following week.

FOLLOW-UP INTERVIEWS (3 MINUTES EACH)

The purpose of the follow-up meetings is to determine whether the children did what they agreed to during the initial interviews. If they did, congratulate them and invite them to the group meeting.

Sometimes the bullying students don't try the suggestions they agreed to try—but they do leave the targeted students alone. If this is the case, congratulate them and invite them to the group meeting. Leaving the targets alone is an important change in behavior.

GROUP MEETING (30 MINUTES)

The purpose of the group meeting is to maintain the changes made since the initial interviews.

1. Meet first with the students who bully. Ask them to think of something positive they can say to the targets.

2. Ask the targets to enter the room. Place their chairs where they won't have to walk past those who bullied them to reach their seats.

3. Have the bullies say their positive statements.

4. Congratulate everyone on their success—they have made the bullying situation better than it was.

5. Ask everyone how they can maintain this new and improved situation.

6. Ask them what they will do if the bullying starts again.

7. Introduce the idea of tolerance—being in the same school and classroom without quarreling, accepting each other's differences, coexisting peaceably (but without necessarily being friends).

It might not be necessary to meet again for several weeks. Monitor the situation and call an interim meeting if needed.

TRY THE NO BLAME APPROACH

Developed by Barbara Maines and George Robinson, the No Blame Approach encourages children to take responsibility for their actions and the consequences of their actions. Like the Method of Shared Concern (see pages 105–106), this is a nonpunitive intervention model that directly involves children in resolving a bullying situation.*

Step 1: Interview the bullied child.

Talk with the child about his or her feelings. Do not question the child directly about the bullying incident(s), but do try to establish who is involved.

Step 2: Arrange a meeting for all the children who are involved.

Include children who joined in but did not directly bully the person.

Step 3: Explain the problem.

Tell the children how the bullied child is feeling. You may want to use a drawing, poem, or other piece of writing by the child to illustrate his or her feelings. Do not discuss the details of the incident or blame any of the bullying students.

Step 4: Share responsibility.

State clearly that you know the group is responsible and can do something about it. Focus on resolving the problem rather than blaming the children.

---

*This description is adapted from *School Bullying: Insights and Perspectives*, edited by Peter K. Smith and Sonia Sharp (London: Routledge, 1994), pp. 88–89. Used with permission.

Step 5: Identify solutions.

Ask each child in turn to suggest a way in which he or she could help the bullied child feel happier in school. Show approval of the suggestions, but don't ask the children to promise to implement them or go into detail about how they will implement them.

Step 6: The students take action themselves.

End the meeting by giving responsibility to the group to solve the problem. Arrange a time and place to meet again and find out how successful they have been.

Step 7: Meet with them again.

After about a week, see each student and ask how things have been going. It is usually better to see them individually in order to avoid any new group accusations about who helped and who didn't. The important thing is to ascertain that the bullying has stopped and the bullied student is feeling better.

ENCOURAGE STRONG FAMILY RELATIONSHIPS

Do as much as you can to support closeness and togetherness in your students' families. *Examples:*

- Work with other teachers and staff to schedule open houses, family nights, and other events that welcome parents and students.

- Bring in speakers who talk about family life and issues.

- Invite students to attend parent-teacher conferences with their parents.

- Regularly call or write to parents. Let them know about their children's progress. Report on something special their children did—something that deserves praise and recognition.

- Have students interview their parents for homework assignments.

ENCOURAGE RELATIONSHIPS WITH OTHER ADULTS

When students develop close relationships with adults—not only their parents, but also other family and community members—they learn important social skills and build their self-confidence and self-esteem. This is important for *all* students, and can be especially beneficial to those who lack social skills and are targets or potential targets of bullying.

SCHOOL STAFF

Do teachers, administrators, and other staff members make the effort to get to know students? Do they sponsor clubs, coach teams, supervise before-school and after-school activities, and/or lead discussion groups for kids? Do they take time to listen to students' concerns and offer support and advice? Talk with your coworkers. What can you do individually and together to form positive, meaningful relationships with students?

Enlist the help of all school employees in making students feel welcome, accepted, and appreciated. Custodians, cafeteria workers, librarians, office personnel, and others can greet students by name, share a kind word with them, and intervene if they see a student being mistreated.

Encourage school staff to find ways for students with low self-esteem or poor social skills to shine. *Examples:* A student could deliver the principal's telephone messages or help younger children do library research.

GRANDPARENTS

Encourage students to spend time with their grandparents, sharing their problems and concerns as well as their achievements.

Because many of your students might not be in regular contact with their grandparents, consider establishing an Adopt-a-Grandparent program in cooperation with a local nursing home or retirement center.

Arrange for your class to visit their adopted grandparents regularly. Bring class plays, presentations, and musical performances to them. Make artwork for the grandparents' rooms and send them cards on special occasions. Invite all grandparents to visit your students at school and volunteer in your classroom and on field trips.

You may also encourage students to spend time with aunts and uncles or other extended family members.

Clubs, Groups, Troops, and Teams

Gather information about local and national clubs, groups, troops, teams, and organizations led by caring adults. *Examples:*

Boy Scouts of America
Contact your local council or visit the website, www.scouting.org.

Boys & Girls Clubs of America
Contact your local club or visit the website, www.bgca.org.

Camp Fire USA
Contact your local council or visit the website, www.campfireusa.org.

4-H
Contact your local program or visit the website, www.4h-usa.org.

Girl Scouts of the U.S.A.
Contact your local council or visit the website, www.girlscouts.org.

Girls Inc.
Contact your local affiliate or visit the website, www.girlsinc.org.

YMCA
Contact your local affiliate or visit the website, www.ymca.net.

Youth Service America
Contact your local affiliate or visit the website, www.ysa.org.

YWCA
Contact your local affiliate or visit the website, www.ywca.org.

You might also invite representatives to visit your class, tell about their organizations, and talk with your students.

Community Members
Start a card file or computer database of community members who are willing to spend time with students—exploring shared interests, helping kids develop their talents, and making a difference in their lives. Pair interested students with caring adults.

IMPORTANT: You'll want to get parents' permission and take all safety precautions. Check with your principal about how to proceed.

Mentors
Kids of all ages have formed strong relationships with mentors—caring adults who make active, positive contributions to their lives. You might find out if teachers, administrators, and other school staff are willing to serve as mentors; match them up with students who share their interests and arrange for them to spend time together. Parents might be available to mentor other students in your class.

To learn more about mentoring and mentorships, contact these organizations:

Big Brothers Big Sisters of America
The oldest mentoring organization serving children in the country, BBBSA has provided one-to-one mentoring relationships between adult volunteers and children at risk since 1904. BBBSA currently serves over 100,000 children in more than 500 agencies throughout the United States. Contact your local office or visit the website, www.bbbsa.org.

MENTOR: National Mentoring Partnership
A resource for mentors and mentoring initiatives nationwide, the National Mentoring Partnership forges partnerships with communities and organizations to promote mentoring. It also educates young people and adults about how to find and become mentors. Write or call: MENTOR: National Mentoring Partnership, 1680 Duke Street, 2nd Floor, Alexandria, VA 22314;

telephone 703-224-2200. Or visit the website, www.mentoring.org.

PROVIDE SAFE HAVENS

Students who are bullied at school need places to go where they feel safe and accepted. Work with other teachers, your principal, and staff to set aside a special room or place where all students are welcome. Provide adequate supervision. Older students can help run a quiet activities room.

If space in your school is tight, you might identify a corner of the media center or cafeteria as a safe haven. Or use your classroom Peace Place (see page 75).

Go Further

Find out about McGruff Houses or block parent programs in the neighborhoods where your students live, then let students know that these havens exist. A McGruff House is a safe place especially for kids who are bullied, followed, or hurt while walking in a neighborhood. It has a picture of McGruff the Crime Dog and the words "McGruff House" in a window or on a door. For neighborhoods that don't have McGruff Houses or programs, talk with parents and encourage them to work with their neighbors or police department to start them. For more information about McGruff, go to www.ncpc.org or call 202-466-6272.

HAVE "WHAT IF?" DISCUSSIONS

Lead class discussions, small group discussions, or role plays around "What If?" questions. *Examples:*

- What if you're walking down the hall and someone calls you a bad name?

- What if someone tries to make you give him (or her) your money?

- What if you get a mean text message?

- What if someone picks a fight with you?

- What if someone pushes you down on the playground?

- What if someone spreads a nasty rumor about you?

Invite students to contribute their own "What If?" questions to talk about or act out. Don't be surprised if this takes an interesting twist. The questions students offer might relate to real bullying incidents they have experienced or witnessed—and you haven't heard about until now.

As students come up with suggestions or role-play possible ways of coping with problem situations, remind them that people who bully enjoy having control over the people they bully. They target individuals who are physically weaker and lack confidence. Guide students to come up with answers that are assertive, confident, and strong—and, at the same time, aren't likely to make things worse.

Tip: If you and your students haven't done the "Explore Ways to Deal with Bullying" activity (page 94), you might want to do this before having "What If?" discussions.

EQUALIZE THE POWER

Bullying relationships always involve the unequal distribution of power. Those who bully have it, their targets don't—or they have most of it and targets have very little.

Look for opportunities to boost the power of students who are bullied or at risk for being bullied. *Examples:*

- Praise them sincerely, appropriately, and publicly.

- Learn their skills and areas of expertise, then suggest that other students consult them as "experts" on a topic.

- Show that you trust them and have confidence in their abilities. From time to time, give them special tasks to do. Make sure these are tasks that other students would find desirable and enjoyable. Assigning "busy work" or "grunt jobs" further stigmatizes them.

Equalizing the power can be a delicate balance. You'll want to offer targets chances to succeed—but without making them "teacher's pets." (See also "Give Them Opportunities to Shine" below.) Be careful not to pit targets and the people who bully them against each other as you're handing out praise and special tasks. This might make the kid bullying even more determined to show the target who's in charge.

GIVE THEM OPPORTUNITIES TO SHINE

Increase students' social contacts by giving them specific responsibilities that are social in nature. *Examples:* tutoring other students on the computer, working in the school office, mentoring younger students, reading aloud to younger students, being in charge of group projects. This offers them opportunities to interact with others, help their peers, and demonstrate their skills. Plus, assigning students these responsibilities shows that you trust and accept them. (See also "Equalize the Power," page 109.)

Help students discover and develop their talents and skills. This boosts their self-confidence and increases their standing among their peers. *Example:* If one of your students enjoys making kites, he or she could bring some examples for show-and-tell, teach other students what he or she knows, and lead a project on kite-making related to a science or geography lesson.

HAVE STUDENTS KEEP JOURNALS

Writing is a way to get in touch with our feelings, record events in our lives, formalize our plans and goals, and explore what's important to us. For students who are bullied, writing is a way to regain some of the power they've lost—and keep track of important details (what happened when, who did or said what) that you and other adults can use to stop the bullying and prevent future bullying. Written records make bullying easier to prove.

If possible, give students spiral-bound notebooks or small blank journaling books.* In one-on-one or small group meetings, explain or demonstrate some of the ways they might use their journals. Or give them a topic to write about each week. *Examples:*

- a time when I was bullied (what happened, who was there, how I felt about it, what I did about it)
- a list of people I can talk to about my problems—people I trust
- a list of people I can count on to help me
- a list of things I can say when someone teases me or calls me names
- a list of funny things I can say to someone who bullies me or others
- ways to build my self-esteem
- good things I can tell myself (positive self-talk)

Students might use their journals to tell you about things that are happening in their lives—things they don't feel comfortable talking about.

TEACH PLANNING SKILLS

Students can learn to dodge potential bullying situations by planning ahead. With the whole class or in small groups, work with students to brainstorm ways to avoid kids who bully them, ways to stay safe in their everyday lives, and ways to be more observant. *Examples:*

- When you're walking down the hall and you see someone who bullies you, don't make eye contact. Stay as far away from the person as you can. Try to keep other people between you. If possible, turn and go in a different direction.

---

*See also "Weekly Journaling" (page 68).

- Travel in groups. When you're on the playground, stay close to a friend or two. When you're in the lunchroom, sit with kids who are friendly to you.

- Make a list of places where you feel unsafe. Plan to stay away from those places. If that's not possible, make sure you never go to those places alone. This might mean changing your route to school, avoiding parts of the playground, or only using common rooms or bathrooms when other people are around.

- If you notice a person coming toward you who bullies you, walk calmly but quickly in the opposite direction.

- Stay away from anyone who makes you feel uncomfortable, anxious, scared, worried, or nervous.

- When you're walking in a public place, don't look at the ground. Look around you and notice who else is there.

- Always let a trusted friend or caring adult know where you're going.

- Stick with a group, even if they aren't your friends.

Distribute copies of "Planning Ahead" (page 125). Students can complete them on their own, or work in pairs or small groups. Afterward, share and discuss responses. Praise students for coming up with good ideas.

TEACH POWER SKILLS

Teach these skills to students you consider ready to go beyond the basics (stay calm, walk away, join a group, tell an adult). Use demonstration, discussion, role playing, and plenty of guided practice. After students use the following strategies, it is often best to calmly and confidently walk away. If that isn't possible, they could start a conversation with someone or join a nearby adult.

Note: Some students may be too timid to try these approaches. If that's the case, don't force it.

1. Agree with everything the bullying student says.

Examples: "Yes, that's true." "You're right." "I see what you mean." "You are absolutely 100 percent correct! I *am* a wimp!"

2. Use humor to disarm the person who bullies.

Laugh and walk away. Or laugh and don't walk away. Act as if the two of you are sharing a good joke. Play along. When the person starts laughing, you can say something like, "Wow, that was fun! See you later. Gotta go!"

Turn a put-down into a joke. *Example:* "You called me a wimp. You're right; I need to lift weights more often."

3. Bore the other person with questions.

Examples: "I'm a wimp? What do you mean by that? How do you know I'm a wimp? Do you know any other wimps? Have you compared me to them? Am I more or less wimpy than they are? What exactly is a wimp, anyway?"

4. Be a broken record.

Whatever the other person says, say the same thing in response . . . over and over and over again. *Examples:*

Other kid: "You're a wimp."

You: "That's your opinion."

Other kid: "Yeah, and I'm right."

You: "That's your opinion."

Other kid: "So what are you going to do about it?"

You: "That's your opinion."

Other kid: "You'd better shut up."

You: "That's your opinion."

Other kid: "I'm getting sick of you."

You: "That's your opinion."

Other kid: "I mean it! Shut up!"

You: "That's your opinion."

Other kid: "Oh, forget it!"

Other kid: "You want to fight?"

You: "I don't do that."

Other kid: "That's because you're a wimp."

You: "I don't do that."

Other kid: "You're too scared to fight. You're chicken."

You: "I don't do that."

Other kid: "I'll bet I can make you fight."

You: "I don't do that."

Other kid: "What's with you? Is that all you can say?"

You: "I don't do that."

Other kid: "Oh, forget it!"

5. Just say no.

Examples: "You can't have this toy. I'm playing with it now." "You can't have my lunch. I'm eating it." "You can't have my money. I need it to buy lunch later." "You can't have my pencil. I need it. Give it back."

6. Use "fogging."

If being assertive and telling someone to stop calling you names doesn't work, try responding with short, bland words and phrases that neutralize the situation. *Examples:* "Possibly." "You might be right." "It might look that way to you." "Maybe." "That's your opinion."

7. Act like you can't hear the teaser.*

Pretend you can't hear what the teaser is saying, and respond to every taunt by saying something like, "Sorry, can't hear you" or "I'm sorry, I didn't hear that. Let's talk some other time." Don't go on and on, and don't let the conversation escalate into an argument or fight—it only takes a few times to show that you're not going to let the teasing bother you.

PROTECT YOURSELF

Teachers can be bullied, too. Maybe you have an intimidating or aggressive student—someone who makes you feel uneasy or threatened. Or maybe the problem is a coworker, a group of your coworkers, or a superior.

1. Check your school or district policies on how to handle students who bully.

There should be guidelines in place. If none exist, talk with your principal and other teachers about this issue.

Go Further

Contact the Crisis Prevention Institute (CPI) and ask about their Nonviolent Crisis Intervention program, which teaches the safe management of disruptive or assaultive behavior. Many schools and districts have benefited from this training. Write or call: CPI, 10850 W. Park Place, Suite 600, Milwaukee, WI 53224; toll-free telephone 1-888-426-2184. On the Web, go to, www.crisisprevention.com.

2. What if you're being bullied by your coworkers or superiors?

Workplace bullying is on the rise, and schools are workplaces, just like businesses or factories. Talk to your principal. Talk to your union representative. You don't have to put up with rude, hostile behavior or putdowns. Learn about the laws that protect you.

---

*Excerpted from *Speak Up and Get Along!* by Scott Cooper, copyright © 2005. Used with permission of Free Spirit Publishing Inc., Minneapolis, MN; 800-735-7323; www.freespirit.com. All rights reserved.

Go Further

Contact the advocates for the anti-bullying Healthy Workplace Bill. The Healthy Workplace Campaign, founded by Gary Namie, Ph.D., and Ruth F. Namie, Ph.D., is a nonprofit organization that acts as a resource for employee and employer solutions. Contact: Healthy Workplace Campaign at 360-656-6630 or email healthyworkplacebill.org. The organization's website offers information, research results, surveys, and news articles about workplace bullying. Go to, www.healthyworkplacebill.org.

3. Meanwhile, here are some commonsense tips you can follow to safeguard yourself:

- Vary your routine. If you walk to and from school, don't always walk the same route at the same time. If you drive, change your route frequently (and try stopping for coffee at a different place now and then).

- Pay attention to your intuition; act on it. It's better to be safe and risk a little embarrassment than stay in an uncomfortable situation that may turn out to be dangerous.

- Don't label keys with your name or any identification.

- Try not to overload yourself with books and other materials when walking down the hall or walking to and from the school building.

- Before or after school hours, check your surroundings before getting out of your car.

- Have your keys ready before you leave the school building. Look inside and under your car before getting in, and always lock your car.

- If your school has an elevator, stay close to the controls and locate the emergency button.

- Get to know your coworkers and look out for each other.

- Walk with confidence. Be assertive. Watch your body language. (See pages 73.)

- Be extra watchful when you're walking between buildings, in poorly lighted areas, etc. Try to have another adult with you.

- If you feel that you're in serious, immediate danger, don't try to defuse the situation on your own. Get help from school security or law enforcement personnel.

WARNING SIGNS

The following behaviors may indicate that a student is being bullied or is at risk of being bullied. For any student you're concerned about, check all that apply.

When any of these behaviors are evident and persistent over time, you should definitely investigate. There's no magic number of warning signs that indicate a student is definitely being bullied—but it's better to be wrong than to allow a student to suffer.

Some of these characteristics are obviously more serious than others. A child who talks about suicide or carries a weapon to school, for example, needs immediate help. Don't wait for the child to come to you (this may never happen). Following the guidelines established by your school or district, contact a professional who is specially trained in dealing with high-risk behaviors.

Student's name: _____ Today's date: _____

SCHOOL AND SCHOOLWORK

_____ **1.** Sudden change in school attendance/academic performance

_____ **2.** Loss of interest in schoolwork/academic performance/homework

_____ **3.** Decline in quality of schoolwork/academic performance*

_____ **4.** Academic success; appears to be the teacher's pet*

_____ **5.** Difficulty concentrating in class, easily distracted

_____ **6.** Goes to recess late and comes back early

_____ **7.** Has a learning disability or difference

_____ **8.** Lack of interest in school-sponsored activities/events

_____ **9.** Drops out of school-sponsored activities he or she enjoys

*True, #3 and #4 are opposites. They are also extremes. Watch for any extremes or sudden changes; these can be signs that something stressful is happening in a student's life.

SOCIAL

_____ **1.** Lonely, withdrawn, isolated

_____ **2.** Poor or no social/interpersonal skills

_____ **3.** No friends or fewer friends than other students, unpopular, often/always picked last for groups or teams

_____ **4.** Lacks a sense of humor, uses inappropriate humor

_____ **5.** Often made fun of, laughed at, picked on, teased, put down, and/or called names by other students, doesn't stand up for himself or herself

_____ **6.** Often pushed around, kicked, and/or hit by other students, doesn't defend himself or herself

_____ **7.** Uses "victim" body language—hunches shoulders, hangs head, won't look people in the eye, backs off from others

CONTINUED ➤

_____ **8.** Has a noticeable difference that sets him or her apart from peers

_____ **9.** Comes from a racial, cultural, ethnic, and/or religious background that puts him or her in the minority

_____ **10.** Prefers the company of adults during lunch and other free times

_____ **11.** Teases, pesters, and irritates others, eggs them on, doesn't know when to stop

_____ **12.** Suddenly starts bullying other students

PHYSICAL

_____ **1.** Frequent illness*

_____ **2.** Frequent complaints of headache, stomachache, pains*

_____ **3.** Scratches, bruises, damage to clothes or belongings, etc. that don't have obvious explanations

_____ **4.** Sudden stammer or stutter

_____ **5.** Has a physical disability

_____ **6.** Has a physical difference that sets him/her apart from peers—wears glasses, is overweight/underweight, taller/shorter than peers, "talks funny," "looks funny," "walks funny," etc.

_____ **7.** Change in eating patterns, sudden loss of appetite

_____ **8.** Clumsy, uncoordinated, poor at sports

_____ **9.** Smaller than peers

_____ **10.** Physically weaker than peers

*A school nurse or other healthcare professional can determine if these physical symptoms might have other causes. A nurse can also gently question a child to learn if he or she is being bullied.

EMOTIONAL/BEHAVIORAL

_____ **1.** Sudden change in mood or behavior

_____ **2.** Passive, timid, quiet, shy, sullen, withdrawn

_____ **3.** Low or no self-confidence/self-esteem

_____ **4.** Low or no assertiveness skills

_____ **5.** Overly sensitive, cautious, clingy

_____ **6.** Nervous, anxious, worried, fearful, insecure

_____ **7.** Cries easily and/or often, becomes emotionally distraught, has extreme mood swings

_____ **8.** Irritable, disruptive, aggressive, quick-tempered, fights back (but always loses)

_____ **9.** Blames himself or herself for problems/difficulties

_____ **10.** Overly concerned about personal safety; spends a lot of time and effort thinking/worrying about getting safely to and from lunch, the bathroom, lockers, through recess, etc.; avoids certain places at school

_____ **11.** Talks about running away

_____ **12.** Talks about suicide

WHAT SHOULD YOU DO?

What should you do when someone bullies you? Read each idea and decide if you think this is something you might do. Check "Yes" if you would, "No" if you wouldn't, or "Not sure."

WHEN SOMEONE BULLIES YOU, YOU SHOULD:	YES	NO	NOT SURE
1. cry			
2. tell a friend			
3. tell the parents of the person who bullies you			
4. run away			
5. try to get even with the person			
6. tell a teacher			
7. stay home from school			
8. hit, push, or kick the person who bullies you			
9. stand up straight, look the person in the eye, and say in a firm, confident voice, "Leave me alone!"			
10. hunch over, hang your head, and try to look so small the person will stop noticing you			
11. laugh and act like you don't care			
12. stand up straight, look the person in the eye, and say in a firm, confident voice, "Stop it! I don't like that."			
13. tell your parents			
14. threaten the person bullying you			
15. call the person a bad name			
16. stay calm and walk away			
17. shout as loudly as you can for the person to stop			
18. ignore the bullying			
19. tell a joke or say something silly			
20. if other people are nearby, join them so you're not alone			

ANSWERS TO WHAT SHOULD YOU DO?

When someone bullies you, you should:

1. **cry**   Best answer: **NO.**
   People who bully love having power over others. They enjoy making people cry. When you cry, you give them what they want. On the other hand, you might be so upset that you can't help crying. If this happens, get away as quickly as you can. Find a friend or an adult who will listen and support you.

2. **tell a friend**   Best answer: **YES.**
   Make sure it's a friend who will listen, support you, and stand up for you. And don't just tell a friend. Tell an adult, too.

3. **tell the parents of the person who bullies you**   Best answer: **NO.**
   Some kids bully because their parents bully them. The kid's parents are more likely to believe their child, not you. They might even get defensive and blame you.

4. **run away**   Best answer: **NOT SURE.**
   If you feel you're in real danger—for example, if you're facing a gang of kids bullying—then run as fast as you can to a safe place. At other times, it might be better to stand your ground and stick up for yourself. Follow your instincts!

5. **try to get even with the person**   Best answer: **NO.**
   The kid bullying might get angry and come after you again. Plus, getting even makes you someone who bullies, too.

6. **tell a teacher**   Best answer: **YES.**
   Especially if the bullying happens at school. Most bullying happens where adults aren't likely to see or hear it. Your teacher can't help you unless you tell (or someone else tells).

7. **stay home from school**   Best answer: **NO.**
   Unless you feel you're in real danger, you should never stay home from school to avoid bullying. Remember, people who bully love power. Imagine how powerful they feel when they can scare someone away from school! Plus, staying home from school gets in the way of your learning and hurts you even more.

8. **hit, push, or kick the person who bullies you**   Best answer: **NO.**
   Since people tend to pick on people who are smaller and weaker than them, chances are you'd get hurt. Plus, you might get in trouble for fighting.

9. **stand up straight, look the person in the eye, and say in a firm, confident voice, "Leave me alone!"**   Best answer: **YES.**
   People who bully don't expect people to stand up to them. They usually pick on people who don't seem likely to defend themselves. So they're surprised when someone acts confident and strong instead of scared and weak. This might be enough to make them stop.

CONTINUED →

10. **hunch over, hang your head, and try to look so small the person will stop noticing you** Best answer: **NO.**
This gives kids who bully what they want—someone who appears even more scared and weak.

11. **laugh and act like you just don't care** Best answer: **NOT SURE.**
Some kids will give up bullying if people don't react to it. But others will bully harder to get the reaction they want.

12. **stand up straight, look the person in the eye, and say in a firm, confident voice, "Stop it! I don't like that."** Best answer: **YES.**
See #9.

13. **tell your parents** Best answer: **YES.**
Tell them what's happening and ask for their help.

14. **threaten the person bullying you** Best answer: **NO.**
The person might get angry and come after you in an even more forceful way.

15. **call the person a bad name** Best answer: **NO.**
This will only make him or her angry—bad news for you.

16. **stay calm and walk away** Best answer: **YES.**
Especially if you can walk toward a crowded place or a group of your friends.

17. **shout as loudly as you can for the person to stop** Best answer: **YES.**
This may surprise the kid who is bullying you and give you a chance to get away. Plus, if other people hear you, they might turn and look, giving the person an audience he or she doesn't want.

18. **ignore the bullying** Best answer: **NO.**
People bully because they want a reaction from the people they're bullying. Ignoring them might lead to more and worse bullying.

19. **tell a joke or say something silly** Best answer: **NOT SURE.**
Sometimes humor can defuse a tense situation. Be careful not to tell a joke about the person bullying you or make fun of him or her.

20. **if other people are nearby, join them so you're not alone** Best answer: **YES.**
People generally don't pick on kids in groups. They don't like being outnumbered.

1. If you think your child is being bullied, *ask your child.* Many children won't volunteer this information; they're ashamed, embarrassed, or afraid. Adults need to take the initiative. Ask for specifics and write them down.

   If you suspect that your child won't want to talk about being bullied, try approaching the topic indirectly. You might ask a series of questions like these:

   - "So, who acts like a bully in your classroom?"
   - "How do you know that person bullies? What does he or she do?"
   - "What do you think about that?"
   - "Who gets picked on most of the time?"
   - "Do you ever get picked on?"
   - "What does [name of student who acts like a bully] say or do to you? How does that make you feel?"

2. If your child tells you that he or she is being bullied, *believe your child.* Ask for specifics and write them down.

3. Please DON'T:
   - confront the bullying student or the student's parents. This probably won't help and might make things worse.
   - tell your child to "get in there and fight." Kids who bully are always stronger and more powerful than those they choose to target. Your child could get hurt.
   - blame your child. Bullying is never the target's fault.
   - promise to keep the bullying secret. This gives those who bully permission to keep bullying. Instead, tell your child you're glad that he or she told you about the bullying. Explain that you're going to help, and you're also going to ask the teacher to help.

4. Contact the teacher as soon as possible. Request a private meeting (no students should be around, and ideally no students except for your child should know that you're meeting with the teacher). Bring your written record of what your child has told you about the bullying, and share this information with the teacher. Ask for the teacher's perspective; he or she probably knows things about the bullying that you don't. Ask to see a copy of the school's anti-bullying policy. Stay calm and be respectful; your child's teacher wants to help.

CONTINUED

Ask what the teacher will do about the bullying. Get specifics. You want the teacher to:

- put a stop to the bullying

- have specific consequences in place for bullying, and apply them

- help the bullying student change his or her behavior

- help your child develop bullying resistance and assertiveness skills

- monitor your child's safety in the future

- keep you informed of actions taken and progress made

IMPORTANT: It takes time to resolve bullying problems. Try to be patient. The teacher will need to talk with your child, talk with the child who bullied your child, talk with other children who might have witnessed the bullying, and then decide the best plan of action for everyone involved.

5. Make a real effort to spend more positive time with your child than you already do. Encourage your child to talk about his or her feelings. Ask your child how the day went. Encourage your child's efforts as often as possible. Give your child opportunities to do well—by helping you with a chore, taking on new responsibilities, or showing off a talent or skill.

6. Help your child develop bullying resistance skills. Role-play with your child what to say and do when confronted with bullying. Here are a few starter ideas:

- Stand up straight, look the other person in the eye, and say in a firm, confident voice, "Leave me alone!" or "Stop that! I don't like that!"

- Tell a joke or say something silly. (Don't make fun of the person bullying you.)

- Stay calm and walk away. If possible, walk toward a crowded place or a group of your friends.

- If you feel you're in real danger, run away as fast as you can.

- Tell an adult.

Ask your child's teacher or the school counselor for more suggestions. Also ask your child for suggestions. It's great if your child comes up with an idea, tries it, and it works!

7. Consider enrolling your child in a class on assertiveness skills, friendship skills, or self-defense. Check with your child's teacher or community resources—your local public library, YMCA or YWCA, or community education.

IMPORTANT: Self-defense classes aren't about being aggressive. They're about avoiding conflict through self-discipline, self-control, and improved self-confidence. Most martial arts teach that the first line of defense is nonviolence.

CONTINUED

8. If your child seems to lack friends, arrange for him or her to join social groups, clubs, or organizations that meet his or her interests. This will boost your child's self-confidence and develop his or her social skills. Confident children with social skills are much less likely to be bullied.

9. Consider whether your child might be doing something that encourages people to pick on him or her. Is there a behavior your child needs to change? Does your child dress or act in ways that might provoke teasing? No one ever deserves to be bullied, but sometimes kids don't help themselves. Watch how your child interacts with others. Ask your child's teachers for their insights and suggestions.

10. Label everything that belongs to your child with his or her name. Things are less likely to be "lost" or stolen if they're labeled. Use sew-in labels or permanent marker.

11. Make sure your child knows that his or her safety is always more important than possessions (books, school supplies, toys, money). If your child is threatened, your child should give up what the other person wants—and tell an adult (you or the teacher) right away.

12. Encourage your child to express his or her feelings around you. Give your child permission to blow off steam, argue, and state opinions and beliefs that are different from yours. If you allow your child to stand up to you now and then, it's more likely that he or she will be able to stand up to someone who bullies them.

13. Check with your child often about how things are going. Once your child says that things are better or okay at school—the bullying has slowed down or stopped—you don't have to keep asking every day. Ask once every few days, or once a week. Meanwhile, watch for any changes in behavior that might indicate the bullying has started again.

14. If you're not already involved with your child's school, get involved. Attend parent-teacher conferences and school board meetings. Join the Parent-Teacher Association or Organization (PTA or PTO). Learn about school rules and discipline policies. Serve on a school safety committee. If you have the time, volunteer to help in your child's classroom.

15. Remember that you are your child's most important teacher. Discipline at home should be fair, consistent, age-appropriate, and respectful. Parents who can't control their temper are teaching their children that it's okay to yell, scream, and use physical violence to get their way. *Tip:* Many children who bully others come from homes where their parents bully *them*.

WAYS TO STAY BULLY FREE

Ways to Stay Bully Free

Avoid people who bully
Act confident
Look confident
Be observant
Tell a friend
Tell an adult
Be assertive
Stay calm
Keep a safe distance
Walk away
Say "Stop it!"
Say "Whatever!"
Use humor
Travel in a group
Join a group
If you're in danger, *run*

Ways to Stay Bully Free

Avoid people who bully
Act confident
Look confident
Be observant
Tell a friend
Tell an adult
Be assertive
Stay calm
Keep a safe distance
Walk away
Say "Stop it!"
Say "Whatever!"
Use humor
Travel in a group
Join a group
If you're in danger, *run*

Ways to Stay Bully Free

Avoid people who bully
Act confident
Look confident
Be observant
Tell a friend
Tell an adult
Be assertive
Stay calm
Keep a safe distance
Walk away
Say "Stop it!"
Say "Whatever!"
Use humor
Travel in a group
Join a group
If you're in danger, *run*

Ways to Stay Bully Free

Avoid people who bully
Act confident
Look confident
Be observant
Tell a friend
Tell an adult
Be assertive
Stay calm
Keep a safe distance
Walk away
Say "Stop it!"
Say "Whatever!"
Use humor
Travel in a group
Join a group
If you're in danger, *run*

INTERVIEWING SOMEONE WHO BULLIES:
GUIDELINES AND SAMPLE SCRIPT

Start by saying:

I hear you have been mean to [student's name]. Tell me about it.

The student will probably deny this. Follow up immediately with:

Yes, but mean things have been happening to [student's name]. Tell me about it.

Listen to what the student tells you. Be patient; give him or her time to think, and don't worry about lengthy silences. If the child doesn't respond after a significant period of time has elapsed, say:

It seems that you don't want to talk today. You'd better go back to class now.

He or she might start talking at this point. If so, just listen. Don't accuse or blame. Avoid asking questions. Try to determine if the child feels justified in his or her behavior toward the target. The child might feel quite angry toward the target. Work toward an understanding that the target is having a bad time, whoever is to blame. Say with force and emphasis:

So, it sounds like [student's name] is having a bad time in school.

By now, the child should assent to this. Move on quickly to say:

Okay. I was wondering what you could do to help [student's name] in this situation.

See what solution the child can come up with. Be encouraging. If the child never offers a solution, ask:

Would you like me to make a suggestion?

If the child offers a solution that depends on someone else's efforts (yours or the victim's), say:

I was thinking about what you could do. What do you think you could do?

If the child makes an impractical suggestion, don't reject it. Instead, ask:

So, if this happened, the bullying would stop?

When the child proposes a practical and relevant solution, say:

Excellent. You try that out for a week, and we'll meet again and see how you've done. Good-bye for now.

INTERVIEWING A TARGET: SAMPLE SCRIPT

Nonprovocative Target

Teacher: Hello, Matthew. Sit down. I want to talk with you because I hear some mean things have been happening to you.

Child: Yes. It's the others in my class. They just keep on picking on me. They won't leave me alone. They mess around with my bag . . . putting stuff in it.

Teacher: You sound as if you're fed up with it.

Child: It just doesn't stop. The rest of the class joins in now.

Teacher: Is there anything you can think of that might help the situation?

Child: I could change schools.

Teacher: Mmm. So you feel it would be better to get out of the situation altogether.

Child: Well, sometimes. But I don't suppose my mother would let me. They're not so bad when I hang around with Simon.

Teacher: So being with someone else helps the situation?

Child: Yes. He backs me up when I tell them to stop it.

Teacher: So he supports you?

Child: Yes. I could sit next to him.

Teacher: Okay. You do that over the next week and then we'll have another chat to see how things have been going. Okay? Good-bye.

Provocative Target

Teacher: Hello, Matthew. Sit down. I want to talk with you because I hear some mean things have been happening to you.

Child: Yes. It's the others in my class. They just keep on picking on me. They won't leave me alone. They mess around with my bag . . . putting stuff in it.

Teacher: You sound as if you're fed up with it.

Child: It just doesn't stop. The rest of the class joins in now.

Teacher: Tell me more about what happens. How does it all start?

Child: It's usually when I go over and sit by them. They just can't take a joke.

Teacher: So you play jokes on them?

Child: Yes, just messing around. I go on really good vacations and they never do so I ask them where they are going . . . it makes them really mad. They're just jealous.

Teacher: Then they get angry with you. What happens when they get angry with you?

Child: Well, that's when they started messing around with my bag.

Teacher: Is there anything you can think of that might help the situation?

Child: I guess I could leave them alone.

Teacher: Okay. You do that over the next week and then we'll have another chat to see how things have been going. Okay? Good-bye.

PLANNING AHEAD

Ways to avoid kids who bully:

Ways to stay safe:

Ways to be observant:

HELP KIDS WHO BULLY

Kids who bully need help—the sooner the better. Bullying among primary schoolage children is recognized as an antecedent to more violent behavior in later grades. If children don't learn to change their behaviors, bullying becomes a habit that carries forward into their teens and their lives as adults.

Although many kids who bully may be popular in the early grades (because they're powerful, others look up to them), their popularity wanes during late adolescence; by the time they reach senior high, their peer group may be limited to other bullies or gangs. They may get in trouble with the law; studies show that one in four kids who bully will have a criminal record before age 30. They may bully their spouses, children, and coworkers and have difficulty forming and sustaining healthy, positive relationships.

The "Create a Positive Classroom" and "Empower Bystanders to Become Allies" sections of this book include many tips and strategies that can help all students—including students who bully—learn better ways of relating to others. Some of the strategies in "Help Targets of Bullying" can be adapted for use with kids who bully and kids with the potential to bully. *Examples:*

- "Encourage a Positive Attitude" (page 102)
- "Build Students' Self-Esteem" (pages 102)
- "Teach Positive Visualization" (page 103)
- "Give Them Opportunities to Shine" (page 110)

One of the strategies in "Help Targets of Bullying" is meant to be used with both targets and the kids who bully them:

- "Try the Method of Shared Concern" (pages 105)

Some of the strategies in "Help Targets of Bullying" will benefit all of your students. *Examples:*

- "Encourage Strong Family Relationships" (page 107)
- "Encourage Relationships with Other Adults" (pages 107)

"Help Kids Who Bully" focuses mainly on suggestions for working with students known to bully or who potentially will bully. As you try these ideas in your classroom, here are some good things you can expect to happen:

Your students will learn how to:

- change their thinking
- know what to expect when they use inappropriate behavior
- accept responsibility for their behavior

- manage their anger
- explore positive ways to feel powerful
- understand why they bully others
- stop bullying

You'll discover how to:

- identify students who bully and potentially may bully
- have clear consequences in place
- work to change the behavior of kids who bully—without acting like a bully yourself
- communicate with parents
- teach students positive ways to feel powerful
- change the thinking of those who bully, not just the behavior

IMPORTANT: Most children can change their behavior with guidance and help from caring adults. Sometimes, however, you might encounter a student who resists your efforts and simply won't change. Find out ahead of time what your school and district are prepared to do in these extreme circumstances. When you truly run out of options—when strategies don't work, the family can't or won't support your efforts, and the student's behavior gets progressively worse—you may have no choice but to take the problem to your principal or other administrators and leave it in their hands. The ideas in this book are not intended to help incorrigible bullies or children with severe behavioral and personality problems.

CATCH THEM IN THE ACT

The first and most important thing you can do to help kids who bully is notice their behavior and respond appropriately.

Obviously, you want to catch them "being bad"—teasing, using hurtful words, intimidating other students, hitting, shoving, kicking, and so on—and put a stop to that behavior as soon as you become aware of it. See "On-the-Spot Responding" (page 95) for specific suggestions on intervening with bullying you witness personally or learn about in another way; see also "Have Clear Consequences in Place" (page 132).

Not as obviously (and sometimes not as easily), you also want to *catch them being good*. No one can bully 24 hours a day; even the most persistent bully takes an occasional break. These students need "strokes" as much as other students—probably more.

- Recognize and reward positive and accepting behaviors whenever you observe them. This will increase the likelihood that such behaviors will be repeated.

Go Further

Contact the Crisis Prevention Institute (CPI) and ask about their Nonviolent Crisis Intervention program, which teaches the safe management of disruptive or assaultive behavior. Many schools and districts have benefited from this training. Write or call: CPI, 10850 W. Park Place, Suite 600, Milwaukee, WI 53224; toll-free telephone 1-888-426-2184. On the Web, go to www.crisisprevention.com.

- Go the extra distance and praise behaviors you might take for granted in other students—waiting one's turn, sharing, saying please or thank you.

- Create situations that give students who bully the opportunity to shine. *Examples:* Ask a problem student to help you with an important project. Or send an older student who bullies to a younger class to help a student practice spelling words or do math problems. Then recognize your student's positive behavior.

Of course, you'll want to notice and praise positive, prosocial behaviors in all of your students. You can do this verbally each day ("Thanks for helping, Evan." "Nice job, class. You're making our new student feel welcome."). You might also award special certificates recognizing specific behaviors. Students will appreciate "You Were Caught Being Good!" certificates (page 147)—and parents will treasure them.

Tip: In one school, students who are seen or reported as displaying positive social interactions (e.g., sticking up for a friend, making a new friend, welcoming or accepting a new student, being a good role model, cooperating, showing empathy) are given a "Gotcha!" card to sign. The cards are entered in a prize drawing at the end of each week.

Finally: Monitor your own interactions with your students. Are they mostly negative, mostly positive, or a mixture of both? Make an effort to increase the number of positives—smiles, acknowledgments, words of praise and approval, thank-yous, nods. The National Association of School Psychologists (NASP) recommends that teachers give approximately five positives for each negative. Keep track of your behavior for a day or two. How close do you come to the five-to-one ratio? Is there room for improvement?

HAVE COMPASSION

Kids who bully can be distracting, disruptive, annoying, frustrating, and even scary at times. But they need as much help, understanding, and compassion as you can give them. Food for thought:

- Many kids who bully have family problems—parents, siblings, or other bigger, stronger people who bully them. They don't know other ways to behave. And even if they learn and observe other ways in your classroom, they experience a sort of "dissonance" when they return home. Like children of divorced parents who alternate between their parents' homes, they must fit into both environments, and it's not easy.

- Many kids who bully are angry all or most of the time. Being angry is no fun—especially if you're not really sure *why* you're angry, you don't have anyone to talk to about your anger (or think you don't, and even if you do, you might not know *how* to talk about it), and your peers avoid and fear you. For some kids, being angry is a vicious circle, and they're caught in the middle with no way out.

- It's hard to be the meanest, toughest kid in the classroom or on the playground. You're always having to prove yourself and fend off other kids who want to take over as meanest and toughest.

- It's hard to feel that you always have to win and can't ever lose. No one likes to lose, but kids who bully can't afford to lose—it's too risky. So they cheat, play dirty, and intimidate anyone who stands in their way. And eventually no one wants to play with them or against them.

GO FURTHER
Work with other teachers and administrators to arrange a special awards ceremony to be held once a month or several times a year. Try to schedule it for a time when parents and grandparents can attend. Instead of handing out the usual awards—for athletic or academic achievement—reserve this ceremony for students whose prosocial behaviors have made a positive difference in your classroom and school.

Help Those Who Bully **129**

- Many bullying kids are jealous of other people's success. Jealousy is a nasty, uncomfortable feeling. It's so overpowering that it can prevent you from enjoying your own successes—or distract you so much that you don't achieve your true potential.

- Some kids never wanted to hurt or harass anyone. They were bullied by someone else into joining a bullying gang and are going along just to stay on the good side of those kids.

- Many kids who cyberbully may do it unintentionally. They may forward mean messages without understanding it is bullying.

- Many kids who bully lack social skills. When you don't know how to get along with others, and when you see groups of friends hanging out, laughing, telling jokes, and enjoying each other's company, you know you're missing out on something important . . . but you don't know how to get it for yourself. Which may be another reason why these kids are so angry.

- Many kids who bully have hangers-on, "henchmen," or "lieutenants," but they seldom have real friends. Life without friends is lonely.

The kids in your classroom who bully other kids may be some of the most unpleasant, least appealing kids you know. The good news is, they're still kids . . . for now. As kids, they have the potential to learn, grow, and change.

IDENTIFY KIDS WHO BULLY OR HAVE THE POTENTIAL TO BULLY

You may know that some students in your classroom bully; either you've seen them in action yourself, or you've heard reports from other students and teachers. But what about students whose bullying actions aren't noticed by adults, whose targets are too intimidated or ashamed to come forward, and whose witnesses either don't want to get involved or fear reprisals if they do? And what about those students who haven't started bullying others but may be heading in that direction?

"Identify Targets or Potential Targets" (pages 91–93) explains how to look for warning signs and seek input from students' parents. You can use similar approaches to identify kids who bully or have the potential to bully.

LOOK FOR WARNING SIGNS

For any student you suspect might be bullying or may start bullying, complete the "Warning Signs" checklist (pages 148–149).

IMPORTANT: These forms should be kept confidential. You may want to share them with other adults—teachers, your principal, the school counselor, the student's parents—but they should never be accessible to students.

GET PARENTS' INPUT

If a student shows some or many of the warning signs, contact the family. Arrange a face-to-face meeting at school. You may want to include the school counselor or psychologist in the meeting.

No parent wants to hear that his or her child might be bullying, so you'll need to handle this *very* carefully. You might start by emphasizing your commitment to creating a positive classroom environment where every student is valued, accepted, safe, and free to learn. Share information about what's being done at your school to reduce and eliminate bullying.

Next, tell the parents about the *positive* behaviors you've observed in their child. (See "Catch Them in the Act," pages 127–128.) Parents love hearing good things about their children, and this sets the stage for a productive meeting.

Then tell the parents that you've noticed some behaviors at school that may indicate their child is bullying others or might be headed in that direction. Give examples. Explain that kids who bully often exhibit other behaviors that don't show up at school, and you need their help identifying those behaviors.

Ask if they have noticed any of the following with their child:

- having more money than he or she can explain

- buying things he or she normally can't afford

- having new possessions (games, clothing, CDs) and claiming that "my friends gave them to me"

- defying parental authority; ignoring or breaking rules; pushing parental boundaries harder than ever

- behaving aggressively toward siblings

- exhibiting a sense of superiority—of being "right" all the time

- being determined to win at everything; being a poor loser

- blaming others for his or her problems

- refusing to take responsibility for his or her negative behaviors

What else can the parents tell you? What else have they noticed that you should know—that might help you help their child?

IMPORTANT: Studies show that kids who bully often come from homes where physical punishment is used, where children are taught to handle problems by striking back physically, and where parental involvement and warmth are minimal or lacking. But never *assume* that this is true for every child. In my experience, most parents of kids who bully are deeply concerned about their children. They want their children to be accepted by others; they want them to develop social skills, friendships, and positive character traits including tolerance, compassion, and empathy. So instead of expecting the worst, hope for the best. Project a sense of optimism; communicate your belief that you and the parents can work together to turn the child around.

You'll also want to talk with the parents about how bullying violates your school and classroom policies and rules. Mention the consequences of such behavior, but don't dwell on these too long. Rather, the purpose of this meeting should be to identify warning signs and reach an agreement that everyone involved—you, the parents, and the counselor (if present)—will work together to help the student. Make it clear that you have high expectations that the problem can and will be resolved successfully. You want the parents to leave your meeting with a desire to work with you on their child's behalf, not the feeling that you and the school are united "against" them and their child.

Toward the end of the meeting, give parents a copy of "Bringing Out the Best in Kids: Tips for Parents" (pages 150–151). Explain that this is a list of suggestions they can try at home. Answer any questions they may have. *Tip:* You may want to find out ahead of time about parenting courses and resources available in your community, so you can give this information to parents who want it.

Thank the parents for coming in and talking with you. Tell them that you'll communicate with them often about their child's behavior and progress, and ask them to do the same for you. Then be sure to follow through.

Make a written record of your meeting. Note any relevant information the parents shared with you, any conclusions you came to, and any agreements you reached.

NEVER BULLY KIDS WHO BULLY

When faced with a student who bullies, and frustrated or angered by his or her behavior, it's easy for adults to "lose their cool." Shouting, spanking, and threats aren't uncommon.

Severe punishment may suppress the current behavior, but it doesn't teach alternate behaviors, including positive ways to act. Here are eight more reasons why "bullying kids who bully" is always a bad idea:

1. Adults who respond to bullying with violence, force, or intimidation are modeling and reinforcing the same behaviors they're trying to change. Children imitate what they see adults do.

2. Severe punishment reinforces the power imbalance and shows kids that bullying is acceptable.

3. Severe punishment may stop one behavior temporarily but stimulate other aggressive behaviors.

4. The child may stop the punished behavior only when adults are around and increase it in other settings.

5. The child may strike back at the adult who's doing the punishing, or strike out at someone else because of displaced anger.

6. Angry children who don't fear authority may become even angrier and focus on getting revenge.

7. Frequent punishment may cause some children to withdraw, regress, and give up. Others may feel a strong sense of shame and low self-esteem.

8. Severe punishment is a short-term "solution" that may cause more problems down the road. ("If adults can hit, why can't I? Maybe I just have to wait until I'm bigger.")

If you feel that you sometimes overreact and would like to learn ways to control your emotions, check with your school psychologist or counselor. Or visit your local library or bookstore and look for books on managing stress and handling challenging kids. Ask other teachers what they do when they feel like they're about to blow up. Meanwhile:

- Remember that you're the adult, then behave like one.

- Tell yourself that you'll stay calm no matter what.

- Learn and practice simple relaxation techniques you can use when students push you to the edge of your patience.

- Make an agreement with another teacher whose classroom is near yours. Whenever one of you reaches the end of your rope, you can ask the other to take over your class for a few minutes while you go to a quiet place and regain control of your emotions. Or you can send a student who's driving you crazy to the other teacher's room for a short period of time.

- Never spank a child—even if your school permits corporal punishment. Why model a behavior you're trying to teach your students never to use? When you swat or paddle a student, you're saying, "It's okay for bigger, stronger people to hit smaller, weaker people."

 GO FURTHER

Many states still permit corporal punishment in schools. Corporal punishment of children is unsupported by educational research, sometimes leads to serious injury, and contributes to a proviolence attitude. If your state still permits corporal punishment in schools and you'd like to do something to change that, the Center for Effective Discipline (CED) can help. This national organization provides educational information to the public on the effects of corporal punishment and alternatives to its use. It coordinates and serves as headquarters for two other organizations: the National Coalition to Abolish Corporal Punishment in Schools (NCACPS) and End Physical Punishment of Children (EPOCH-USA). Write or call: The Center for Effective Discipline, 327 Groveport Pike, Canal Winchester, OH 43110; telephone 614-834-7946. On the Web, go to www.stophitting.com.

What if a student threatens you? Try not to look angry, upset, or afraid. Don't grab the student. Don't raise your voice. Don't set up a power struggle by challenging him or her. Don't cross your arms and shout across the room. Don't verbally attack the student and back him or her into a corner by demanding immediate compliance.

Instead, remain calm, confident, assertive, and under control. Keep your body language and facial expression neutral. Speak clearly in your normal tone of voice as you move closer to the student (no closer than arm's length), state your expectations, and give the student a choice: stop the behavior and accept the consequences, or continue the behavior and bring on worse consequences. If the student wants to argue, simply restate the choice.

Tip: If you feel that you might be in real danger, get reinforcements—another teacher, an administrator, the school security officer, or local law enforcement.*

---

*See also "Protect Yourself" (page 112).

HAVE CLEAR CONSEQUENCES IN PLACE

If your school or district already has consequences in place for bullying behaviors, familiarize yourself with them. Communicate them to students and parents so everyone knows what they are.

- You might summarize the consequences simply and clearly on a poster for your classroom.

- Create a handout for students; send copies home or give them to parents during conferences, open houses, or parents' night.

- If your school publishes a student or parent handbook, the consequences should be included there.

Consequences are essential because they tell you exactly how to follow through when a student behaves inappropriately. You will know which behaviors are grounds for a reprimand, time-out, in-school detention, dismissal, suspension, and (a last resort) expulsion. You won't have to decide what to do each time a bullying situation arises; uncertainty is replaced by consistency, and there are no surprises for anyone.

What if your school or district hasn't spelled out specific consequences for bullying behaviors? Form a team of other teachers and administrators and work together to determine consequences that are:

- *practical* (doable where you are and with the resources available to you)

- *logical* (they make sense and are related to specific bullying behaviors)

- *reasonable and fair* (excessively punitive consequences "bully the kid who bullies")

- *inevitable* (if a student does A, then B happens—no exceptions)

- *predictable* (everyone in the school community knows that A leads to B)

- *immediate* (consequences are applied at the earliest possible opportunity)

- *escalating* (continuing the behavior leads to more serious consequences)

- *consistently enforced* (if two students do A, then B happens for both)

- *developmentally appropriate and age appropriate* (the consequences for name-calling in first grade will be different from the consequences for name-calling in sixth grade)

Tip: Consider including students on your team. Since bullying affects them directly, they'll have a personal interest and commitment to the process, and they'll bring their unique perspective to the table.

APOLOGIES AND AMENDS

Although opinions differ on whether students should apologize to the students they have bullied, saying "I'm sorry" is the first step toward recognizing that a behavior is inappropriate and taking responsibility for that behavior. Many kids blame the target ("he made me do it," "he deserved it") and see no need to apologize. Don't listen to excuses; simply insist that the student apologize—verbally or in writing. If he or she refuses, apply appropriate consequences for his or her lack of cooperation.

Beyond apologizing to the target, the student should also make amends for his or her behavior. *Examples:*

- For every "put-down" comment the student makes about another, he or she should make one or more "build-up" comment.

- If the student extorted money, he or she should pay it back as soon as possible. Also consider having the student do work around the school (e.g., in the media center, office, gym) for a half hour every day for one week.

- If the student damaged or destroyed something belonging to another, he or she should repair or replace it as soon as possible.

TIME-OUTS

The time-out is a time-honored way to modify students' behavior—or at least put a stop to inappropriate behavior and give tempers a chance to cool.

Tell students when time-outs will be used, and describe the specific behaviors that will lead to a time-out. Establish a time-out place in your classroom—a special area away from the group where students can be seen and supervised. In contrast to the rest of your classroom, try to keep the time-out place relatively dull and boring—no fun posters, no books or toys.

As you use time-outs with your students, keep these general guidelines in mind:

- A time-out is not a detention. Rather, it's time spent away from the group and its activities, social feedback, and rewards.

- A time-out is not a punishment. It's an opportunity for a student to calm down and ponder his or her behavior.

- A time-out is brief. A few minutes is usually sufficient—longer for more serious or disruptive behaviors, but no more than 10–15 minutes. For younger students (kindergarten or first grade) it should be much shorter.

- A time-out is not to be used for classwork or homework. (Nor should it be used by the student as an opportunity to get out of an assignment or classwork he or she doesn't want to do.)

- A time-out is not a battleground. Don't argue with the student. Don't engage in any kind of conversation with the student. Simply say, "You [broke a particular class rule, or violated a guideline], and that results in a time-out. Please go to the time-out place right now."

- What if a student refuses to go to the time-out place? Try adding one or two minutes to the time-out for each minute the student delays going. Or you might say, "For every minute you put off going to time-out, that's five minutes you'll have to stay in from recess."

- When a time-out is over, it's over. The student returns to the group without criticism, comments, or conditions.

Tip: Consider giving students the option to put *themselves* on a time-out when they feel they are about to behave inappropriately. This empowers students to make good choices on their own behalf and teaches them to remove themselves from a potentially volatile situation.

CHANGE THEIR THINKING

As you work to help kids who bully, it's as important to change their *thinking* as it is to change their behavior. These kids often deny that they've done anything wrong and refuse to take responsibility for their behavior. They believe that their actions are someone else's "fault." Or they dismiss them as "no big deal" or insist that they were "misinterpreted."* You'll need to challenge their thinking without preaching.

1. Ask them to consider this question and respond verbally or in writing:

   If you think you're not bullying another person, but that person thinks you are, who's right?

   Lead students to understand that bullying is in the "eye of the beholder"—that the other person's feelings and fears are real to him or her.

2. Suggest that there are three ways to look at any situation involving two people:

   - my interpretation—what I think happened and why

   - your interpretation—what you think happened and why

   - the facts—what really happened

   Sometimes it helps if there's a third person present (a bystander or witness) who's objective and can give his or her view of the facts.

---

*See "Warning Signs" (pages 148–149).

3. Have students keep a daily journal of events that upset, frustrate, or anger them.* For each event, they should write a brief, factual description, followed by their own interpretation of what happened.

   Review and discuss their journal entries one-on-one or in small group discussions. Encourage students to look for possible errors in their interpretations. *Example:* Maybe what happened was an accident. Maybe they misinterpreted something that wasn't meant to upset them. Maybe *they* caused the problem.

4. When dealing with specific bullying situations, use the Method of Shared Concern (page 105) or the No Blame Approach (page 106), both of which encourage children to take responsibility for their actions.

Go Further

For a list of thinking errors and the correct social thinking, see *Bully-Proofing Your School: A Comprehensive Approach for Elementary Schools* by Carla Garrity, Kathryn Jens, William Porter, Nancy Sager, and Cam Short-Camilli (Sopris West, 2000).

5. Help students self-identify. The "Do You Bully?" handout (page 152) will start them thinking about their own behavior. You might give these only to students you know or suspect are bullying others. Or make this a whole-class exercise, followed by discussion. Even students who don't bully can benefit from examining some of their own attitudes and behaviors.

 IMPORTANT: Collect the completed handouts and keep them confidential.

COMMUNICATE WITH PARENTS

Once you've informed a student's parents that their child is or may be bullying others, it's essential to follow through with regular communication and updates on their child's progress. It's normal for parents to be defensive at first, perhaps even angry that their child has been identified as a "problem" student. You can help allay their fears, calm their worries, lower their defenses, build trust, and increase their willingness to cooperate by promising to stay in touch—and keeping your promise.

You probably already communicate with your students' parents—in conferences, at open houses and parents' nights, with notes home, and in other ways. Here are a few more ideas to consider:

- Pick up the phone and call parents, or let them know the best times to call you. Offer alternatives—before school, after school, during lunch or break times.

- Each day, write comments on a note card about the child's behavior in school and send it home with the child. (For privacy, put the card in a sealed envelope.) Make sure to write at least as many positive comments as negative comments (if possible, write *more* positives than negatives). You might put a star by each positive comment. Suggest to parents that when a child has earned a certain number of stars for the week, they might offer the child a reward—doing something special with Mom or Dad, choosing a video to watch, having a friend spend the night. *Tip:* For the first few days, you might follow through with a phone call to make sure your notes are getting into parents' hands and not being "lost" on the way home from school.

- If both you and the parents have access to email, this is a fast and easy way to stay in touch.

Depending on the situation, you can also have the student communicate directly with his or her own parents. *Example:* If Kevin calls Marcus a name, have Kevin write a note describing what he said and what happened afterward. Kevin might write, "I called Marcus a bad name in school. First Ms. Sellick said to apologize to Marcus. I said I was sorry. Then she put me on a time-out. I thought about how Marcus felt when I called him the bad name. I won't do it again." Read the note before it goes home; check to make sure that the student has taken responsibility for his or her behavior (as opposed to "Marcus is a !@#$%" or "I got in trouble because Stefan ratted on me"). Follow through with a phone call to make sure parents receive the note.

As the student progresses, daily communication can eventually become weekly communication, then twice monthly, and so on until the problem behaviors have greatly improved or stopped altogether.

GET PARENTS TOGETHER

When you first inform parents that their children are bullying others or are being bullied, you'll want to meet *separately* with each set of parents (or guardians). It's hard enough for parents to hear this kind of news without having to face the parents of the child who is hurting their son or daughter (or being hurt by him or her). It's tempting for them to go on the offensive or become defensive, and suddenly you have another set of problems on your hands.

In time, however, and especially if you're making progress helping both students, you might want to consider getting the parents together for a face-to-face meeting. You might want to include the school counselor or psychologist.

IMPORTANT: Use your judgment, follow your instincts, and ask the parents (separately) how they feel about this. Are they ready to sit down and talk to each other? Can they set aside their negative feelings—anger, disappointment, fear, hostility—and keep an open mind? Can they agree to hear both sides? Can they present a united front of caring adults who all want the best for their children?

When parents are willing to communicate and work together, this brings a special energy to the situation. Students who are having difficulty getting along see a good example: adults on opposite sides of a problem who are willing to talk and work together. This gives both sets of parents the opportunity to serve as positive role models.

KEEP THE FOCUS ON BEHAVIOR

In your interactions with a student who bullies others, be sure to emphasize that the problem is the *behavior*, not the student himself or herself.

Never label the student a "bully." Instead of saying, "I've noticed that you're a bully," or "People tell me you're a bully," or "You must stop being a bully," say something like "Hitting [or kicking, teasing, excluding, name-calling, etc.] are bullying behaviors, and they are not allowed in our classroom." Or "There are lots of good things I like about you—your smile, your talent for drawing, and your sense of humor. But I don't like it when you tease other students, and we need to work on that behavior." For every negative statement you make to point out an undesirable behavior, try to include one or more positives.

When you need to remove a student from a situation, be specific about your reasons for doing so. *Example:* "Jon, I'm putting you on time-out because you shoved Tracy, and shoving isn't allowed." Make sure the student knows why he or she is being removed. Ask, "Why am I putting you on time-out?" If the student offers excuses ("Tracy shoved me first" or "I didn't mean to shove her" or "It was an accident"), calmly restate your reason ("I'm putting you on time-out because you shoved Tracy, and shoving isn't allowed"). Ask the student to reflect on his or her reasons for being removed. You might even use an old-fashioned technique and have the student write the reason on paper. ("I'm on time-out because I shoved Tracy, and shoving isn't allowed.")

Take every opportunity to show your approval and acceptance of the student as a person. Separate the student from the behavior. *Example:* "Shawna, you know I like you a lot. But I don't like it when you pick on kids who are smaller than you. Let's talk about ways you can change that behavior."

TEACH STUDENTS TO MONITOR THEIR OWN BEHAVIOR

Have students who bully others monitor their own behavior. Work with each student to identify and list inappropriate behaviors he or she needs to change. The student then keeps a tally of how often he or she engages in each behavior. Or, to cast this in a more positive light, the student can record the amount of time (in 15-minute intervals or number of class periods) during which he or she doesn't engage in the behavior. Either way, this deliberate, conscientious record-keeping usually leads to greater control over one's behavior. *Tip:* The student must want to change the behaviors, or self-monitoring won't work.

PROVIDE COUNSELING

Students who bully others need help learning how to relate to their peers in more positive, productive ways. If at all possible, they should have access to some type of counseling—by a school psychologist, guidance counselor, or another trained adult. In some cases, peer counseling can also be useful. Some experts feel that counseling or discussion with students involved in bullying should occur *before* consequences are applied.

Counseling groups have a big advantage over punishment or other disciplinary tactics, although they shouldn't take the place of reasonable and consistent consequences for specific behaviors. Rather than driving the problem underground, groups bring it out in the open where students can discuss it and adults can offer their input and advice. Rather than making kids who bully feel even more excluded and socially inept, groups offer opportunities for students to talk about what's bothering them, explore reasons for their behavior, and learn alternatives to bullying others.

In general, kids who bully don't "outgrow" their problem without some type of professional help. Often, it's not enough to counsel only these students—especially if their inappropriate behaviors were learned at home. During your discussions with the student's family, you might suggest they consider family counseling. Have a list of local and community resources available for parents who seem willing to give it a try.

GET OTHER STUDENTS INVOLVED

Never underestimate the power of peer pressure! As you're helping kids change their behavior, get the whole class involved.*

In some schools, students have formed "good gangs" to defend kids who are bullied. When they see someone being mistreated (perhaps when the teacher's back is turned), they shout in unison at the student who's doing the bullying: "Leave [target's name] alone!" You might role-play this with your class to see how it works.

Have students practice things they might say to friends who bully others. *Examples:* "If you want me to keep being your friend, you have to stop teasing Paul." "I don't like it when my friends hurt other people." "When you hit Raisa, that makes *me* feel bad and I don't want to be around you."

When you notice bullying behavior, call students' attention to it. You might say, "Look at what Ben just did to Alex. He threw Alex's notebook on the floor. That's not fair, is it? What can we do to help?" Then encourage students to act on a valid suggestion (helping Alex pick up his notebook; telling Ben to cut it out).

Give students permission to point out when someone is breaking a class rule (see "Set Rules," page 15). *Example:* A student might say, "Class Rule Number Two! We don't tease people."

Go Further

Have students brainstorm ways to express their intolerance for bullying behavior. Write their ideas on the whiteboard or chart paper and invite class discussion. They might vote for their top five ideas, then create a poster titled "Ways to Be a Bully Buster."

---

*See also "Mobilize Bystanders" (page 63).

SET UP A BULLY COURT

Some schools have set up "bully courts"—forums in which kids who bully are tried and sentenced by their peers. Half of the court's members are elected by the student's classmates, and half are appointed by the teacher. The teacher serves as chairperson to ensure fair play. "Sentences" have included banning students from a school trip or the playground, and having them perform service-related tasks such as tidying classrooms.

Bully courts might be more appropriate for older students than younger students. But if you want to explore the possibility for your classroom, check out these resources on teen and student courts:

American Bar Association
Division for Public Education
321 North Clark Street
Chicago, IL 60654
1-800-285-2221
www.abanet.org
Request a free packet of information about teen/youth/student courts.

Office of Juvenile Justice and Delinquency Prevention
202-307-5911
www.ojjdp.gov
Request a copy of "Guide for Implementing Teen Court Programs."

HELP STUDENTS IDENTIFY AND PURSUE THEIR INTERESTS

It's often true that students who bully others don't have special interests or hobbies. They spend much of their time picking on others, planning ways to pick on others, or responding to imagined slights or offenses. Because they tend to be very competitive and are poor losers, they may choose not to get involved in activities where there's a chance they won't excel or win.

Identify students who are bullying or at risk to start bullying (see page 129), then make time to talk with them one-on-one. Explain that you'd like to get to know them better. Ask them what they like to do in their free time; don't be surprised if they can't (or won't) answer right away. They may be suspicious or defensive. Be patient, friendly, welcoming, and warm; back off if you sense that a student feels uncomfortable.

You might guide them with questions like the following.* *Tip:* Along the way, share information about your own interests and hobbies, as appropriate. The discussion shouldn't be about *you*, but if you're willing to reveal a little about your life, students might follow your example and let you in on theirs.

1. Do you like to read books or magazines? What are your favorites? Do you have a favorite time to read? A special place where you like to curl up or sprawl out and read?

2. What do you like to watch on TV?

3. Do you like video games? Which ones do you like best?

4. What websites do you visit most often? Why?

5. Have you seen any good movies lately? What are your favorite movies or videos? What do you like about them?

6. What's your favorite kind of music? Who are your favorite groups or bands?

7. What's your favorite way to let off steam? Do you run? Bike? Skate? Shoot hoops?

8. When you have free time at home, what do you like to do best? Do you have a hobby? Tell me about it.

9. How much time to you spend on your hobby? What do you like most about it?

10. Imagine that you have all the money and all the freedom in the world. What's one thing you'd really like to do?

11. What do you think you might want to be when you grow up?

12. Imagine that you could go anywhere in the world. Where would you like to go? Why? What would you do there?

---

*See also "Learn More About Your Students" (page 68).

13. Imagine that you could be anyone in the world—past, present, or future. Who would you be? Why would you want to be that person? What would you do if you were that person?

14. Is there something you've always wanted to try? What about [acting in a play, starting a collection, singing in a band, playing on a team, joining a club, playing a musical instrument, dancing, working with animals]?

If you learn that the student has a hobby, encourage him or her to tell you more about it. If it's a collection, maybe the student can bring all or part of it to school and share it with the class.

If you learn that the student has a special interest (or the potential to develop a special interest), offer to help him or her pursue it. Put the student in touch with people or organizations in your school and community.* Offer encouragement and follow through by asking questions about his or her progress and experiences as the year goes on.

TEACH LEADERSHIP SKILLS

Students who bully are skilled at getting and using power over others. They do it for the wrong reasons (to intimidate and control), in the wrong ways (with physical force, verbal abuse, or emotional manipulation), and to the wrong ends (making others miserable), but clearly they possess real ability. Why not channel all that talent into something worthwhile?

Consider offering leadership training especially for students who have been identified as kids who bully or who have the potential to bully. Find out whether your school already offers a leadership program, or check to see what's available in your community through Family and Children's Services and other organizations that serve children and youth.**

Good leadership training promotes and strengthens many positive character traits and skills. *Examples:*

- activism
- admitting mistakes
- assertiveness
- being a good sport
- caring
- citizenship
- coaching
- communication
- compromise
- concern
- confidence
- conflict resolution
- cooperation
- courage
- creativity
- credibility
- decision-making
- dedication
- delegating
- dependability
- endurance
- enthusiasm
- fairness
- follow-through
- goal-setting
- honesty
- imagination
- independence
- influencing others
- ingenuity
- initiative
- inspiring others
- integrity
- judgment
- justice
- learning
- listening
- loyalty
- motivating others
- patience
- perseverance
- planning
- positive attitudes
- positive risk-taking
- pride
- purpose
- resiliency
- resourcefulness
- respect for others
- responsibility
- self-awareness
- self-esteem
- self-improvement
- self-respect
- service to others
- setting a good example
- tact
- team-building
- thoughtfulness
- trustworthiness
- unselfishness

Imagine what might happen if we could turn kids who bully into leaders! It's worth a try . . . and it could turn troublemaking students into contributing assets to our schools and communities.

---

*See also "Encourage Relationships with Other Adults" (page 107).
**See "Clubs, Groups, Troops, and Teams" (page 108).

HELP STUDENTS FIND MENTORS

Students who bully others are students at risk for serious problems now and in the future. It's a proven fact that students at risk can be helped to improve their behavior and stay out of trouble by being matched with mentors—adults or teens who care about them and spend time with them.

In 1994 and 1995, Public/Private Ventures (P/PV), a national research organization based in Philadelphia, studied the effects of mentoring during an 18-month experiment involving nearly 1,000 boys and girls ages 10–16 in eight states.* Half of the children were matched with mentors through Big Brothers Big Sisters of America (BBBSA) agencies; half were assigned to a waiting list, or control group. The children in the first group met with their Big Brothers/Sisters about three times a month for at least a year. All these years later, this study is considered foundational to the mentoring field.

At the end of the study, P/PV found that the mentored students were:

- 46 percent less likely than the students in the control group to start using illegal drugs
- 27 percent less likely to start using alcohol
- 53 percent less likely to skip school
- 37 percent less likely to skip a class
- almost 33 percent less likely to hit someone
- getting along better with their peers
- getting along better with their parents

You can make a big difference in the life of any student by matching him or her with a mentor. For more information about BBBSA, contact your local office or visit the website (www.bbbsa.org).

You can also ask other teachers in your school if they would be willing to mentor students in your classroom who need more positive interaction with adults. (At the same time, you might offer to mentor a student in another teacher's classroom.)

For more about mentoring, see page 108.

LEARN MORE ABOUT YOUR STUDENTS

Learn as much as you can about the kids who bully or who have the potential to bully in your classroom.** Show interest in them as individuals—as people worth knowing. Make it clear that even though you don't like some of their behaviors,[†] you still value them as human beings. You want them to succeed, and you care about their future.

LEARN ABOUT THEM

- Meet with them individually or in small groups as often as you can. You might start by meeting weekly, then twice a month, then monthly.

- Show interest in their lives and be a good listener (see page 99).

- Communicate your high expectations for them—and your confidence that they can meet your expectations.

- Point out and praise the positive behaviors you've noticed, and encourage them to keep up the good work. Let them know that you're keeping an eye on them—and you want to "catch them being good."[‡]

- You might also mention the negative behaviors you've noticed and remind them of why these behaviors are not acceptable, but don't dwell on these. This isn't the time. "Learn More" meetings should focus on positive qualities, characteristics, and behaviors as much as possible.

---

*SOURCE: "Making a Difference: An Impact Study of Big Brothers Big Sisters" by Joseph P. Tierney and Jean Baldwin Grossman with Nancy L. Resch. (From the Big Brothers Big Sisters website, www.bbbs.org, accessed April 21, 2011.)

**See also "Learn More About Your Students" (page 68) and "Help Students Identify and Pursue Their Interests" (page 137).

†See also "Keep the Focus on Behavior" (page 135).

‡See also "Catch Them in the Act" (page 127).

LEARN ABOUT THEIR FAMILIES

- Ask students about their families. You might have them write essays, poems, stories, songs, or skits about their families. If your students are keeping journals (see page 68), you might ask them to write about their families in their journals.

- Hold regular conferences with their parents; you might include the students, too. Observe the interactions between parents and children. If you sense that the parents don't like you or trust you—perhaps because they see you as part of the problem—try to find out if there's another teacher or administrator they do like and trust. Ask if they're willing to meet with that person instead.

- Ask the parents if it's okay to visit them at home. This will give you a better understanding of how the students' family experiences might be affecting their behavior at school.

CAMPAIGN AGAINST BULLYING

One way to help kids who bully change their behavior is to make it clear that bullying won't be tolerated in your classroom. When you and the majority of your students present a united front against bullying, kids find it harder to behave in ways that are obviously unwanted, undesirable, and unpopular.

The "Create a Positive Classroom" section of this book includes many tips and strategies that can discourage kids from bullying—and encourage them to explore more positive ways of relating to others. You might also conduct an all-out campaign against bullying. Have your students work together (as a class or in small groups) to create posters, banners, jingles, skits, raps, or songs around one or more anti-bullying themes. *Examples:*

- Bullying isn't cool.
- Kindness is cool.
- Acceptance is cool.
- Tolerance is cool.
- We stand up for ourselves and each other.
- In our classroom, no one is an outsider.
- In our classroom, everyone is welcome.
- We treat others the way we want to be treated.
- Spreading rumors isn't cool.
- Gossip isn't cool.
- Name-calling isn't cool.
- New students are welcome here.
- No one ever deserves to be bullied.
- Everyone is unique.
- Hurray for differences!
- No teasing allowed.
- If we see someone being bullied, we're telling!
- Telling isn't tattling.
- Reporting isn't ratting.
- Bullying? No way! There's always a better way.

 GO FURTHER

Have groups of students research successful advertising campaigns, then try to determine what made them successful. Did the campaigns have catchy slogans? Appealing graphics? Popular spokespersons? Songs or jingles that were easy to remember? Ask students to create anti-bullying campaigns based on what they learned from their research. You might even have a schoolwide competition, with the winning campaign adopted by the whole school. Keep your local media (newspapers, magazines, radio stations, TV stations) informed about the competition and the winner.

Or have students brainstorm anti-bullying themes, then choose one they'd like to work on.

HELP STUDENTS MANAGE THEIR ANGER

Students who bully others have a hard time managing their anger. That's one reason they bully. They need help learning how to control their temper, curb violent or aggressive impulses, and resist taking out their anger on others.

Have one-on-one conversations with students who bully others—or who might not be bullying yet but seem to have difficulty managing their anger. Or you might have a class discussion on this topic.

Ask questions like the following eight. If you prefer, you might adapt these questions for a worksheet. Have students complete it in class or as a homework assignment. Then review their responses and meet individually or in small groups with students who seem to need help.

1. How can you tell when you're angry? What do you do?

2. How do you feel when you're angry? Hurt? Misunderstood? Frustrated? Sad? Hot all over? Like you're about to explode? Like you want to strike out at someone else?

3. Describe a time when you were very angry. How did you feel? What did you do? What happened next? How did you feel afterward?

4. How do you feel when someone gets angry at you? Are you scared? Upset? Do you wish you could just disappear?

5. Do you think it's fair when someone else takes out his or her anger on you?

6. How does your anger affect the people around you? What about your family? Friends? The person or people you're angry at? How do you think they feel when you take out your anger on them?

7. Is there anything you'd like to change about the way you feel and act when you get angry?

8. Would you like to learn different ways to act when you get angry?

With your students, brainstorm ideas for managing anger. Write their ideas on the whiteboard or chart paper. Afterward, have students choose one idea to work on for the next few days, then report back to you on whether it works for them. Here are some starter ideas:*

- Learn to recognize the signs that you're about to explode. Do something *before* you explode.

- Walk away from the person or situation that's making you angry. You're not running away. You're doing something positive to make sure things don't get worse or out of control.

- Take five deep breaths. Take five more.

- Count to 10 s-l-o-w-l-y. Do it again if you need to.

- Let off steam in a safe, positive way. Go for a run. Shoot some hoops. Take a bike ride. Jump up and down.

- Make yourself relax and cool down. Think calm, peaceful thoughts. Try tensing and then relaxing every muscle in your body, from your head to your toes.

- Pretend that you're not angry. You may do such a good acting job that you convince yourself.

- Ask yourself, "Why am I angry?" Maybe the person didn't mean to make you angry. Maybe it was an accident or a misunderstanding.

- Try not to take things so personally. Understand that the whole world isn't against you.

Go Further
Talk with your school psychologist or counselor about starting an anger management group for students. The group might meet during recess or lunch—times that are otherwise unstructured.

*See also "Teach Anger Management Skills" (page 23).

GET OLDER STUDENTS INVOLVED

Often, students who bully others find it easier to talk and work with older students than with adults. See if your local high school trains students to serve as peer mediators and peer counselors. If the answer is yes, ask if one or more students might be available to work with bullying students at your school.

USE "STOP AND THINK"

Most teachers have developed a "sixth sense" when it comes to student behavior. They can detect a problem before it occurs and act quickly to prevent it. Sometimes all it takes is a look or a word from the teacher to get students back on track.

"Stop and Think" takes this a step further. Not only does it interrupt inappropriate behavior, it also invites students to consider what they're doing (or about to do) and make a better choice.

Here are three ways to use "Stop and Think" in your classroom:

1. Tell your students, "You have the power to *stop and think* before you speak or act. This is a way to keep yourself from saying or doing something that might get you in trouble or hurt someone else. Whenever I say 'Stop and Think,' I want the person or people I'm addressing to do just that. *Stop* whatever you're saying or doing. Then *think* about what you're about to say or do. Decide if you should say or do something else instead."

   Once you've introduced the concept of "Stop and Think," use the short, simple phrase whenever necessary. Keep your voice calm and your expression positive or neutral. (This is a great alternative to yelling or other emotional responses.)

2. Distribute copies of the handout on page 153. Have students color in the stop sign and thought bubble, then cut along the dark solid line, fold along the dotted line, and tape or staple the top together.

Younger students might want to wear their "Stop/Think" signs as necklaces (punch two holes in the top corners, then weave a length of yarn or string through the holes). Older students can carry their signs in their pockets.

Tell your students, "You have the power to *stop and think* before you speak or act. Your 'Stop/Think' sign can remind you to do this."

3. Give students permission to use "Stop and Think" with each other. Enlist their help in interrupting impulsive or negative behaviors.

GIVE STUDENTS MEANINGFUL RESPONSIBILITIES

As you're planning special class projects and events, try giving some of the most meaningful and desirable tasks to students who might otherwise use their time and energy bullying others.* Make sure these are tasks that really matter, and let students know you're counting on them to do their best.

Tip: If you know that a younger student is being bullied on the playground, consider assigning another child who bullies as that child's protector. Talk this over with your student ahead of time; emphasize that he or she is not to bully or be aggressive toward the student who is bullying the younger student. Your student's presence might be enough to dissuade that student from picking on him or her.

TEACH THEM TO "TALK SENSE TO THEMSELVES"

Schools can have rules and anti-bullying programs, and adults can determine and apply consequences, but ultimately each student must learn to control his or her own inappropriate and/or impulsive behaviors.

Just as students can learn positive self-talk (see page 104), they can also learn to "talk sense

---

*See also "Give Them Opportunities to Shine" (page 110).

to themselves"—to talk themselves *out of* behaviors that are likely to hurt someone else or get themselves *into* trouble, and into behaviors that are more desirable and acceptable.

Work with your students one-on-one or in small groups to come up with brief, powerful, easy-to-remember words and phrases they can use to "talk sense to themselves." *Examples:*

- I don't have to do this.
- I can make a better choice.
- I can keep my hands to myself.
- I can walk away.
- I can control myself.
- There's a better way.
- I'm better than this.
- I'm in charge of me.
- I can stop and think.
- I can put on the brakes.

Have students choose their favorite word or phrase, then write it on a 3" x 5" card and carry it in their pocket. Tell them to think (or whisper) their phrase whenever they feel they might say or do something to hurt another person.

COMPILE BEHAVIOR PROFILES

For each student who exhibits bullying behaviors, create a Behavior Profile in a special folder.

Throughout the day or at the end of the day, jot down detailed notes about the student's behavior.

 IMPORTANT: Be sure to include positive as well as negative behaviors.

Use the folder to collect and store notes and reports you receive from other students, teachers, and staff about the student's behavior; notes taken during meetings and conversations with the student's parents; and anything else you feel is meaningful and relevant.

Toward the end of each week, review and summarize the Behavior Profile. Has the student's behavior improved during the week? Are there areas that still need work? What strategies and techniques did you try to help the student? Which ones were most effective? If the student behaved inappropriately, what consequences were applied? Did the consequences have the desired effect?

Share pertinent information from your Behavior Profile with the student, his or her parents (through a phone call, an email, or a note home), and other staff members involved in helping the student improve his or her behavior.

Tip: Careful notes can be very useful during parent-teacher conferences and meetings with school officials.

HELP STUDENTS SELF-ASSESS CYBERBULLYING TRAITS

It is important to give students an opportunity to examine their online and cell phone behavior to determine if they engage in cyberbullying. Many students are unaware that some of the activities they do online—often without a second thought—can be considered bullying. Review what cyberbullying is (pages 16–19) and have a class discussion about how it can be easier to bully people online because of the lack of actual human interaction. When people interact online, they can't see each other's facial expressions or hear the tone of their voice. That sometimes makes it hard to judge the intent of people's messages, and it can make it easy to be hurtful when you don't have to face the pain someone may feel.

Distribute the "Cyber Survey" handout (page 154) and review the instructions together. Then give students 10 to 15 minutes to complete it. Let them know whether you will be collecting the surveys, but remind them not to put their names on the sheets either way. After they are done, collect the sheets so you can take note of any (anonymous) cyberbullying issues that may be happening in your class or suggest to students that they keep their surveys for a future comparison of their online behavior.

Go Further

A Smart Kid's Guide to Online Bullying by David J. Jakubiak (PowerKids Press, 2009).

Cyberbullying: Deal with It and Ctrl Alt Delete It by Robyn MacEachern (Lorimer, 2011).

Consider asking students to make cyber-behavior goals, such as "I will not forward rumors, mean messages, or rude pictures"; "I will not harass anyone by sending repeated messages"; or "I will not post or send any mean messages." You may want to review proper online behaviors with the group (again, see pages 16–19).

TEACH POSITIVE WAYS TO FEEL POWERFUL

Offer bullying students positive ways to channel their need for power. Here are 10 examples and ideas to try:

1. In one school, officials learned that an older student was harassing younger students. The school counselor took this student aside, told him that someone was picking on the little kids in the school, and asked him to help. The older student became a guardian.

2. In another school, students who bullied were sent to clean up the kindergarten classroom as a subtle form of punishment. The kindergartners then wrote thank-you notes to the older students—a not-so-subtle form of praise that made them feel good about themselves.

3. Consider having students who bully hand out awards to students who have done good deeds, taken part in social service projects, helped other students, or otherwise set positive examples for others to emulate.

4. There's power in correcting mistakes and righting wrongs. Emphasize that mistakes are for learning and wrongs are opportunities to step forward, be a leader, and win well-deserved admiration from peers and adults.

5. Assign students who bully to watch out for and help students who are especially timid or shy. Encourage them to feel good about protecting their new friends.

6. Some experts suggest holding students responsible for the safety and well-being of kids they've bullied. If something happens to their targets, the kids who bullied them suffer the consequences—even if someone else did the deed.

7. Encourage bullying students to get involved in school activities—plays, sports, or clubs. Do everything in your power to ensure that their experiences are positive and successful. If they aren't interested in any of the activities currently available, offer to help them start a club or group of their choosing (within reason). Participating gives students a sense of belonging, which helps them feel valued—and powerful.

8. Ask your school counselor or psychologist to assess students' self-esteem. It's a myth that all kids who bully have low self-esteem (in fact, some have *high* self-esteem), but it's worth checking into. If kids are found to have low self-esteem, start a group or program to help them.

9. Doing good by helping others is a powerful feeling. See "Get Students Involved in Service" (pages 32–33).

10. Invite students who bully to brainstorm their own ideas for being powerful without hurting or intimidating others. Express confidence in their ability to come up with good strategies.

PROVIDE A PLACE FOR STUDENTS TO GO

If at all possible, set aside a room in your school where students who bully others can be sent or can choose to go to calm down and consider their behavior.

You might call this the Resource Room, the Learning Room, the Quiet Room, the Thinking Room, or anything else that sets it apart from a regular classroom (and doesn't obviously label it "the place where bullies go"). Staff it with a full-time, trained professional who can work with students, talk with them, provide structured activities, listen to their concerns, and help them learn and practice positive ways of relating to others.

Going to this special room might be a consequence for bullying behavior, or a choice students can make for themselves when they feel they're losing control.

START A CLUB

Once you've identified the kids who bully or who have the potential to bully in your classroom (see pages 129–130), start a club exclusively for them. Have it meet during recess or lunch—times when students' activities usually aren't structured and bullying can be a problem.

You might run the club yourself or train someone else to run it. Or see if another teacher or staff person at your school has experience in this area. If you've identified only one kid who bullies or potentially could bully in your classroom, ask other teachers if they have students who might benefit from belonging to the club.

Use meeting times to discuss inappropriate versus appropriate behaviors, role-play various situations, teach empathy, reiterate the consequences of bullying behaviors, invite students to think about the consequences, practice prosocial skills, teach anger management, and more. All three sections of this book include activities you might try in the club; many activities in the "Help Targets of Bullying" section can be adapted to fit. *Tip:* From time to time, let students set the agenda.

HELP STUDENTS UNDERSTAND WHY THEY BULLY OTHERS

If you can help students *recognize* that they behave inappropriately and take *responsibility* for their behavior,* you can start to help them *realize* why they do the things they do.

This activity and the "Reasons Why" questionnaire (page 155) may not be appropriate for some students. Some questions may be too complex or confusing for their age or developmental level. Use your judgment and your knowledge of your students; adapt where appropriate—or come up with other questions you think will work better. If you use this questionnaire, be sure to tell your students this isn't a test. There are no "right" or "wrong" answers—only answers that are true for them and may not be true for anyone else.

BULLY FREE **IMPORTANT:** Consider inviting the school counselor or psychologist to join you for this activity. He or she will be a valuable resource. Also: This activity should precede "Help Students Stop Bullying" (following). If you decide to use the "Reasons Why" questionnaire, be sure to follow through with "Reasons Why (Guidance Questions)" (pages 156–157).

Depending on your students' ages and abilities, they can complete the "Reasons Why" handout and turn it in to you, or you might choose to go over the questions one at a time during a face-to-face meeting or small-group discussion.

HELP STUDENTS STOP BULLYING

This activity should follow "Help Students Understand Why They Bully Others" (preceding). If you haven't yet done that activity, please read through it carefully. If you choose not to do that activity, skip this one, too.

"Help Students Stop" returns to the questions in "Help Students Understand," with the addition of more questions designed to start students thinking about alternatives and solutions. If a student has identified one or more "Reasons Why" as true for him or her, you can refer to "Reasons Why (Guidance Questions)" (pages 156–157) for ideas on where to go next.

---

*See "Change Their Thinking" (page 133).

BULLY FREE **IMPORTANT:** The "Guidance Questions" aren't meant to be comprehensive or conclusive, and you'll notice they don't have "the answers." Read them, think about them, then add your own notes and ideas. Be sure to consult your school counselor or psychologist; he or she will be a valuable resource.

STARTER TIPS FOR HELPING THEM STOP

A few possibilities to consider:

- Pair each student with a partner—an older student he or she respects, admires, and would like to be friends with. The older student can offer advice, just listen, and monitor the younger student's behavior (speech, actions, body language). The older student can praise positive changes and point out when the younger student reverts to bad habits or negative behaviors.

- When a student commits to making a change, suggest the "one-day-at-a-time" approach rather than a blanket promise for the future. *Example:* Instead of "I'll never pick on anyone ever again," try "I won't pick on anyone today."

- If possible, have students apologize and make amends to students they've bullied. Have them keep trying, even if the former targets are suspicious or don't believe the students are serious.

- Pair students with newcomers to your classroom or school. The newcomers won't know about the students' past, which will help clear the way for a possible friendship.

- Help students find and pursue interests outside of school and away from their former targets (and reputations). Encourage them to make new friends.

- Help students find and pursue physical sports or disciplines (biking, blading, softball, martial arts) as a way to let off steam and use their strength in positive ways.

- Try to form a "safety net" of adults (teachers, administrators, playground supervisors, lunchroom supervisors) the students can go to when you're not available. These people should know that the students have had behavior problems and sincerely want to change. The students can go to their "safety net" people when they feel angry, upset, or about to lose control.

YOU WERE CAUGHT BEING GOOD!

Today's date: _____

Your name: _____

Teacher's comment:

Teacher's Signature: _____

WARNING SIGNS

The following behaviors and traits may indicate that a student is bullying others or, if bullying isn't yet evident or hasn't been reported, has the potential to begin bullying. For any student you're concerned about, check all that apply.

Student's name: _____ Today's date: _____

- **1.** Enjoys feeling powerful and in control.
- **2.** Seeks to dominate and/or manipulate peers.
- **3.** May be popular with other students, who envy his or her power.
- **4.** Is physically larger and stronger than his or her peers.
- **5.** Is impulsive.
- **6.** Loves to win at everything; hates to lose at anything. Is both a poor winner (boastful, arrogant) and a poor loser.
- **7.** Seems to derive satisfaction or pleasure from others' fear, discomfort, or pain.
- **8.** Seems overly concerned with others "disrespecting" him or her; equates "respect" with fear.
- **9.** Seems to have little or no empathy for others.
- **10.** Seems to have little or no compassion for others.
- **11.** Seems unable or unwilling to see things from another person's perspective or "walk in someone else's shoes."
- **12.** Seems willing to use and abuse other people to get what he or she wants.
- **13.** Defends his or her negative actions by insisting that others "deserved it," "asked for it," or "provoked" him or her; a conflict is always someone else's fault.
- **14.** Is good at hiding negative behaviors or doing them where adults can't notice.
- **15.** Gets excited when conflicts arise between others.
- **16.** Stays cool during conflicts in which he or she is directly involved.
- **17.** Exhibits little or no emotion (flat affect) when talking about his or her part in a conflict.
- **18.** Blames other people for his or her problems.
- **19.** Refuses to accept responsibility for his or her negative behaviors.
- **20.** Shows little or no remorse for his or her negative behaviors.
- **21.** Lies in an attempt to stay out of trouble.
- **22.** Expects to be "misunderstood," "disrespected," and picked on; attacks before he or she can be attacked.

CONTINUED

_____ **23.** Interprets ambiguous or innocent acts as purposeful and hostile; uses these as excuses to strike out at others verbally or physically.

_____ **24.** "Tests" your authority by committing minor infractions, then waits to see what you'll do about it.

_____ **25.** Disregards or breaks school and/or class rules.

_____ **26.** Is generally defiant or oppositional toward adults.

_____ **27.** Seeks/craves attention; seems just as satisfied with negative attention as positive attention.

_____ **28.** Attracts more than the usual amount of negative attention from others; is yelled at or disciplined more often than other students.

_____ **29.** Is street-smart.

_____ **30.** Has a strong sense of self-esteem. _Note:_ This is contrary to the prevailing myth that kids who bully have low self-esteem. In fact, there's little evidence to support the belief that kids bully because they feel bad about themselves.

_____ **31.** Seems mainly concerned with his or her own pleasure and well-being.

_____ **32.** Seems antisocial or lacks social skills.

_____ **33.** Has difficulty fitting into groups.

_____ **34.** Has a close network of a few friends (more accurately described as "henchmen" or "lieutenants"), who follow along with whatever he or she wants to do.

_____ **35.** May have problems at school or at home; lacks coping skills.

Cyberbullying Warning Signs (you may need to consult with the student's parents):

_____ Uses the computer a lot, often late at night.

_____ Quickly changes screens or closes windows when you come near him or her or avoids talking about what he or she is doing online.

_____ Has multiple email addresses or online accounts.

BRINGING OUT THE BEST IN KIDS
TIPS FOR PARENTS

1. Have regular home meetings with your child. Show interest in what he or she is doing. Ask questions and be a good listener. Who are your child's friends? What are your child's likes and dislikes? How does your child spend his or her time at school, and away from school when he or she isn't with the family? *Tip:* Some of the best family discussions happen around the dinner table.

2. Make a real effort to spend more positive time with your child than you already do. Try to do things together that your child enjoys. Encourage your child to talk about his or her feelings. Ask how the day went. Praise your child as often as possible. Give your child opportunities to do well—by helping you with a chore, taking on new responsibilities, or showing off a talent or skill.

3. Monitor the television shows your child watches and websites he or she frequents, and reduce the amount of screen violence he or she is exposed to. Experts have found that watching violence has a negative effect on children. Also limit the amount of violence your child encounters in video and computer games and on devices such as iPods and smart phones.

4. Set and discuss rules around electronic communications (computers, smart phones, etc.) with friends and peers. Be clear about what is okay and what is not, and what are the consequences of cyberbullying.

5. Supervise your child's whereabouts and activities even more closely than you already do. Set reasonable rules and limits for activities and curfews. Make it a point to always know where your child is and whom he or she is with.

6. Consider enrolling your child in a class on conflict resolution, stress management, anger management, friendship skills, or self-defense. Check with your child's teacher or community resources—your local public library, YMCA or YWCA, or community education.

   BULLY FREE **IMPORTANT:** Self-defense classes aren't about being aggressive. They're about avoiding conflict through self-discipline, self-control, and improved self-confidence. Most martial arts teach that the first line of defense is nonviolence.

7. If your child's teacher has told you that your child is bullying others, take it seriously. Kids who bully often have serious problems later in life.

   - Talk with your child. Be aware that your child might deny or minimize his or her behavior; this is normal. Don't blame; don't ask "why" something happened or "why" your child acted in a certain way, because this may lead to lies and excuses. Stay calm and make it clear that bullying is *not* okay with you.

CONTINUED →

From *The New Bully Free Classroom®* by Allan L. Beane, copyright © 2011. Free Spirit Publishing Inc., Minneapolis, MN; 800-735-7323; www.freespirit.com. This page may be reproduced for individual, classroom, and small group work only. For all other uses, contact www.freespirit.com/company/permissions.cfm.

- Reassure your child that you still love him or her. It's the bullying *behavior* you don't like. Tell your child that you'll work together to help change the behavior—and you won't give up on him or her.

- Talk with your child's teacher(s) and other adults at the school—in private, when no other students are around. Get the facts on your child's behavior. Ask them to keep you informed.

- Work with the school to modify your child's behavior. Stay in touch with teachers, administrators, and playground supervisors so you know how your child is progressing. Let them know about your efforts at home.

- Apply reasonable, age-appropriate, and developmentally appropriate consequences (withdrawing privileges, giving time-outs, assigning extra chores around the house) for bullying behavior. Avoid corporal punishment, which sends your child the message that "might is right."

- Talk with your child about how bullying affects the targeted student. If you remember times from your own childhood when you were bullied, you know how much it hurts.

- Help your child learn and practice positive ways to handle anger, frustration, and disappointment. (How do you handle those feelings at home? Remember: You're an important role model for your child.) Try role-playing new behaviors with your child.

- Praise your child's efforts to change. Praise your child for following home and school rules. The more positives you can give your child, the better. *Tip:* Try giving your child five positive comments for every negative comment.

8. If you think you might need a refresher course on parenting skills, you're not alone. Many parents today seek advice and insights from other parents and trained professionals. Check your local bookstore or library for parenting books or do an online search for websites devoted to parenting, such as KidsHealth (www.kidshealth.org). See if your child's school sponsors parenting discussions, programs, or workshops; find out what's available in your community. The more you learn, the more you know!

9. If you think you might need more help than you can get from a book, website, program, or workshop on parenting, and especially if you feel that your child is developing problem behaviors, get professional help. Ask the school counselor, psychologist, or social worker for recommendations. Check with the children's mental health center in your community. There's no shame in this; it takes wisdom and courage to acknowledge that you can't do it all. (If money is an issue, many resources offer free services or sliding fee scales.)

DO YOU BULLY?

Read each question and circle "**Y**" (for yes) or "**N**" (for no). When you're through, give this handout to the teacher.

Be honest! Your answers will be kept private.

1. Do you pick on people who are smaller than you, or on animals? **Y   N**

2. Do you like to tease and taunt other people? **Y   N**

3. If you tease people, do you like to see them get upset? **Y   N**

4. Do you think it's funny when other people make mistakes? **Y   N**

5. Do you like to take or destroy other people's belongings? **Y   N**

6. Do you send or post mean messages online? **Y   N**

7. Do you want other students to think you're the toughest kid in school? **Y   N**

8. Do you get angry a lot and stay angry for a long time? **Y   N**

9. Do you blame other people for things that go wrong in your life? **Y   N**

10. Do you like to get revenge on people who hurt you? **Y   N**

11. When you play a game or sport, do you always have to be the winner? **Y   N**

12. If you lose at something, do you worry about what other people will think of you? **Y   N**

13. Do you get angry or jealous when someone else succeeds? **Y   N**

Read this *after* you answer all of the questions!

If you answered "Yes" to one or two of these questions, you may sometimes bully others. If you answered "Yes" to three or more questions, you probably bully others often, and you need to find ways to change your behavior. Good news: Kids who bully can get help dealing with their feelings, getting along with other people, and making friends. Parents, teachers, school counselors, and other adults can all give this kind of help. *Just ask!*

1. Cut along the dark line.

➡️

2. Fold on the dotted line.

➡️

CYBER SURVEY

Do not write your name on this sheet. Read each statement and check "Yes," "No," or "More than once" in the columns on the right. **All questions refer to actions done using text messages, emails, chat or discussion room posts, social networking sites such as Facebook, and any other electronic or Internet communications.**

When you are finished, read the follow-up instructions at the bottom of the page.

Be truthful! (The survey is anonymous.)

BEHAVIOR	YES	NO	MORE THAN ONCE
1. I have sent a message that contained an embarrassing secret about someone.			
2. I have sent or posted a mean picture of someone.			
3. I have used profanity or angry language with someone online.			
4. I have sent someone a hurtful or mean message.			
5. I have sent someone hurtful or mean messages over and over again.			
6. I have forwarded a hurtful message that someone sent me.			
7. I have used a cell phone or computer to spread gossip, rumors, or lies.			
8. I have used cell phones or computers to play cruel jokes on someone.			
9. I have used cell phones or computers to threaten someone.			
10. I have pretended to be someone else online in order to embarrass that person or get that person in trouble.			

If you answered "Yes" or "More than once" to any of the above questions, you may have cyberbullied someone. What specific goal can you set for yourself in order to reduce or stop cyberbullying?

_____

_____

_____

_____

REASONS WHY

You know that you sometimes bully other people. Have you ever wondered why? When we know the reasons for our behaviors, this can give us the power to change our behaviors.

Maybe one or more of these reasons are true for you. Read them, think about them, and decide for yourself. Write answers only if you want to.

1. Is there someone in your life who picks on you?
2. Do you feel lonely at school?
3. Are you afraid of being picked on?
4. When other people hurt you, do you feel you have to get back at them?
5. Do you feel you have to prove that you're tougher and stronger than other people?
6. Do you just like to show off and get a reaction? Do you like lots of attention?
7. Do you always have to win at everything? Do you get angry when you lose?
8. Are you jealous of other people?
9. Is there someone who irritates you so much you just can't stand it?
10. When you say or do something to hurt someone else, does that make you feel strong and important?
11. Is there something in your life that makes you feel unhappy or afraid?
12. When you feel sad, frustrated, angry, or afraid, does it seem like the only way to get rid of your bad feeling is to take it out on someone else?
13. Is there something in your life that makes you feel angry much of the time?
14. Is school really hard for you?
15. Do you feel like you're always letting other people down? Are their expectations just too high?
16. Are you bigger and stronger than other people your age? Does this make you feel powerful?
17. Do you hang around with other kids who bully? Do you feel you have to go along with whatever they do?
18. Is it very hard for you to control your temper? Does it seem impossible sometimes?

One more thing to think about . . .

Is there an adult you trust and respect—someone you think you could talk to? Would you be willing to talk to that person? If you can't think of anyone, would you be willing to meet someone who's a really good listener?

REASONS WHY: GUIDANCE QUESTIONS

1. Is there someone in your life who picks on you? ***Go further:*** Do you want to tell me who it is? Would you like me to help you do something about it?

2. Do you feel lonely at school? ***Go further:*** Would you like to feel less lonely and more like you belong here? Are you willing to try some ideas for fitting in?

3. Are you afraid of being picked on? ***Go further:*** Do you feel the only way to protect yourself is to get other people before they get you? Would you like to learn other ways to feel safe and not worry so much?

4. When other people hurt you, do you feel you have to get back at them? ***Go further:*** Would you like to learn other ways to deal with the hurt? And maybe avoid feeling hurt? Is it possible that people aren't hurting you on purpose?

5. Do you feel you have to prove that you're tougher and stronger than other people? ***Go further:*** Are you willing to try other ways to feel powerful and important?

6. Do you just like to show off and get a reaction? Do you like lots of attention? ***Go further:*** If you knew other ways to get attention—positive ways—would you try them?

7. Do you always have to win at everything? Do you get angry when you lose? ***Go further:*** Would you like to learn how to enjoy things more and not worry so much about winning or losing?

8. Are you jealous of other people? ***Go further:*** Why are you jealous? What do they have that you want? Is it really that important? Would you like to learn ways to be happy with who you are and what you have?

9. Is there someone who irritates you so much you just can't stand it? ***Go further:*** Would you like to learn ways to avoid the person—or not let him or her "get to you" as much?

10. When you say or do something to hurt someone else, does that make you feel strong and important? ***Go further:*** Are you willing to try other ways to feel good about yourself?

11. Is there something in your life that makes you feel unhappy or afraid? ***Go further:*** What would make you feel better? Would you like someone to help you?

12. When you feel sad, frustrated, angry, or afraid, does it seem like the only way to get rid of your bad feeling is to take it out on someone else? ***Go further:*** If you knew other ways to get rid of bad feelings, would you try them instead?

13. Is there something in your life that makes you feel angry much of the time? ***Go further:*** Would you like to know how to handle your anger—maybe even get rid of some or all of your anger?

CONTINUED ➜

14. Is school really hard for you? **Go further:** If you knew ways to make school easier and more fun, would you try them?

15. Do you feel like you're always letting other people down? Are their expectations just too high? **Go further:** Would you like to tell them how you feel? Would you feel better if they backed off a bit and accepted you the way you are?

16. Are you bigger and stronger than other people your age? Does this make you feel powerful? **Go further:** Do you ever wish you weren't so big and strong? Would you like to know positive ways to use your size and strength?

17. Do you hang around with other kids who bully? Do you feel you have to go along with whatever they do? **Go further:** If you had a chance to get out of that group (or gang), would you?

18. Is it very hard for you to control your temper? Does it seem impossible sometimes? **Go further:** Would you like to learn ways to control your temper, or how to get help when you can't?

Finally . . .

Is there an adult you respect and trust—someone you think you could talk to? Would you be willing to talk to that person? If you can't think of anyone, would you be willing to meet someone who's a really good listener? **Go further:** If you know someone and tell me who it is, I can help get the two of you together. Would that be okay? OR: May I suggest someone you might want to meet?

RESOURCES

BOOKS FOR ADULTS

Asperger Syndrome and Bullying: Prevention Strategies and Solutions by Nick Dubin (London: Jessica Kingsley Publishers, 2007). This book explains why kids with Asperger's syndrome are often bullied and provides strategies for parents, professionals, schools, and targets to address the bullying. The author emphasizes the important role of bystanders.

The Bully, the Bullied, and the Bystander by Barbara Coloroso (New York: HarperCollins, 2009). For teachers, parents, and others concerned about bullying, this book teaches adults to empower students against mistreatment.

Olweus Bullying Prevention Program: Teacher Guide by D. Olweus and S. Limber (Center City, MN: Hazelden, 2007). This psychologist, the world's leading authority on bullying, gives good practical advice on how to stop bullying in schools.

Bullying Beyond the Schoolyard: Preventing and Responding to Cyberbullying by Sameer Hinduja and Justin W. Patchin (Thousand Oaks, CA: Corwin Press, 2008). With a focus on protecting teens, this book addresses the evolving issue of cyberbullying and how technology can magnify bullying that is already happening.

Bully Prevention: Tips and Strategies for School Leaders and Classroom Teachers by Elizabeth A. Barton (Thousand Oaks, CA: Corwin Press, 2006). For use in both elementary and secondary classrooms, this resource provides updated research and the tools for building a successful schoolwide anti-bullying program.

The Challenge to Care in Schools by Nel Noddings (New York: Teachers College Press, 2005). Noddings emphasizes that caring and being cared for are fundamental human needs, then calls on schools to address these needs and nourish students' growth.

Childhood Bullying and Teasing by Dorothea M. Ross, Ph.D. (Alexandria, VA: American Counseling Association, 2003). This book includes a review of literature and a variety of strategies that can be used by guidance counselors and others.

Emotional Intelligence by Daniel Goleman (New York: Bantam, 2006). This fascinating book discusses the importance of empathy, social deftness, and other forms of emotional intelligence for success in life, and includes information about how children develop these skills.

How to Handle a Hard-to-Handle Kid by C. Drew Edwards, Ph.D. (Minneapolis: Free Spirit Publishing, 1999). Clinical child psychologist C. Drew Edwards explains why some children are especially challenging, then spells out clear, specific strategies that parents can use to address and correct problem behaviors with firmness and love.

How to Talk So Kids Will Listen and Listen So Kids Will Talk by Adele Faber and Elaine Mazlish (New York: Avon Books, 1999). Filled with practical suggestions and examples, this is one of the best books ever written on how to talk with kids of all ages.

Learning the Skills of Peacemaking by Naomi Drew (Rolling Hills Estates, CA: Jalmar Press, 1999). This book teaches specific skills as well as a general problem-solving process by which elementary-age children can begin to create a peaceful future. The 56 lessons use creative writing, role playing, the arts, music, and class discussion to teach children to resolve conflicts, accept themselves and others, and communicate effectively.

Let's Be Friends: A Workbook to Help Kids Learn Social Skills & Make Great Friends by Lawrence E. Shapiro, Ph.D., and Julia Holmes (Oakland, CA: Instant Help Publications, 2008). The activities in this book offer tools for helping children become better friend-makers by teaching a wide variety of social skills.

Little Girls Can Be Mean: Four Steps to Bully-Proof Girls in the Early Grades by Michelle Anthony, M.A., Ph.D., Reyna Lindert, Ph.D. (New York: St. Martin's Griffin, 2010). This guide offers practical tips and personal anecdotes aimed at alleviating female "relational aggression" in elementary grades. In each chapter, the authors, both developmental psychologists, illustrate how adults can guide girls through a four-step process to identify and deal with tough social situations.

No Kidding About Bullying by Naomi Drew (Minneapolis: Free Spirit Publishing, 2010). This flexible resource gives educators and youth leaders a diverse range of activities to help kids in grades 3–6 build empathy, manage anger, work out conflicts, and be assertive.

The Power of Positive Talk by Douglas Bloch with Jon Merritt (Minneapolis: Free Spirit Publishing, 2003). Written for parents, teachers, and counselors, this book teaches adults how to speak more affirmatively to children and how to teach children to speak more affirmatively to themselves.

See Jane Hit: Why Girls Are Growing More Violent and What We Can Do About It by James Garbarino, Ph.D. (New York: Penguin Press, 2007). Through voluminous research and brief first-person statements from teens, Garbarino uncovers a steadily increasing trend toward violence among America's girls.

Teaching Your Kids to Care by Deborah Spaide (Secaucus, NJ: Citadel Press, 2002). The founder of the Kids Care Clubs, Deborah Spaide believes that children have a natural instinct to help others. In this practical, inspiring book, she describes 105 projects that develop the charity instinct in children from preschool through high school.

Training Peer Helpers: Coaching Youth to Communicate, Solve Problems, and Make Decisions by Barbara B. Varenhorst (Minneapolis: Search Institute Press, 2010). Based on Search Institute's 40 Developmental Assets, this handy guide includes 15 peer-training sessions that help prepare them for resolving peer conflicts. Includes a CD-ROM with handouts.

Understanding Girl Bullying and What to Do About It: Strategies to Help Heal the Divide by Julaine E. Field, Jered B. Kolbert, Laura M. Crothers, and Tammy L. Hughes (Thousand Oaks, CA: Corwin Press, 2009). This book covers the causes and characteristics of girl bullying; outlines assessment, prevention, and intervention methods; and provides an original 10-session curriculum for small groups.

BOOKS FOR CHILDREN

All I Really Need to Know I Learned in Kindergarten by Robert Fulghum (New York: Ballantine Books, 2004). This entertaining book says a lot about respect, sharing, playing fair, not hitting people, and saying you're sorry when you hurt someone. For all ages.

Bailey the Big Bully by Lizi Boyd (New York: Penguin Books, 1992). All the kids are afraid of Bailey, who's big and mean and always gets his way, except Max, the new boy in town. For grades K–3.

Best Enemies Again by Kathleen Leverich (New York: Greenwillow, 1999). Wealthy Felicity continues to complicate Priscilla's life both in and out of school, until one day the tables are turned. For grades 2–5.

BOOKS FOR CHILDREN, CONTINUED

Bootsie Barker Bites by Barbara Bottner (New York: Putnam Publishing, 1997). A little girl finds her life made miserable by the torments devised by the nasty, mischievous Bootsie Barker, until the terrible Bootsie receives her just punishment. For grades preschool–3.

Bullies Are a Pain in the Brain by Trevor Romain (Minneapolis: Free Spirit Publishing, 1997). This book blends humor with serious, practical suggestions to help children learn what to do if a bully picks on them. Also included are tips to help kids who bully get along with others. For grades 3–8.

Bullies Never Win by Margery Cuyler (New York: Simon & Schuster Children's Publishing, 2009). Brenda is a bully and she won't leave Jessica alone. Brenda teases Jessica about her homework and her skinny legs. It worries Jessica so much, she can't even sleep! Can Jessica stop worrying and stand up to Brenda? For grades preschool–3.

Bully by Janine Amos (Tarrytown, NY: Benchmark Books, 1994). Different stories about kids being bullied or bullying others provide questions for a discussion about bullying. For grades K–4.

Bully B.E.A.N.S. by Julia Cook (Chattanoga, TN: National Center for Youth Issues, 2009). *Bully B.E.A.N.S.* focuses on the "other" side of bullying: being a bystander to bullying. It teaches kids what they can—and should—do if they witness bullying. For grades preschool–3.

The Bully Buster Book by John William Yee (Toronto: Outgoing Press, 1997). This book provides boys and girls with hints on how to keep new kids who bully from bothering them as well as how to get rid of an existing kid who bullies. It is about how you can shift the odds in your favor by merely talking to the kid who bullies, making yourself more visible, and invading the kid's personal space. For grades 7–9.

The Bully of Barkham Street by Mary Stolz (New York: Harper & Row, 1963). Martin's parents are threatening to take away his dog, Rufus, and Martin is having a rough time in school. Something must change. For grades 4–8.

Bully on the Bus by Carl W. Bosch (Seattle: Parenting Press, 1988). Jack is being teased by a fifth-grader on the school bus. Readers help Jack decide whether to ignore him, ask an adult for help, or fight back. For grades 2–6.

Bully Trouble by Joanna Cole (New York: Random House, 1990). Arlo and Robby, finding themselves bullied by a neighborhood kid, work out a red-hot scheme for discouraging him. For grades preschool–3.

Cliques, Phonies, & Other Baloney by Trevor Romain (Minneapolis: Free Spirit Publishing, 1998). Cliques exist because everyone wants to have friends. This book explains what cliques are and why they exist, and gives important self-esteem tips that will help kids feel good about themselves. For grades 3–8.

Confessions of a Former Bully by Trudy Ludwig (New York: Tricycle Press, 2010). Ten-year-old Katie was caught bullying a friend on the school playground, and now she must meet with the school counselor once a week and figure out how to atone for her actions. As Katie learns more about herself and her options, she keeps a diary-like notebook of reflections and advice as well as facts about physical, emotional, and cyberbullying; why people bully others; and what tools kids can use when they experience or witness bullying. For grades 4–7.

Dear God, Help! Love, Earl by Barbara Park (New York: Yearling, 2006). Tired of being picked on and having to pay protection money to Eddie McPhee, wimpy Eddie Wilber and his friends Maxie and Rosie come up with an ingenious scheme to seek revenge. For grades 3–5.

Don't Pick on Me: Help for Kids to Stand Up to & Deal with Bullies by Susan Eikov Green (Oakland, CA: Instant Help Books, 2010). This book contains 10-minute activities and exercises adults and children can do together to learn how to effectively and safely stand up to a person who bullies. For grades 4–7.

The 18th Emergency by Betsy Byars (New York: Puffin Books, 1981). When the toughest boy in school swears to kill him, 12-year-old Mouse finds little help from friends and must prepare for this emergency alone. For grades 4–7.

Ellie McDoodle: New Kid in School by Ruth McNally Barshaw (New York: Bloomsbury USA Children's Books, 2009). When Ellie's family moves to a new town, she's sure she won't fit in. But when the students need someone to help them rally against unfair lunch lines, it's Ellie to the rescue—and if shorter lines and better food prevail, can friendship be far behind? For grades 4–7.

Fighting Invisible Tigers by Earl Hipp (Minneapolis: Free Spirit Publishing, 2008). This book discusses the pressures and problems encountered by teenagers and provides information on life skills, stress management, and methods of gaining more control over their lives. For grades 6 and up.

First Grade King by Karen L. Williams (New York: Clarion Books, 1992). This book relates the experiences first-grader Joey King has at school: making friends, learning to read, and dealing with the class bully. For grades K–3.

Fourth Grade Rats by Jerry Spinelli (New York: Scholastic, 1991). Suds learns that his best friend is wrong. You don't have to be a tough guy to be a grown-up fourth-grader. For grades 4–7.

Freak the Mighty by W. Rodman Philbrick (New York: Blue Sky Press, 1993). Dumb, stupid, and slow. All Max's life, he'd been called these names, and it didn't help that people were afraid of him. So Max learned to be alone—at least until Freak came along. Together, they were Freak the Mighty. For grades 4–7.

Good Friends Are Hard to Find by Fred Frankel (Glendale, CA: Perspective Publishing, 1996). This book has step-by-step ideas to help children ages 5–12 make friends and solve problems with other kids. Includes concrete help for teasing, bullying, and meanness, both for the child who is picked on and for the tormentor. For grades K–6.

Harriet the Spy by Louise Fitzhugh (New York: Harper & Row, 1964). The revelation of Harriet's secret journal, recording the activities of her neighbors and schoolmates, causes chaos. For grades 4–7.

Hot Issues, Cool Choices: Facing Bullies, Peer Pressure, Popularity, and Put-Downs by Sandra McLeod Humphrey (Amherst, NY: Prometheus Books, 2007). This is a collection of stories about the students at the fictional Emerson Elementary, in which they face and make decisions about situations of bullying, social aggression, and harassment. For grades 4–7.

Howard B. Wigglebottom Learns About Bullies by Howard Binkow (Sarasota, FL: Thunderbolt Publishing, 2008). Howard was being bullied at school, and his intuition told him to let the teacher know. Instead he chose different strategies and they all failed. He finally told the teacher and she took action to make him feel okay and safe. Tips and lessons are included. For grades preschool–3.

How to Handle Bullies, Teasers and Other Meanies by Kate Cohen-Posey (Highland City, FL: Rainbow Books, 1995). This book provides information on what makes people who bully and tease tick, how to handle them, how to deal with prejudice, and how to defend oneself when teased. For grades 6–10.

How to Lose All Your Friends by Nancy Carlson (New York: Viking Penguin, 1994). With colorful pictures and tongue-in-cheek humor, Carlson pokes fun at bullies, grumps, whiners, poor sports, and other kids who alienate others. For grades K–3.

BOOKS FOR CHILDREN, CONTINUED

How to Take the GRRRR Out of Anger by Elizabeth Verdick and Marjorie Lisovskis (Minneapolis: Free Spirit Publishing, 2003). Kids learn how to recognize when they are angry and strategies for calming down. With sound advice, jokes, and funny cartoons, this book helps readers understand that anger is normal and can be expressed in healthy ways. For grades 3–4.

I Am Not a Short Adult! by Marilyn Burns (Boston: Little, Brown, 1977). This nonfiction book talks about what kind of person a kid might want to be and has an excellent section on what tone of voice, body language, and facial expression say about a person. For grades 4–6.

I Like Being Me: Poems for Children About Feeling Special, Appreciating Others, and Getting Along by Judy Lalli, photographs by Douglas L. Mason-Fry (Minneapolis: Free Spirit Publishing, 2007). Simple rhyming poems and eloquent photographs explore issues important to the everyday lives of young children. For grades preschool–3.

I Like Me! by Nancy L. Carlson (New York: Puffin, 2009). By admiring her finer points and showing that she can take care of herself and have fun even when there's no one else around, a charming pig proves the best friend you can have is yourself. For grades preschool–3.

I'm Like You, You're Like Me: A Book About Understanding and Appreciating Each Other by Cindy Gainer (Minneapolis: Free Spirit Publishing, 2011). Warm, simple words and appealing illustrations invite young children to discover, accept, and affirm individual differences. Includes activity guide for adults. For grades preschool–3.

Joshua T. Bates Takes Charge by Susan Richards Shreve (New York: Knopf, 1993). Remembering how a mean gang used to tease him for being held back in the third grade, Joshua sees the same boys teasing a new student and fears that helping will bring the attention back to him. For grades 4–7.

The Juice Box Bully: Empowering Kids to Stand Up for Others by Bob Sornson and Maria Dismondy (Northville, MI: Ferne Press, 2010). The students in *The Juice Box Bully* don't just stand by while others are bullied: they step in and stand up for what's right. For grades 3–7.

The Kids' Guide to Working Out Conflicts by Naomi Drew (Minneapolis: Free Spirit Publishing, 2004). Conflict is a part of life, but kids can learn to solve problems without resorting to violence. This book is full of strategies for resolving disputes with others. For grades 5–9.

King of the Playground by Phyllis Reynolds Naylor (New York: Atheneum, 1991). With his dad's help, Kevin overcomes his fear of the "King of the Playground," who has threatened to tie him to the slide, put him in a deep hole, or put him in a cage with bears. For grades K–3.

Liking Myself by Pat Palmer (Oakland, CA: Uplift Press, 2009). This book introduces kids to the concepts of feelings, self-esteem, and assertiveness. For grades K–4.

Loudmouth George and the Sixth Grade Bully by Nancy L. Carlson (Minneapolis: Carolrhoda Books, 2003). After having his lunch repeatedly stolen by a bully twice his size, Loudmouth George and his friend Harriet teach the bully a lesson he'll never forget. For grades preschool–3.

Make Someone Smile and 40 More Ways to Be a Peaceful Person by Judy Lalli, photographs by Douglas L. Mason-Fry (Minneapolis: Free Spirit Publishing, 1996). Children model the skills of peacemaking and conflict resolution throughout this book. An ideal read-aloud book and discussion starter. For all ages.

My Secret Bully by Trudy Ludwig (Berkeley, CA: Tricycle Press, 2005). When Kate uses name-calling, humiliation, and exclusion to bully her, Monica doesn't know what to do. When she gets the help of an adult, though, Monica is able to take back her power and feel better. For grades K–6.

Nothing's Fair in Fifth Grade by Barthe DeClements (New York: Puffin, 2008). A fifth-grade class, repelled by the overweight new student who has serious problems at home, finally learns to accept her. For grades 4–7.

Push & Shove by Jim and Joan Boulden (Weaverville, CA: Boulden Publishing, 1994). Bullies cannot exist without targets and both participate in the bullying relationship. The reader will discover how both a bully and a target feel. For grades 2–4.

Random Acts of Kindness, More Random Acts of Kindness, and *Kids' Random Acts of Kindness* by the editors of Conari Press (Berkeley, CA: Conari Press, 2002, 1994, and 1994). Check out these books for inspiring true stories of people who have been the givers or recipients of caring and compassion. For all ages.

The Rat and the Tiger by Keiko Kasza (New York: Puffin, 2007). In Rat and Tiger's friendship, Tiger always gets the bigger piece and the most desired part. Rat, who is much smaller, finally has to stand up for himself. For grades K–3.

Reluctantly Alice by Phyllis Reynolds Naylor (New York: Atheneum, 1991). Disgusted with the seventh grade after only her first day, Alice finds her troubles compounded when she encounters Denise "Mack Truck" Whitlock. For grades 4–7.

Say Something by Peggy Moss (Gardiner, ME: Tilbury House, 2004). This book encourages kids to "say something" when bullying occurs. Bright illustrations make it an inviting read with an important message. For grades K and up.

The Shorty Society by Shery Cooper Sinykin (New York: Viking, 1994). Three seventh-graders, the victims of nasty pranks, turn the tables on their tormentors but run the risk of becoming bullies themselves. For grades 4–8.

The Skin You Live In by Michael Tyler (Chicago: Chicago Children's Museum, 2005). This picture book takes a cheerful look at human diversity by focusing on skin. For grades preschool–3.

Spaghetti in a Hot Dog Bun: Having the Courage to Be Who You Are by Maria Dismondy (Northville, MI: Ferne Press, 2008). How can Ralph be so mean? Lucy is one of a kind and Ralph loves to point that out. Lucy's defining moment comes when Ralph truly needs help. Because she knows what she stands for, Lucy has the courage to make a good choice. For grades preschool–3.

Stand Up for Yourself and Your Friends: Dealing with Bullies and Bossiness and Finding a Better Way by Patti Kelley Criswell (Middleton, WI: American Girl, 2009). This book helps girls learn how to spot bullying and stand up and speak out against it. Quizzes, quotes from real girls, and "what would you do?" scenarios give readers lots of ideas for dealing with bullying, including clever comebacks and ways to ask adults for help. Includes an anti-bullying pledge for girls to sign, plus tear-out tips to share with their parents. For grades 3–6.

Stick Up for Yourself! Every Kid's Guide to Personal Power and Positive Self-Esteem by Gershen Kaufman, Ph.D., Lev Raphael, Ph.D., and Pamela Espeland (Minneapolis: Free Spirit Publishing, 1999). Written for any kid who's ever been picked on at school, this book provides practical, encouraging advice through simple words and real-life examples. A teacher's guide is also available. For grades 3–7.

Stone Soup for the World: Life-Changing Stories of Ordinary Kindness and Courageous Acts of Service (Berkeley, CA: Conari Press, 1998). Inspiring stories by or about Nelson Mandela, Mother Teresa, Christopher Reeve, Ram Das, Steven Spielberg, and more than 100 others are included in this book, plus an extensive resource guide and directory to service groups and social organizations around the country. For all ages.

Teen Esteem by Pat Palmer (San Luis Obispo, CA: Impact Publishers, 2010). This book provides guidance on developing self-esteem and the positive attitude necessary to cope with such adolescent challenges as peer pressure and substance abuse. For grades 7–12.

BOOKS FOR CHILDREN, CONTINUED

The Way I Feel by Janan Cain (New York: Scholastic, 2000). This book gives kids the language they need to express feelings. Beautiful color illustrations accompany this vocabulary of feelings. For grades preschool–3.

We Can Get Along: A Child's Book of Choices by Lauren Murphy Payne, M.S.W. (Minneapolis: Free Spirit Publishing, 1997). This book teaches essential conflict resolution skills—think before you speak or act, treat others the way you want to be treated—in a way that young children can understand. For grades preschool–3.

What Do You Stand For? For Teens by Barbara A. Lewis (Minneapolis: Free Spirit Publishing, 1997). This book empowers children and teens to identify and build the character traits that are most important to them. True stories profile kids who exemplify positive traits, and inspiring quotations set the stage for kids to think about, discuss, and debate positive traits. For grades 4–7.

What Do You Think? A Kid's Guide to Dealing with Daily Dilemmas by Linda Schwartz (Santa Barbara, CA: The Learning Works, 1993). This inviting book encourages young people to consider issues from more than one perspective. For grades 3–7.

What Would You Do? A Kid's Guide to Tricky and Sticky Situations by Linda Schwartz (Santa Barbara, CA: The Learning Works, 1991). This commonsense guide prepares children to handle more than 70 unexpected, puzzling, and frightening situations at home, at school, or out on their own. For grades 3–7.

Why Is Everybody Always Picking on Me: A Guide to Handling Bullies by Terrence Webster-Doyle (Middlebury, VT: Atrium Society, 1991). Stories and activities show how to resolve conflicts nonviolently. For grades K–5.

You Can Be a Friend by Tony Dungy and Laura Dungy (New York: Little Simon Inspirations, 2011). Jade has a dilemma: Should she have her birthday party at a water park as planned, or should she change her plans in order to include and accommodate her new friend, who is in a wheelchair? For grades preschool–3.

You're Dead, David Borelli by Susan M. Brown (New York: Atheneum, 1995). After his mother dies and his father absconds with company funds, David is sent to a foster home, an inner-city school, and a new life. Threatened by bullies and confronted by uncaring teachers, David must find his own way into a life that he can accept. For grades 3–5.

VIDEOS

Bully Girls (20 minutes). This program focuses on increasing awareness of bullying among girls and educating viewers about how, when, and why it occurs. Understanding the difference between teasing and bullying, identifying specific female bullying techniques and tactics, recognizing warning signals that help is needed, knowing the best ways to report incidents, and getting school officials involved to combat the problem are all subjects thoroughly explored in the video. A viewable/printable instructor's guide is available online. Correlates to all applicable state and national standards. Available from Films Media Group, 1-800-257-5126, www.films.com.

Coping with Fighters, Bullies, and Troublemakers (22 minutes). This video is helpful for all students, but especially for those who are frequently the target of bullies and troublemakers. The program also offers specific techniques for coping with disruptive classmates. Students learn how to avoid being a victim; the best defense against fighters, bullies, and troublemakers; how to stand up to bullies without making matters worse; and when to ask for help. For middle school students, high school students, and adults. Available from various distributors.

Cyberbullies (19 minutes). Using dramatizations and Q&A sessions, this video addresses the issue of cyberbullying, including warning signs, online activities children and teenagers should avoid, and possible legal repercussions. An instructor's guide is available online. Available from Films Media Group, 1-800-257-5126, www.films.com.

Cyberbullying: Cruel Intentions (40 minutes). An *ABC News* program, this video illustrates how teens use cell phones, digital cameras, and social networking sites to bully their peers. Reports on a Brigham Young University experiment in which the behavior of a group of teenage girls was researched and analyzed; they fought for attention and social power through online verbal and emotional abuse. Available from Films Media Group, 1-800-257-5126, www.films.com.

Disrespect, Rudeness, and Teasing (22 minutes). This video will help students learn what being disrespectful and rude tells us about a person and why teasing is never a good solution to a problem. They will also learn how to disagree without being rude. For middle school students, high school students, and adults. Available from Impact Publications, 1-800-361-1055, impactpublications.com.

Don't Pick on Me! (20 minutes). This program examines the dynamics behind teasing and models effective responses to being harassed. A teacher's guide is included. For grades 3–8. Available from National Professional Resources, 1-800-453-7461, nprinc.com.

Got Empathy? (13 minutes). For grades 4–7. Students learn what empathy means and how they can act on this important feeling. Includes DVD and CD-ROM with a complete lesson plan. Available from NIMCO, 1-800-962-6662, www.nimcoinc.com.

Groark Learns About Bullying (28 minutes). Groark is a pleasant, childlike dragon puppet playing with his friends when two of them start teasing and picking on a third friend. As the situation escalates, Groark gets drawn in, and before he realizes it, Groark is picking on his best friend. Groark then convinces his friends that they have been cruel and unfair, and they should make peace with the friend they teased. For elementary school students. Available from various distributors.

How to Cope with School Violence (17 minutes). This video helps youngsters understand how to cope with violent confrontations that could arise in or around school. They learn effective ways to avoid violence and what to do when a confrontation seems unavoidable. For middle school students, high school students, and adults. Available from Impact Publications, 1-800-361-1055, impactpublications.com.

Hurting on the Inside: Girls & Bullying. Gossip, whispers, nasty looks, shunning—this video looks at how girls bully, why they do it, and how it can be dealt with successfully and brought under control. For grades 6–12. Available from NIMCO, 1-800-962-6662, www.nimcoinc.com.

INBOX (25 minutes). What starts out as a seemingly simple tale of a love triangle involving students Susan, Scottie, and Amanda soon turns serious. Amanda, Scottie's girlfriend, begins tormenting Susan via email; in the meantime, a girl from a neighboring town has been kidnapped, and it turns out it all began with threatening emails. For middle school students. Available from the Educational Media Corporation, 1-800-966-3382, www.educationalmedia.com.

The "In" Crowd and Social Cruelty (41 minutes). In this *ABC News* special, correspondent John Stossel visits middle and high schools to discover why kids dish out abuse, why they take it, and what parents and school administrators can do to make it better. He also visits schools with successful anti-bullying programs. Discussions with students, as well as with psychologist Michael Thompson, author of *Best Friends, Worst Enemies*, reveal a number of factors that cause popularity or unpopularity among children, adolescents, and even adults. Available from Films Media Group, 1-800-257-5126, www.films.com.

Internet Bullies (14 minutes). This video focuses on the use of the Internet in conveying strong emotions, and how such use can cause problems. Includes DVD and CD-ROM with a complete lesson plan. For grades 4–7. Available from NIMCO, 1-800-962-6662, www.nimcoinc.com.

It's Not Funny! Teasing Is a Real Bummer for Everyone. For grades 5–9. Why do kids tease each other? Examining the reasons is a good first step toward resolving the problem of peer teasing and bullying. This video touches on teasing based on obesity, stuttering, and learning difficulties, and also address sexual harassment. Includes a study guide. Available from NIMCO, 1-800-962-6662, www.nimcoinc.com.

No More Teasing! (14 minutes). Students in this video introduce common teasing situations and offer solutions. Included with the video are seven student worksheets and a teacher's guide. For grades 2–4. Available from National Professional Resources, 1-800-453-7461, nprinc.com.

The Power of One (24 minutes). By following the stories of three different kids who are new to their school, this video aims to teach kids about fairness, kindness, and respect. For elementary students. Available from the Educational Media Corporation, 1-800-966-3382, www.educationalmedia.com.

Real Life Teens: Bullies and Harassment (17 minutes). This program discusses bullying and harassment on campus and some of the motivations behind a bully's behavior. Subjects covered include the existence of bullying; student harassment; how to deal with a bully; the law and its involvement with bullying; school rules to protect students from harassment; how to stand up for oneself; and where to turn for help with a harassing situation. Interviews with teens who bully and teens who have been bullied are included. A viewable/printable instructor's guide is available online. Available from Films Media Group, 1-800-257-5126, www.films.com.

Real Life Teens: Teens and Disabilities (17 minutes). This program explores the different ways that disabilities can impact a teen's life and how the general student population can support people with disabilities. Subjects covered include what a disability is; how to understand a disabled student; why those with disabilities are called "special"; how to show respect and help people with disabilities; and special education. A viewable/printable instructor's guide is available online. Available from Films Media Group, 1-800-257-5126, www.films.com.

Resisting Pressure to Join Gangs (22 minutes). This video will help students see the pressure to join gangs for just what it is—negative peer pressure—and offers them realistic alternatives. Students will also learn how to feel like they "belong" without joining a gang. For middle school students, high school students, and adults. Available from Impact Publications, 1-800-361-1055, impactpublications.com.

7 Ways to Block a Cyberbully (20 minutes). Email, social networking, and text messaging have made it easier for kids to be cruel anonymously and to feel more empowered to bully. Using seven strategies (understanding the e-bully; protecting passwords; guarding personal information; using safety software; cutting off communications; saying "no" to revenge; and telling someone about the cyberbullying), this video teaches students how to avoid being cyberbullied and how to deal if they are already being cyberbullied. Also included is a section especially for parents and educators. Available from Films Media Group, 1-800-257-5126, www.films.com.

Why Do Bullies Bully? (14 minutes). Students will gain a better understanding of bullying and build a stronger foundation for dealing with bullies. Includes DVD and CD-ROM with a complete lesson plan. For grades 4–7. Available from NIMCO, 1-800-962-6662, www.nimcoinc.com.

OTHER MATERIALS

Anger Management: From Mad to Worse. An activity book, reproducible activity pages, a facilitator's guide, and lesson plans in this package teach students positive ways to handle anger. For grades 3–4. Available from Marco Products, 1-800-448-2197, marcoproducts.com.

Beyond Hate. This two-DVD set takes us beyond hate by exploring its origins and dimensions, with perspectives from world leaders, human rights activists, students, youth gangs, Arabs and Israelis, and an American white supremacist group. For middle school students, high school students, and adults. Available from Guidance Associates, 1-800-431-1242, www.guidanceassociates.com.

Bully Free® Card Game. Bullying is not a game—but helping kids learn anti-bullying concepts can be. This Crazy Eights–style game asks kids to respond to questions about bullying; they get rid of cards (and move closer to being "bully free") by offering reasonable suggestions. Meant to be played with adult supervision. For grades K–8. Available from Free Spirit Publishing, 1-800-735-7323, www.freespirit.com

It's Not Okay to Bully. This program explains what bullying is and suggests ways to prevent bullying behaviors, including knowing when to stand up for yourself and when to tell an adult. The 12-minute video mixes real children and animation with a simple, original, and easy-to-sing song. The 16-page coloring book (10 copies are provided with each video) includes stills from the video and song lyrics as text. For grades K–3. Available from Hazelden, 1-800-328-9000, www.hazelden.org.

No-Bullying Curriculum. This program includes system-wide strategies to involve all school personnel, students, parents, and concerned community members. The kit includes a program director's manual; teacher's manuals for grades K–1, 2–3, 4–5, and middle school; 100 No-Bullying stickers; and 50 overview booklets. Available from Impact Publications, 1-800-361-1055, impactpublications.com.

Second Step. Empathy, anger management, and impulse control are the main lessons taught in this violence prevention curriculum. Age-appropriate lessons are available for students in preschool/kindergarten, grades 1–3, grades 4–5, and middle school/junior high. At all grade levels, the lessons include opportunities for modeling, practice, and reinforcement of the new skills. A guide for families can also be purchased. Available from the Committee for Children, 1-800-634-4449, www.cfchildren.org

Student Workshop: Handling Your Anger. A hands-on workshop designed to teach anger management techniques to middle school students, this program helps students understand that while they cannot control angry feelings, they *can* control angry behavior. Includes a 33-minute video, 18 student handbooks, and a teacher's guide. For grades 5–9. Available from SR Publications, 1-888-879-5919, srpublications.com.

Take Action Against Bullying. Included in this program are a book, a video, bookmarks, and a poster set designed to teach students about the dangers of bullying. Visit the website for interesting facts and stories about bullying. For middle school students. Available from Bully B'ware Productions, 1-888-552-8559, www.bullybeware.com.

Working with Hostile and Resistant Teens. This set of two 45-minute videos and a discussion guide teaches hands-on survival skills for dealing with hostile teens in any setting. The DVDs include role plays with actual at-risk teens, who in many cases are acting out their own personal histories. Dr. Steven Campbell leads the role plays, then provides an analysis of each one, showing viewers how to work effectively with this challenging population. Appropriate for middle and high school teachers and staff members. Available from the Attainment Company, 1-800-327-4269, www.attainmentcompany.com

ORGANIZATIONS

Center for Effective Discipline (CED)
327 Groveport Pike
Canal Winchester, OH 43110
614-834-7946
www.stophitting.com
Corporal punishment of children is unsupported by educational research, sometimes leads to serious injury, and contributes to a pro-violence attitude. CED provides educational information to the public on the effects of corporal punishment and alternatives to its use.

Center for the Prevention of School Violence
1810 Mail Service Center
Raleigh, NC 27699
1-800-299-6054
www.cpsv.org
The Center focuses on ensuring that schools are safe and secure, creating an atmosphere that is conducive to learning. Newsletters, research bulletins, and special feature articles provide current information about Center activities and school violence prevention.

Children's Creative Response to Conflict (CCRC)
PO Box 271
521 North Broadway
Nyack, NY 10960
914-353-1796
www.planet-rockland.org/conflict
CCRC provides conflict resolution training based on peer leadership to children, adolescents, teachers, and parents. This training emphasizes cooperation, communication, affirmation, problem solving, mediation, and bias awareness. The CCRC also conducts workshops and publishes other materials useful for training in conflict resolution.

Crisis Prevention Institute (CPI)
10850 W. Park Place, Suite 600
Milwaukee, WI 53224
1-888-426-2184
www.crisisprevention.com
CPI offers training in the safe management of disruptive and assaultive behavior, as well as other topics.

Educators for Social Responsibility (ESR)
23 Garden Street
Cambridge, MA 02138
1-800-370-2515
www.esrnational.org
ESR's primary mission is to help young people develop the conviction and skills to shape a safe, sustainable, and just world. The Resolving Conflict Creatively Program (see page 173) is ESR's largest initiative. ESR is nationally recognized for promoting children's ethical and social development through its leadership in conflict resolution, violence prevention, group relations, and character education. The website includes resources and activities for teachers and students.

Eunice Kennedy Shriver National Center for Community of Caring
c/o University of Utah
1901 E. South Campus Drive, #1120
Salt Lake City, UT 84112
801-587-8990
www.communityofcaring.org
Contact this organization for well-developed educational materials for grades K–12 and excellent consulting. Endorsed by the National Association of Secondary School Principals. A project of the Joseph P. Kennedy, Jr. Foundation.

Giraffe Heroes Project
PO Box 759
Langley, WA 98260
360-221-7989
www.giraffe.org
This powerful program helps teachers and youth leaders build courage, caring, and responsibility in kids from 6 to 18 years old, then guides kids in designing and implementing their own service projects. Businesses, service clubs, and other organizations can become Giraffe Partners.

Heartwood Institute
1133 S. Braddock Avenue, Suite C
Pittsburgh, PA 15218
1-800-432-7810
www.heartwoodethics.org
This organization produces educational materials to support children's books about courage, loyalty, justice, respect, hope, honesty, and love. Mainly for elementary grades.

National Association for Community Mediation
1959 South Power Road, Suite 103-279
Mesa, AZ 85206
602-633-4213
www.nafcm.org
A membership organization for mediators and other community advocates. Provides funding opportunities, networking, and research materials.

National Crime Prevention Council (NCPC)
2001 Jefferson Davis Highway, Suite 901
Arlington, VA 22202
202-466-6272
www.ncpc.org
NCPC is a national nonprofit organization dedicated to helping America prevent crime and build safer, stronger communities. Their website includes useful information about crime prevention, community building, and comprehensive planning, along with fun activities for kids.

National PTA
1250 N. Pitt Street
Alexandria, VA 22314
1-800-307-4782
www.pta.org
The mission of the National PTA is to support and speak on behalf of children and youth in the schools, assist parents in developing the skills they need to raise and protect their children, and encourage public involvement in public schools. Visit their website for information on a variety of topics, including safeguarding children in schools.

National School Safety Center (NSSC)
141 Duesenberg Drive, Suite 7B
Westlake Village, CA 91362
805-373-9977
www.schoolsafety.us
The NSSC offers helpful booklets and videos addressing violence prevention, bullying, and conflict resolution for educators and parents. Call or write to request a free catalog.

Office of Safe and Drug-Free Schools
550 12th Street SW, 10th Floor
Washington, DC 20202
202-245-7896
www2.ed.gov/osdfs
This federal program supports initiatives designed to prevent violence in and around schools, and to strengthen programs that involve parents; the program also works to prevent the illegal use of alcohol, tobacco, and drugs. It is coordinated with other federal, state, and local efforts and resources.

PeaceBuilders
741 Atlantic Avenue
Long Beach, CA 90813
1-877-473-2236
www.peacebuilders.com
PeaceBuilders is a long-term, community-based program designed to help create a school environment that reduces violence. Four basic principles are at the heart of the program: praise people, give up put-downs, notice hurts and right wrongs, and seek wise people. This program is in use in nearly 400 elementary schools across the country, and the number continues to grow.

Resolving Conflict Creatively Program (RCCP)
23 Garden Street
Cambridge, MA 02138
1-800-370-2515
www.esrnational.org
An initiative of Educators for Social Responsibility (see page 171), RCCP is a pioneering school-based conflict resolution and intergroup relations program that provides a model for preventing violence and creating caring learning communities.

Teaching Tolerance
c/o Southern Poverty Law Center
400 Washington Avenue
Montgomery, AL 36104
334-956-8200
www.teachingtolerance.org
Teaching Tolerance is a national education project dedicated to helping teachers foster equity, respect, and understanding in the classroom and beyond. *Teaching Tolerance* magazine is available free to teachers.

WEBSITES

Angries Out
Talk, Trust & Feel Therapeutics
www.angriesout.com
Talk, Trust & Feel and the Angries Out website were developed to give people alternatives to conflict and violence when they are upset. The mission of Angries Out is to help people learn to use their anger in ways that empower them. From their website, you can download free articles about peace-building skills and learn more about bully behavior.

BullyStoppers
www.bullystoppers.com
Use this site to report bullying, find state resources, and check out current resources being used by educators.

Cyberbullying.ca
www.cyberbullying.ca
A kid-friendly site with lots of info on bullying that uses new technologies.

Family.com
www.family.go.com
This site contains useful information for parents and other adults, including articles on helping children learn to face bullies and be kind to one another.

Kidscape
www.kidscape.org.uk/kidscape
Visit this site for information about keeping kids safe. The ideas and materials here focus on preventing bullying before it happens.

McGruff
www.mcgruff.org
This is a fun site for kids, and an informative one for adults. Click on "Parents & Educators" for info on helping kids stay safe and bully free.

Mental Help
www.mentalhelp.net
This site is home to the oldest and largest online mental health community and indexes over 9,000 mental health resources, including articles on aggression and behavior disorders.

Safety Awareness and Family Education Network
www.safenetwork.org
You'll find articles, a message board, and advice from experts on keeping children safe at school and in the community.

Stop Bullying Now!
www.stopbullying.gov
A fun and interactive site for kids, and packed full of information on bullying for adults.

INDEX

Page numbers in **bold** indicate reproducible pages.

R

S

ABOUT THE AUTHOR

Allan L. Beane, Ph.D., is an internationally recognized expert on the topic of bullying. He has over 30 years of experience in education that include teaching special and regular education, directing a school safety center, and serving as vice president of a university. Author of the Bully Free® Program, Allan has spoken and trained staff in many schools on bullying and has served as an expert witness in criminal cases involving student mistreatment.

Allan and his wife, Linda, operate Bully Free Systems, LLC, a company dedicated to preventing bullying in schools. After bullying played a part in the death of their son, Curtis, they have devoted their lives to creating safe and supportive learning environments where all students can be and achieve their best. For information on speaking, training, and workshop opportunities, visit www.bullyfree.com.

Other Bully Free® Products from Free Spirit

Bully Free® Bulletin Boards, Posters, and Banners

For grades K–8. 144 pp., softcover, illust., 8½" x 11"

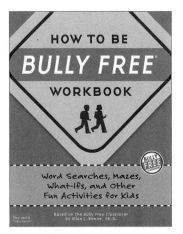

How to Be Bully Free® Workbook

For grades 3–5. 32 pp., softcover, illust., 8½" x 11"

Bully Free Zone® In a Jar

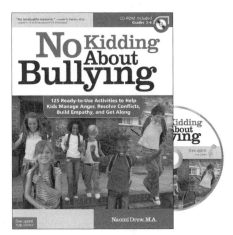

No Kidding About Bullying

For educators, group leaders, and caregivers, grades 3–6. 296 pp., softcover, 8½" x 11"

Bully Free® Card Game

For grades K–8. Pack of 60 cards and 12-page fold-out insert, full color, 3" x 4½"

Bully Free Zone® Poster

17" x 22"

Good-Bye Bully Machine

For ages 8 & up. 48 pp., softcover, color illust., 8" x 8" or 48 pp., hardcover, color illust., 8¼" x 8¼"

Good-Bye Bully Machine Card Game

For ages 8 & up. Pack of 60 cards and 12-page fold-out insert, full color, 3" x 4½"

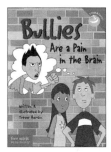

Bullies Are a Pain in the Brain

For ages 8–13. 112 pp., softcover, illust., 5⅛" x 9"

JOIN THE FREE SPIRIT ADVISORY BOARD

Teachers, administrators, librarians, counselors, youth workers, and social workers,
help us create the resources you need to support the kids you serve. In order to make our books and other products even more beneficial for children and teens, the Free Spirit Advisory Board provides valuable feedback on content, art, title concepts, and more. You can assist us in our mission to help kids think for themselves, succeed in school and life, and make a difference in the world. Apply today! For more information, go to **www.freespirit.com/educators.**

See It, Be It, Write It
For educators, grades 3–8. 192 pp., softcover, 8½" x 11"

**Teaching Kids to Be
Confident, Effective Communicators**
For educators, grades K–6. 240 pp., softcover, 8½" x 11"

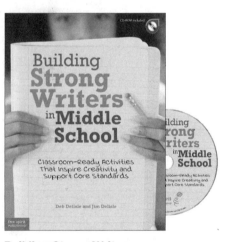

**Building Strong Writers
in Middle School**
For educators, grades 4–8. 176 pp., softcover, 8½" x 11"

The Complete Guide to Service Learning
For educators, grades K–12. 288 pp., softcover, 8½" x 11"

Interested in purchasing multiple quantities?
Contact edsales@freespirit.com or call 1.800.735.7323 and ask for Education Sales.

Many Free Spirit authors are available for speaking engagements, workshops, and keynotes.
Contact speakers@freespirit.com or call 1.800.735.7323.

For pricing information, to place an order, or to request a free catalog, contact:

Free Spirit Publishing Inc.
217 Fifth Avenue North • Suite 200 • Minneapolis, MN 55401-1299
toll-free 800.735.7323 • local 612.338.2068 • fax 612.337.5050
help4kids@freespirit.com • www.freespirit.com